Perspectives on Trust in the History of Philosophy

Perspectives on Trust in the History of Philosophy

Edited by
David Collins, Iris Vidmar Jovanović, and
Mark Alfano

LEXINGTON BOOKS
Lanham • Boulder • New York • London

Published by Lexington Books
An imprint of The Rowman & Littlefield Publishing Group, Inc.
4501 Forbes Boulevard, Suite 200, Lanham, Maryland 20706
www.rowman.com

86-90 Paul Street, London EC2A 4NE

Copyright © 2024 by The Rowman & Littlefield Publishing Group, Inc.

All rights reserved. No part of this book may be reproduced in any form or by any electronic or mechanical means, including information storage and retrieval systems, without written permission from the publisher, except by a reviewer who may quote passages in a review.

British Library Cataloguing in Publication Information Available

Library of Congress Cataloging-in-Publication Data Available

ISBN 9781666931075 (cloth)
ISBN 9781666931082 (ebook)

Contents

List of Abbreviations		vii
Introduction *David Collins*		1
1	A Confucian Account of Trustworthiness *Winnie Sung*	15
2	Aristotle on Friendship and Trust *Corinne Gartner and Wania Ahmad*	35
3	How the Buddha Earns His Disciples' Trust (According to *Some* Pāli Nikāya Texts) *Antoine Panaïoti*	55
4	Mutual Trust and the Foundations of African Communalism *Polycarp Ikuenobe*	77
5	Credulity, Diffidence, and Civil Trust in Hobbes *Erfan Xia*	95
6	David Hume and Adam Smith on the Nature and Functions of Trust and Trustworthiness *Christel Fricke*	111
7	The Obligation to be Trustworthy and the Ability to Trust: An Investigation into Kant's Scattered Remarks on Trust *Esther Oluffa Pedersen*	133

8	Nietzsche on Trust and Mistrust *Mark Alfano*	157
9	Løgstrup and the Sovereignty of Trust *Patrick Stokes*	179
10	Iris Murdoch: Trust in the World *Silvia Caprioglio Panizza*	197

Index	213
About the Contributors	217

List of Abbreviations

CHAPTER 2

EE	Aristotle, *Eudemian Ethics*
NE	Aristotle, *Nicomachean Ethics*

CHAPTER 3

AN	*Aṅguttara Nikāya*
DN	*Dīgha Nikāya*
MN	*Majjhima Nikāya*
SN	*Saṃyutta Nikāya*
Sn	*Suttanipāta*

CHAPTER 6

LJ	Adam Smith, *Lectures on Jurisprudence*
T	David Hume, *A Treatise of Human Nature*
TMS	Adam Smith, *The Theory of Moral Sentiments*
WN	Adam Smith, *An Inquiry into the Nature and Causes of the Wealth of Nations*

CHAPTER 8

Nietzsche's Works

A	*The Antichrist*
AOM	*Assorted Opinions and Maxims* (in part two of *HH*)
BGE	*Beyond Good and Evil*
CW	*The Case of Wagner*
D	*Daybreak*
DS	*David Strauss, the Confessor and the Writer* (in *UM*)
EH	*Ecce Homo*
GM	*On the Genealogy of Morals*
GS	*The Gay Science*
HH	*Human, All-too-human*
HL	*On the Uses and Disadvantages of History for Life* (in *UM*)
SE	*Schopenhauer as Educator* (in *UM*)
TI	*Twilight of the Idols*
WS	*The Wanderer and His Shadow* (in part two of *HH*)
Z	*Thus Spoke Zarathustra*

CHAPTER 10

Iris Murdoch's Works

IP	"The Idea of Perfection"
MGM	*Metaphysics as a Guide to Morals*
OGG	"On 'God' and 'Good'"
SGC	"The Sovereignty of Good Over Other Concepts"
VCM	"Vision and Choice in Morality"

Introduction
David Collins

It is not surprising that philosophers throughout the ages, and across cultures, have had much to say on the topic of trust, given its importance for human life both individually and communally. It is also unsurprising that philosophers' interest in the topic of trust has grown in recent years, given the increasing public concerns with the trustworthiness—or the lack thereof—of a number of institutions, including governments, the media, policing and justice systems, scientific and medical establishments, education, banking and corporations, and the online world of "big tech," in light of events and actions that have called the credibility of these institutions into question. (Within the world of academia, consider the current "replication crisis" in the sciences, or recent scandals involving "hoax" articles published by journals in the humanities.) While it is perhaps premature to declare anything as strong as a "crisis of trust" in modern society, evidence pointing to such a crisis can be found in the rise of conspiracy theories and similar patterns of thinking across the political spectrum, and in the number of public voices either calling for controls meant to restore public trust (or to staunch its hemorrhaging)—for example, controls on online discourse, or on voting procedures—or warning against these due to the apparent untrustworthiness of the governments and corporations who would implement and oversee them. Given these current concerns with trust within and outside of academic philosophy, what *is* surprising is the comparative lack of attention to what past thinkers have said about the moral and social dimensions of trust, and to how their views might usefully inform current scholarship on the topic, with the work that has been done on trust in relation to certain philosophers—for example, the theme of trust in the thought of Confucius, or Hobbes, or Løgstrup—having remained largely internal to the scholarship on those thinkers, with little influence on contemporary philosophers of trust.

This collection brings together ten chapters that examine the varied conceptions of trust found in the work of several historically important philosophers and traditions, ranging from ancient China, Greece, and India to twentieth-century anglophone and continental philosophy. It grew out of our work on another volume, *The Moral Psychology of Trust*, published earlier this year (also from Lexington Books). We had initially planned for that volume to feature a section focusing on historical views of trust to provide a background for the contemporary chapters, but it soon became apparent that this was too much to include in a single volume while doing justice to the temporal and cross-cultural range of thinkers who have something to say about the importance of trust for human life. Accordingly, we decided to add to the intended historically focused section and publish it as the current book, which is meant to work both as a stand-alone collection of chapters and as a companion volume to *The Moral Psychology of Trust*.

Even the present volume can only scratch the surface of the variety of views on trust to be found throughout the history of philosophy, including both Western philosophy and non-Western philosophical traditions from Africa, Asia, and elsewhere. Rather than aiming to give an exhaustive catalog of what philosophers have said about trust over the ages, we have sought instead to highlight the important place that trust has—together with closely related notions such as distrust, trustworthiness, etc.—in the discussions of a selection of thinkers, from different times and places, of the moral, social, and cultural dimensions of human existence. We have also sought to focus on the moral and social dimensions of trust rather than its epistemological dimensions—for instance, issues of trust in others' testimony in relation to the role testimony plays in knowledge acquisition—since the latter have been written on more extensively, although not always with an explicit focus on trust.

One example of a significant work in the history of philosophy that is not usually framed in terms of trust, but in which trust plays a central role, is Descartes's *Meditations on First Philosophy* (1641): here, Descartes's method of radical doubt might well be redescribed as a matter of distrust—specifically, of sensory experience as a justifiable source of knowledge—and the line of reasoning following from his *cogito* argument as Descartes coming to ground the general trustworthiness of our senses in his trust in God. In the same light, the conflict between views that fall broadly under what could be called empiricism and rationalism, running from Plato up to the present day, could be reframed as a matter of trust versus distrust in perception and appearances, although where rationalists tend to distrust the senses to at least some degree, empiricists have not shown the same kind of distrust in reason, and the few philosophers who express what might be called a mistrust of reason—for example, Kierkegaard, or Nietzsche, or Bergson—do so in a limited rather than a "global" way.

The accounts of trust examined in the following ten chapters are taken both from explicit discussions of trust by the philosophers in question and from their discussions of other topics—ethics, friendship, community, political authority, education, and so on—in which the idea of trust is implicit, even if it goes unnamed. The fact that philosophers' accounts of trust are often to be found in their articulations of views on other topics goes some way toward explaining why the importance of trust in the history of philosophy has been relatively neglected, at least in comparison to the attention that has been paid to the histories of concepts such as duty or freedom. It also suggests the extent to which trust is bound up with other facets of our existence as social beings. This accords with anthropological research showing that a propensity to trust others in ever-widening "in groups"—extending from family units to tribes small enough for their members to know each other, to larger communities such as cities and nations and, ultimately (and perhaps ideally), to humanity as a whole—is central to the cooperation that is necessary for human evolution, both biological evolution, or the survival and development of the species, and societal evolution, or the development of civilizations (see Stanish 2023).

Due to the inherent limitations of what might be called the human form, where these include our physical vulnerabilities—for example, our lack of natural defenses or "weaponry" on par with, say, a turtle's shell or a bear's claws—and our epistemic limitations as situated and fallible knowers reliant on finite cognitive capacities—for example, our memories—we are inherently dependent on one another in order to survive, let alone flourish. This aspect of the human condition is recognized by Aristotle in his observation that we are by nature "political animals," and that being able to exist separately from a community—that is, being wholly self-sufficient and not reliant in any way on others of one's kind—is possible only for "either a beast or a god" (Aristotle 2017, I.2 1256a2–3, 27–29). This vulnerability and dependency entails that our own lives are intrinsically bound up with the lives of others in ways that go beyond our survival. We depend on and so must trust others in order to act ethically toward them: for instance, doing something generous for another requires one to trust that the other is genuinely in need of what one will give them in order for one's intention to be generous to be fulfilled.

At the most basic level, treating others ethically requires us to be vulnerable to them, to lower our guard, as it were, and to leave ourselves open to being taken advantage of or even harmed, where doing this presupposes trusting them not to betray us. This trust is so ingrained in our social relations that we are not often consciously aware of it: for example, stopping to give someone directions makes us more vulnerable to their mugging us, but it would be overly paranoid to refrain from doing so for that reason, and when paying for items at a shop, it does not normally occur to us that the salesperson might refuse to give us what we pay for, although giving them our money before we have the items in our possession allows for this. The intertwining of our lives and possibilities for action with those of others is no less true when it comes to betrayals of trust: for an attempt at deception to succeed, the deceived party must initially trust the deceiver—as Kant notes in his argument against the permissibility of lying (see Kant 1785, 4:422; 1797, 6:429)—with whatever benefit the deceiver gains from the deception resulting from, and depending on, the deceived party's loss.

The possibilities of betrayal to which trusting leaves us open, even while trust is a necessary part of human life and flourishing, suggest that this necessary trust is initial and defeasible as opposed to a kind of "blind faith," and that distrust is sometimes called for and, when warranted, is even necessary for the very same flourishing for which trust is: one will not do well in life as a social being if one is continually being taken advantage of. This in turn suggests that something like an Aristotelian "mean," between being overly trusting to the point of naïveté on one hand, and being overly distrusting to the point of paranoia on the other, is the ideal to aim for when it comes to trust. It also points to two separate though related dispositions involving trust, with one being a disposition to trust appropriately—that is, with the right balance of faith and suspicion for a given occasion—and the other a disposition to be trustworthy with respect to others' trust in us. Even if we do not treat them as Aristotelian means between excesses and deficiencies (and it is not clear what it would mean to be *excessively* trust*worthy*), trusting and being trustworthy are the two basic dimensions of the domain of trust, where most of what has been said on the topic by philosophers relates to one dimension or the other: for example, what the conditions are under which we are justified in trusting or distrusting others, what is involved in being a trustworthy person, and how to cash out the various relations in which we stand to others when we trust or are trusted by them.

In chapter 1, Winnie Sung looks at how trust and trustworthiness are understood in the Confucian tradition of Classical Chinese philosophy. She focuses on three interrelated concepts—*xin*, *zhong*, and *cheng*—which have to do with straightforwardness and honesty in how one presents oneself to others, impartiality and a commitment to another's good when speaking or giving advice, and harmony between one's "internal" or mental states and one's "external" states; for example, one's bodily comportment. Together these form the Confucian account of what it is to be trustworthy, with *cheng* being the most fundamental and grounding the other two: it is difficult to be honest in one's self-presentation if the self that one is presenting is conflicted, and one's mental states, including one's motivations, being in harmony is important for the self-awareness needed to ensure that one is truly acting in another's best interests rather than in one's own. Sung outlines each of these concepts in depth, explains their fundamentally social and relational nature, and discusses how this account of trustworthiness compares with modern conceptions of trust. The chapter ends with a consideration of how applicable the Confucian account is to contemporary society, given our comparative lack of clearly established social roles, norms, and expectations, with Sung arguing that it still has much to say to us today despite our different social context.

There are a number of similarities between the Confucian account of trustworthiness and the place of trust in Aristotle's remarks on friendship, on which chapter 2, by Corinne Gartner and Wania Ahmad, focuses. As with the Confucian account, Aristotle takes trustworthiness to involve accurate self-presentation and a commitment to acting for the sake of the person with whom one is in a trusting relationship, rather than seeing the relationship as an occasion to further one's own interests. Gartner and Ahmad connect Aristotle's remarks on trust to his virtue of truthfulness, which, in another parallel with the Confucian account, requires self-knowledge. Complete friendship, that is, friendship between people who are virtuous or who are at least on their way to virtue, which for Aristotle is the kind of friendship that partly constitutes a flourishing life, only comes about with the development of mutual trust. This suggests that trusting some others and being trusted by them in return—and being worthy of their trust—is crucial to well-being. Gartner and Ahmad draw on both the *Nicomachean* and *Eudemian Ethics*, finding that although these texts overlap in many places, the Eudemian account of friendship says more about trust and the difficulties of trusting others to the extent that is required for complete friendships. These difficulties are partly a matter of the time it takes to come to know another person well enough for genuine mutual trust to develop, and Gartner and Ahmad show the importance of the temporal aspect of Aristotle's account, while arguing against reducing friendship to reciprocal goodwill and addressing the seeming paradox that knowledge of self and other is necessary for, but comes from, friendship.

In chapter 3, Antoine Panaïoti turns to examine the place of trust in Classical Indian Buddhism, and specifically its place in the pedagogical relation between Buddhists and their spiritual teachers, with the ultimate teacher being the historical Buddha, Siddhārtha Gautama. Navigating the tangled and thorny debates concerning which interpretations of Buddhism are more authentic or "purer," Panaïoti argues for an antimetaphysical "empiricist-cum-pragmatist" reading that can be gleaned from certain texts and which, he argues, suggests that the trustworthiness of the Buddha as a spiritual teacher is grounded in his ability to cut through abstract metaphysical disputes and to steer his pupils toward fruitful practical action. The trustworthiness of the Buddha, on Panaïoti's reading, is based partly on his encouragement of *self-trust* in his pupils, where they are urged not to follow external authorities or even the apparent authority of purely theoretical reasoning, but instead to adopt a view or accept a claim only when they have verified it for themselves. It is also partly based on the pupil's judgment that the Buddha—or, by extension, any teacher—is free of mental states that lead one's awareness away from truth, such as attraction, aversion, and delusion, since what one who has these mental states says cannot be trusted to be correct. This point is similar to the Confucian concern with the harmony of inner states discussed in chapter 1, and with the requirement of self-knowledge shared by the Confucians and Aristotle as seen in chapter 2.

In chapter 4, Polycarp Ikuenobe outlines a kind of communalism commonly found in many African societies and considers how trust is central to the interpersonal relations that comprise these communities of shared values, practices, and ways of living. He argues that this African form of communalism is not merely a matter of group solidarity between individuals, and that the idea of personhood in these traditions is bound up with trustworthiness, where the trust that other community members place in one, and one's worthiness of this trust, is required for being a *full* person. Full personhood in this sense is largely correlated with being an elder in one's community, with elders seen as trusted authorities with respect to preserving and passing on the values and norms of their communities, and to upholding institutions and traditions. What emerges from Ikuenobe's discussion is a view of individuals that is, like the Confucian view, fundamentally social and relational, with persons and their communities being mutually inter-entailing: in the words of John Mbiti, the self exists as a self because the community exists, and the community exists because its members exist. It is also clear from Ikuenobe's discussion that the view of trust that is found in African communal traditions is not only local but global, with analogues in different traditions and views on trust across all cultures[1]—where this can be seen in Ikuenobe's use of contemporary analytic philosophers of trust, such as Carolyn McLeod, to draw parallels between current Anglo-American views on trust and the traditional African views on which the chapter focuses.

The next three chapters examine the views on trust found, explicitly or implicitly, in a handful of key thinkers from the modern Western philosophical canon. In chapter 5, Erfan Xia argues that trust is important in the philosophy of Thomas Hobbes, not only in his political philosophy—in which civil society depends on citizens' learned dispositions to be trustworthy, as well as their trust in their political authority (or "sovereign") to uphold and enforce the law fairly and effectively and to provide the education necessary to develop into responsible, trustworthy, and civic-minded citizens—but also his epistemology and philosophical psychology, where Hobbes ties both trust and distrust (or "diffidence") to natural human passions, and in his critiques of religious authority. Xia contends that Hobbes was responding to an apparent dilemma, which is that (i) social stability and prosperity require trust, (ii) trust should take into account, and be based on a knowledge of, human emotions or "passions," and (iii) humans, in their natural state, are untrustworthy—and so, untrusting—due to their natural emotional dispositions, primarily their self-interest. Hobbes's solution to this dilemma, according to Xia, is to posit fear of punishment and of social disapproval as an adequate motivation for people to develop a disposition to be trustworthy, which in turn will allow citizens to trust each other since they know that they all share this motivation. Ultimately, Hobbes develops a theory of reasonable or justified trust and reasonable distrust—or enlightened skepticism—in contrast to both unreasonable "credulity," or gullibility, and the irrational or automatic distrust, or "diffidence," that is found in the state of nature.

Chapter 6 compares the understandings of trust and trustworthiness that are implicit in the work of two figures of the Scottish Enlightenment, David Hume and Adam Smith, with Christel Fricke linking the points of divergence in their understandings to the difference between their moral psychologies. According to Hume, people are basically selfish and learn to cooperate out of self-interest; for Smith, however, humans are motivated both by sympathy for others and by self-love. Hence, for Hume, trusting others and being trustworthy are things that need to be learned, whereas Smith holds that we are naturally disposed to trust others. On Hume's view, members of a community collectively create and agree to follow "conventions of justice" from mutual self-interest: for example, people refraining from simply taking things they want away from others who are using them so that others will be less likely to take *their* possessions away from *them*. Because these conventions of social behavior cannot be established by, say, formal promises or contracts, since these depend on just such conventions for their force, some degree of trust in others to act in accordance with a common interest—here, our shared interest in mutual cooperation—is necessary for such conventions to "get off the ground." Because we come to have this common interest in cooperating through reasoning about what is best for us, trusting others and being trustworthy ourselves are, for Hume, fundamentally rational and not a product of our passions, as would be, say, a feeling of goodwill.

For Smith, on the other hand, a feeling of sympathy is what inclines us to limit our selfishness and to act justly and in a trustworthy way while also inclining us to initially trust others, attributing to them a reciprocal sense of goodwill toward us, where what needs to be learned and cultivated is not to trust others and to be trustworthy oneself, but how to do so wisely and impartially. Fricke draws from both Smith's *Theory of Moral Sentiments* and *The*

Wealth of Nations to show that, in the latter work, Smith treats commercial society and the drive toward increased wealth as undermining our natural sympathies and inclination to be trustworthy, thereby inducing the conditions that Hume took to be our natural state in which conventional agreements, enforced by law, are necessary for people to cooperate and not work against each other's interests. In such conditions, government becomes a kind of necessary evil for Smith, who requires politicians to trust the citizens over whom they legislate to make their own decisions whenever possible.

In chapter 7, Esther Oluffa Pedersen draws on Kant's various remarks on trust, which are scattered throughout a number of his works, in order to argue that together they constitute a full-blown Kantian theory of trust that has much to offer modern work on trust. Pedersen argues that, when approached from a Kantian perspective, trust must be understood, like persons themselves, from the "double perspective" of the noumenal and the phenomenal—that is, both as relating to the moral character of persons and as based on empirical observations of human behavior. Part of the Kantian view of trust that Pedersen argues for is the importance of self-trust for living morally; we must trust that the maxims we act upon have been chosen from a pure intention, or with a goodwill, and not from self-interest, since we cannot observe our motives to check whether this is the case, as our wills stand outside the empirical world in which, and only in which, we can obtain evidence. Taking empirical sources such as adherence to social customs and formalities or approval by others to confirm that we are morally good people is decried by Kant as "lazy trust." However, since we can easily deceive ourselves as to the purity of our motivations and intentions, Pedersen notes that Kant warns that the self-trust which is necessary must be balanced to avoid both blind faith and self-skepticism. This point, along with Kant's insistence on our having moral obligations to be trustworthy persons with respect to all other persons, and on the importance of having an honest and accurate view of oneself, is notably similar to ideas found in Confucius and Aristotle discussed in the first two chapters. The emphasis here on the importance of self-trust and the problem of lazy trust in customs and in others as authorities also ties into Kant's ideas of autonomy, maturity, and the need to think for oneself. After showing the centrality of trust for Kant's ideas of morality and distinguishing between moral and prudential trust, Pedersen considers how this Kantian view of trust applies to such topics as friendship and international relations.

In chapter 8, Mark Alfano turns to examine Nietzsche's remarks on trust and mistrust, noting that where trust is addressed in the existing Nietzsche scholarship the focus is only on a handful of places in Nietzsche's corpus where he mentions trust or mistrust, with the result that most of Nietzsche's writing on the topic has so far gone undiscussed. Alfano finds three distinct insights into trust and two that deal specifically with mistrust spread across Nietzsche's writings; the concern with self-trust is not surprising because of its connection with individual self-reliance, but what is perhaps more surprising—given Nietzsche's reputation for pioneering a "hermeneutics of suspicion"—is Nietzsche's negative view of generally mistrustful people, with his positive views of mistrust being limited to specific domains: namely, morality and science. With regard to interpersonal trust, Nietzsche argues against the idea that reciprocal trust is owed—that is, if I trust you, this does not entitle me to expect that you will then trust me—and instead views trust as a gift that must be freely given on the basis only of one's esteem for another's competence, reliability, or trustworthiness. Trusting as and where appropriate is connected to nobility of character and a capacity for joy or life-affirmation, with indiscriminate or generalized mistrust being grouped with resentment and envy as signs of the poverty or "sickness" of a person's character. Regarding self-trust, Nietzsche is primarily concerned with a person's unjustified loss of trust in their own abilities, affective responses, and intuitions, seeing this as a matter of being disconnected from one's instinctive nature, where Alfano shows that this, for Nietzsche, is a kind of vice. Indeed, one of the (many) things for which Nietzsche condemns resentful people—those who operate in terms of "slave morality"—is their propensity to infect others with their own self-mistrust. And regarding the mistrust of others, Nietzsche sees this as positive when it allows one to critically question "received" perspectives, whether from traditional morality—especially as found in religion—or from what might be called "establishment science," and to submit all claims to rigorous testing and committed attempts at falsification.

The final two chapters consider the importance of trust in the thought of two twentieth-century philosophers, both of whom occupy positions at the intersection of analytic and continental traditions. In chapter 9, Patrick Stokes discusses Danish philosopher and theologian K. E. Løgstrup's account of trust. Unlike most of the thinkers covered in previous chapters, Løgstrup did not view trust primarily as a kind of relation between people, instead seeing it as what he calls a "sovereign" expression of life or a primordial part of the "framework" of human social existence. Trust, on this view, is prior to distrust, being a condition for the possibility of interpersonal relations and social (inter-)actions, and with instances of suspicion or mistrust arising only against a background of a more generalized trust that others do not seek to harm us. Trust is thus a necessary condition for everything that comprises human well-being or flourishing, which is why exceptional circumstances, such as war, that disrupt this background are not merely moral and political but *metaphysical* problems, according to Løgstrup, being forms of violence against human life itself that call for resolute (self-)defense—a view that is unsurprising given that Løgstrup was writing in the context of World War II and the debate between resistance or appeasement. Hence, for Løgstrup, any condition in which a "hermeneutics of suspicion" becomes the default mode of interaction is so far forth analogous to wartime, and so ought to be resisted so that the background of generalized trust can be restored. As well as laying out the essential elements of Løgstrup's account of trust, Stokes responds to challenges that have been raised against it and considers how Løgstrupian trust fits with standard conceptions of trust in contemporary analytic philosophy: for example, trust's relation to agency, or whether it is a two- or three-part relation—or something else that goes beyond currently dominant understandings of trust to offer a genuinely new alternative perspective.

Finally, in chapter 10, Silvia Caprioglio Panizza finds in the philosophy of Iris Murdoch another perspective on trust as not just one type of relation that can obtain between people, but as part of the background conditions of human existence—where for Murdoch this is not limited to social life, and where the trust in question is not primarily in other people so much as a trust in the world. Positioning the implicit view of trust found in Murdoch's work within Murdoch's broader challenge to modern moral philosophy and its ideal of the autonomous individual agent—what she calls "the man of liberal culture"—and her desire to recover the "inner," private lives of individuals as an important part of the moral sphere, Panizza argues that Murdoch's move away from impersonal ethical principles to personal moral perception arising from individual acts of attention presupposes self-trust. That is, in the absence of external criteria by which we could verify that our perception is true—for example, that someone really is how they seem to us when seen with the kind of loving attention that Murdoch illustrates in her famous example of a mother and daughter-in-law—we can only trust that it is. As Panizza shows, this is both a trust that what (or whom) we are attending to has certain features or qualities that are not immediately apparent, and that we can come to apprehend them correctly through the kind of attention that we are able to pay.

While this is important for Murdoch's idea of moral perception, Panizza argues that this trust operates in ordinary perception as well, which, to put it simply, presupposes that there is a world, that it is a certain way, and that we can come to know it through observation using the capacities we possess. This kind of trust is the alternative to Descartes's distrust of the senses and is required if there is to be any middle position between foundationalist theories of knowledge (here, moral knowledge, with the foundation being universal ethical principles) and skepticism. In terms of the analogy of Neurath's boat (or Sosa's raft), when we are "at sea" without "stable ground" and can only use the parts of the boat we are sitting in as resources with which to advance, we must trust both the capacity of these parts—the beams, planks, and so on—to continue to support us when rearranged, and our own ability to so rearrange them.[2]

Certain patterns can be seen, and common views found, in these ten chapters. For one thing, the topics of concern move outwards, as it were, from a focus on the individual and questions of self-trust and trustworthiness, to issues concerning trusting others within interpersonal relations, to a more generalized social trust over and above any particular relationship and, ultimately, to a broad sense of trust in the world. For another, there is widespread agreement to be found between thinkers from various times, cultures, and traditions on the necessity of trust for personal and communal wellbeing and for the proper and beneficial functioning of social institutions. There are also affinities to be found between certain thinkers on particular points, such as between Aristotle and the Confucian tradition on the relation between trustworthiness and accurate self-presentation, and the importance of self-knowledge for this, or between Smith and Løgstrup on trust in others being our natural or default attitude—or, in contrast, between Hobbes and Hume on self-interest being our default motivation, with trust coming about only through the establishment of social conventions. What will also be apparent to those familiar with the contemporary literature on trust is how much of this literature is prefigured in the ideas of thinkers from the past. (Consider, for example, how many of the historical accounts surveyed in this volume overlap with the views and arguments found in the seminal text for contemporary work on trust, Annette Baier's 1986 paper "Trust and Antitrust.")

By bringing together chapters that discuss these historical and cross-cultural perspectives on trust, our aim is not only to allow affinities and differences like these to emerge, but to make these various accounts of trust (and trustworthiness) more easily accessible to those currently working on trust in order to provide a historical background for their inquiries on the topic. If philosophers such as Collingwood and Gadamer are right to insist that concepts develop historically, with the ways in which we now think about a phenomenon (such as trust) being shaped by—and bearing the traces of—past thinking on the subject, then a historical background of this kind is crucial, since one will not be able to fully understand contemporary thought without also understanding where it has come from.[3] *Good* philosophy, they would argue, must be historically informed philosophy.

Good philosophical work on trust—work that not only illuminates the place of trust in our lives and our social practices and relations, but which can tie back into and usefully inform these practices—is important in our present context. Exploring the moral and social dimensions of trust, and not only its epistemological dimensions, is crucial for understanding and responding intelligently to a number of contemporary issues and challenges: for example, widespread political polarization, with people on different "sides" of an issue distrusting each other to the point of demonization, or the balance between transparency and privacy, and accompanying questions of accountability, with respect to freedom of information and practices of data collection and use.[4] To the extent that knowing and considering the views on trust that have been developed by important thinkers in the past can aid in this work, we hope that the chapters collected in this volume will make a useful contribution.

NOTES

1. Cf. Oliver Scott Curry's work on morality as cooperation, which is similar in several respects to the view of trust that Ikuenobe outlines and which is global in its scope, applying to human social evolution in all cultures and places.
2. See Neurath (1921) and Sosa (1980).
3. See Collingwood (1939, chapter 9) and Gadamer (1989, especially Part II, 4.1 .B.iv) on the idea of *Wirkungsgeschichte* or "history of effect."
4. On these points, see MacGilvray (2022) and Brin (1998).

REFERENCES

Aristotle. 2017. *Politics*. Translated by C.D.C. Reeve. Indianapolis: Hackett.
Baier, Annette. 1986. "Trust and Antitrust." *Ethics* 96: 231–60.
Brin, David. 1998. *The Transparent Society*. New York: Perseus/Basic Books.
Collingwood, R.G. 1939. *An Autobiography*. Oxford: Clarendon Press.
Collins, David, Iris Vidmar Jovanović, and Mark Alfano, eds. 2023. *The Moral Psychology of Trust*. Lanham: Lexington Books.
Curry, Oliver Scott. 2016. "Morality as Cooperation: A Problem-Centred Approach." In *The Evolution of Morality*, edited by Todd Shackelford and Ranald Hansen, 27–51. Cham: Springer International Publishing.
Descartes, Rene. 1996 [1641]. *Meditations on First Philosophy: With Selections from the Objections and Replies*. Translated by John Cottingham. Cambridge: Cambridge University Press.
Gadamer, Hans-Georg. 1989. *Truth and Method*, second edition. Translated by Joel Weinsheimer and Donald Marshall. London: Continuum.
Kant, Immanuel. 2002 [1785]. *Groundwork for the Metaphysics of Morals*. Translated by Mary Gregor and Jens Timmermann. Cambridge: Cambridge University Press.
———. 2006 [1797]. *The Metaphysics of Morals*. Translated by Mary Gregor. Cambridge: Cambridge University Press.
MacGilvray, Eric. 2022. *Liberal Freedom: Pluralism, Polarization, and Politics*. Cambridge: Cambridge University Press.
Neurath, Otto. 1973 [1921]. "Anti-Spengler." In *Empiricism and Sociology*, edited by Marie Neurath and Robert S. Cohen, 158–213. Dordrecht: D. Reidel Publishing Co.

Sosa, Ernst. 1991 [1980]. "The Raft and the Pyramid: Coherence versus Foundations in the Theory of Knowledge." In Sosa, *Knowledge in Perspective: Selected Essays in Epistemology*, 165–91. Cambridge: Cambridge University Press.

Stanish, Charles. 2023. "Trust, Demographic Thresholds, and Cooperation in Social Evolution." In *The Moral Psychology of Trust*, edited by David Collins, Iris Vidmar Jovanović, and Mark Alfano, 16–36. Lanham: Lexington Books.

Chapter 1

A Confucian Account of Trustworthiness

Winnie Sung

This chapter outlines a Confucian account of trustworthiness by discussing three key Confucian concepts: *xin* 信, *zhong* 忠, and *cheng* 誠. My development of this account might go beyond what the early thinkers themselves have thought about trustworthiness. Nonetheless, the account of trustworthiness I present here is characteristically Confucian and compatible with the general contours of Confucian thinking.

I will primarily draw on Confucian texts in the pre-Qin period from around the sixth century BCE to the third century BCE. The three key texts that are crucial to my account are the *Analects*, the *Mencius*, and the *Xunzi*.[1] The *Analects* is a book of recorded sayings of Confucius (c. 551–479 BCE). It was compiled and edited by Confucius's disciples approximately sixty to seventy years after his death. The *Analects* contains sayings of Confucius's disciples and conversations between them and Confucius, as well as between the disciples themselves. The *Mencius* is also a book of recorded sayings of Mencius (c. 385–312 BCE). Scholars generally think the *Mencius* was edited by Mencius's disciples. The *Xunzi* is a book that is believed to be mostly written by Xunzi (c. 310–215 BCE), with some parts edited and written by his own disciples. It is worth noting that Mencius and Xunzi never directly studied under Confucius; it is also worth noting that Xunzi vehemently disagreed with Mencius on some core issues, such as whether human nature is good and what the function of ritual is. That said, there are certain core concerns and values they share, so much so that the later Han grand historian Sima Qian would group Confucius, Mencius, and Xunzi all under the philosophical family of *Ru* 儒 (Confucians).

In trying to understand the early Confucian conception of trustworthiness, it might be tempting to focus on the concept of *xin* 信, which is often translated as "trustworthiness" (see, e.g., Lau 2002; Slingerland 2003; Ni 2017).

Although *xin* might overlap with much of what we nowadays think about trustworthiness, it alone is too narrow to capture the Confucian conception of trustworthiness. The early Confucian concepts are intimately linked as clusters, which usually only approximate our contemporary understanding of a certain attribute, psychological phenomenon, or state. In the early texts, *xin* 信 as an ethical attribute is often discussed alongside two other concepts: *zhong* 忠 (loyalty)[2] and *cheng* 誠 (sincerity/wholeheartedness) (*Mencius* 4A:12, 5A:2).[3] In order to have a better understanding of the Confucian conception of trustworthiness, we will need at least to consider *xin*, *zhong*, and *cheng* together. Since each of these concepts is complex and all three are closely linked, it is challenging to isolate one from the others. In what follows, I will focus on the aspects that are relevant to the characteristics of the Confucian conception of trustworthiness that I highlight in my fourth section and try to weave these ideas together into a larger picture. This should present at least the rough contours of the Confucian conception of trustworthiness.

XIN 信

The character "xin" comprises the radical *ren* 人 (human beings/person) and *yan* 言 (speech/words). *Xin* is often discussed in connection with speech (see, e.g., *Analects* 5.10, 15.5, 7.25), which suggests that *xin* has to do with speech acts and verbal commitments.[4] The term "xin" also has the connotations of being straightforward or forthright and is used in a literal sense to mean straight without a bend. For example, there is a reference in the *Mencius* that one's finger is not "xin," meaning that one's finger is not straight (*Mencius* 6A:12). This suggests that *xin* also has to do with honesty in a way that goes beyond saying what is true. Since *xin* is a multifaceted concept, it is very difficult to use a single word to translate this term. Translators often use different English words for different usages of "xin" in the same text depending on the context. In addition to "trustworthiness," *xin* is often also translated as "truthfulness" (Legge 1971), "trust" (Lau 2002; Ni 2017), "making good on one's word" (Ames and Rosemont 1998), and "being true to one's word" (Waley 1992). Here, I focus on a feature of *xin* that is significant to our thinking about trustworthiness.

Xin requires one to present herself in a way that matches the way she in fact is.[5] *Xin* necessarily involves self-presentation. Self-presentation occurs when expression of oneself is made available to others. If I watch the sunset with my friend but I think that he cannot hear me, and I say, "That's beautiful," I am not presenting myself; however, if I am watching the sunset with my friend and I think that he *can* hear me, and I say, "That's beautiful," then I am presenting myself. It counts as self-presentation as long as the presenter is aware that her words or actions are made available to others. To borrow Erving Goffman's distinction, someone who is *xin* is not only aware of the expression that she "gives," she is also aware that these expressions convey certain information. In other words, she is aware of the expression that "she gives off," and that others will take these expressions to reveal or indicate something about her (Goffman 1959, 15). Self-presentation is unavoidable whenever one interacts with others. It can take the form of speech acts, actions, facial expressions, and other forms of bodily comportment such as posture, looks, gestures, demeanor, tone of voice.[6]

Since *xin* necessarily involves self-presentation, there must also be someone who the presenter thinks will receive her self-presentation. By the presenter's lights, they are her audience. It is possible they are not, in fact, her audience (e.g., they have not paid attention to what she said). To see someone as one's audience is not the same as seeing someone as a trustor. A trustor is necessarily an audience, but an audience is not necessarily a trustor. Suppose I order a vegetarian meal on a plane and I am aware that the passenger sitting next to me might think I am a vegetarian. In this case, I see the passenger sitting next to me as my audience or potential audience, but not my trustor. I do not think that she depends on me or makes any demands of me, but I think she receives or might receive my self-presentation in a certain way.

The way in which a self-presentation is received depends on a range of factors, from the context to the receiver's expectations. From the perspective of someone who is *xin*, she reasonably expects that her self-presentation will be received positively or that the withholding of a certain self-presentation will lead to a positive reception. By "positive reception," I mean that the audience will come to regard or relate to the presenter in a positive way. It could be that the audience comes to depend on the presenter in some way. It could also be that the audience makes herself dependable for the presenter.

Since *xin* requires one to form reasonable expectations of her self-presentation, one who is *xin* is necessarily a competent communicator and is able to form reasonable expectations of how her self-presentation might be received. Hence, one who is unable to form reasonable expectations—such as a young child, or someone who finds herself with a group of beings who have completely different psychologies or cultural practices that she is unable to comprehend and so cannot form expectations about—is not capable of being *xin*. That the expectation has to be reasonable rules out cases where the presenter's self-presentation is received in a way that differs drastically from what she can reasonably expect. If I use a blue pen to write a memo and my colleague takes me to mean that I am taking a progressive political stance and comes to like me, but there is no context for me to reasonably expect this favorable uptake, then I cannot be faulted for not being *xin*.

It should be clarified that a person who is *xin* is not necessarily overly concerned with how others view her. Self-presentation is different from self-promotion. Sometimes, being *xin* will require a person to correct others' positive views of her. One who is *xin* does have some reasonable expectations about how their audience will receive their self-presentation and is sensitive to others' views. However, this does not amount to anything like mindreading or manipulation. It only requires a level of sensitivity to others' views that does not exceed what is required of competent communicators in everyday social interactions. A competent communicator who is capable of communicating with others, verbally or nonverbally, should have some reasonable expectations about how her words or actions will be taken by the audience. *Xin* requires the presenter to be sensitive to what her self-presentation communicates in the manner Bernard Williams would call "informatively."[7] This level of sensitivity is required of an average competent social agent who is able to communicate informatively.

One who is *xin* is also not necessarily overly self-conscious. If "self-consciousness" means something like being uncomfortable or nervous with the way one appears to others, then one who is *xin* is not self-conscious in this sense. As discussed above, one who is *xin* is not concerned with whether others like her. *Xin* also does not require one to self-monitor when she presents herself. There might be situations where one has to self-consciously present oneself as *x* when one is in fact *x*. For example, someone in a cultural context in which nodding one's head down means "Yes" might move to a different cultural context where shaking one's head side-to-side means "Yes." Here she has to self-consciously shake her head to mean "Yes." Once she has learned and gotten used to communicating that she agrees with something by shaking her head, she will not need to constantly monitor her presentation at this higher-order level.[8] Hence, a competent communicator will not need to be always self-monitoring when she presents herself.

ZHONG 忠

The term "zhong" is often translated as "loyal" or "loyalty" in English-language studies. This is somewhat misleading because the connotation of loyalty was only acquired much later. It is thus anachronistic to understand *zhong* in the early Confucian texts as loyalty.[9] Scholars who are sensitive to the different early meaning of *zhong* translate the term as "doing one's best" (see Lau 2002, xvi, note 6) and "wholeheartedly devoted" (see Ni 2017). In the early texts, *zhong* is frequently related to speech. For example, in about a third of the passages in the *Analects* where *zhong* appears, *zhong* concerns speech and offering advice to others (see *Analects* 12.23, 14.7, 15.6, 16.10).

Zhong is also not restricted to any hierarchical or special relationship. In the *Analects*, there is one passage that says that the ministers should serve the lord with *zhong* and another passage that describes a minister as *zhong* (*Analects* 3.19, 5.19). But even in these two cases, it is not clear that *zhong* is an attitude that someone in a lower hierarchical position should assume toward those who are superior. In other passages, such as *Analects* 13.19 and 1.4, it is said that one has to be *zhong* in interacting with people (*ren* 人) in general.

Here, I will focus on discussing *zhong* as a state of mind that one is in when one interacts with others in the context of offering advice to them. One who is *zhong* is someone who would offer advice or strategic plans for others; moreover, she will offer whatever advice she sincerely believes is good for them, even if the consequence of doing so is costly to herself. In a state of *zhong*, one's respect for one's advisees' epistemic positions is tied to one's concern for their goals. One who is *zhong* might give what is in fact bad advice but, from the perspective of one who is *zhong*, she has done her best to offer the best advice possible to her advisee. In *Analects* 5.19, we see an example of a minister's *zhong* advice leading to his removal from office; this however does not deter him from saying what he thinks is the right way to safeguard the interests of the state. In this chapter, I will only focus on how *zhong* requires one to endeavor to put one's advisees in a better epistemic position.

Zhong requires more than just honest opinion. One who is *zhong* does not simply report one's true beliefs to the recipient. Imagine if a friend asks me if she should accept a job offer that comes with a higher salary, and without asking for more information I suggest that she accepts the job. I could be very honest and sincerely believe that accepting a job with a higher pay is good for her. But I will not count as being *zhong* in this case because I have not bothered to learn about and take into consideration other factors that will allow for her to make an informed decision, such as whether she likes her existing job or the location of the new job. One who is *zhong* has to make the effort to work out and take into account the various factors at play and to think carefully about what is good for the recipient.

Recall that *zhong* is not directed only at those who stand in a hierarchical or special relationship to the one who is *zhong*. Although *zhong* can be directed toward people in general, in practice, the circumstances that call for *zhong* are more likely to be those that involve people with whom one is in some kind of special relationship. Suppose I were approached by a stranger on the street who happens to ask me for advice on whether she should quit her job: I am not in a position to give advice because I do not think that I am able to put her in a better epistemic position. In order to be positioned to give *zhong* advice, one must have adequate knowledge of the other person, the circumstances she is in, and the different factors at play.

Although the circumstances that call for *zhong* usually involve special relationships, it is not only in special relationships that one can be *zhong*. The regard for others' epistemic positions shown in a state of *zhong* is not further defined in terms of a regard for something that is "mine." A person who is *zhong* will not let any consideration pertaining to herself affect her judgment of what really is good for others. It is precisely because *zhong* does not focus on the "mine" component that it also extends to non-special relationships. There is not necessarily a specific individual that is holding her in the state of *zhong*. A person who is *zhong* holds herself responsible for offering good advice and does not require a mutual acknowledgment of her obligation to do so.

CHENG 誠

Cheng 誠 is usually translated as "true to oneself" (Lau 2003, 82), "integrity" (Hutton 2014, 19), or "sincerity" (Chan 1963, 108). Compared with *xin* and *zhong*, *cheng* is rarely discussed as an ethical attribute in the early texts. In texts before the *Mencius*, the term *cheng* is often used as an adverb to mean "indeed" or "wholly." Since the *Mencius*, we see more discussions of *cheng* as an ethical state or an attribute (e.g., *Mencius* 4A:12, 5A:2; *Xunzi* 3, 16).[10] However, compared with the extensive discussion of *cheng* in the Song-Ming period, the early Confucian discussion of this concept is still nascent and vague.[11] Although discussions of *cheng* are relatively scant, there are two conspicuous ideas about *cheng* that are discussed in the early texts and which are relevant to our understanding of *xin* and *zhong*.

One idea is that, if there is *cheng* within the person, there will be a noticeable manifestation of this that can be observed from the outside.[12] If one likes *p*, it will be noticeable from the outside that one likes *p*, for example, from her actions, countenance, and posture. Likewise, if one dislikes *q*, this will be noticeable from the outside. A second idea is that *cheng* is an ideal state of the body (*shen* 身) and the heart/mind. The earlier discussions of *cheng* often concern whether one's body is *cheng* (see *Mencius* 4A:12, 7A:4).[13] While there are discussions about the importance of making one's thoughts (*yi* 意) *cheng*,[14] the idea that one's body has to be *cheng* seems more prevalent in the early Confucian texts. In the context of such usages, the term *shen* does not only refer to the physical body but to the person as a whole, including their thoughts, desires, dispositions, and actions. These two ideas altogether suggest that *cheng* is the state of being devoid of conflicts.[15] While the first idea is concerned with the absence of inner and outer conflicts, the second idea further suggests that one who is *cheng* does not have any inner conflicts.

The requirement that there is no inner-outer conflict is quite straightforward. One who is *cheng* does not present herself as being in a certain state, for example, believing, desiring, or wishing that p when in fact she believes, desires, or wishes that not-p. However, even if one does not intentionally deceive or mislead her audience, in cases where one has conflicting beliefs, desires, or wishes it is not clear whether this will count as insincerity.[16] For example, suppose I consciously believe that my sister loves me, and I tell my friend that my sister loves me. However, further suppose that I have an unconscious belief that my sister does not love me. In such a case, although there is no discrepancy between what I believe that I believe and what I assert, there is still a discrepancy between what I unconsciously believe and what I assert.[17] Or, for example, suppose I desire to stay at home and I also desire to meet up with my friend. The desire to stay at home could be unconscious, or I could be vaguely aware that I also desire to stay at home, or I could be fully aware of a faint desire to stay at home. In any case, I deliberate about what I should do and decide to meet up with my friend. Although there is no discrepancy between my action and my desire to meet up with my friend, it may still be said that there is a discrepancy between my action and my other desire to stay at home. If we go by the inner-outer discrepancy alone, it is difficult to assess whether these cases count as sincere. In the contemporary literature, it has been suggested that even though these cases are not sincere, they are also not insincere (see Chan and Kahane 2011). Putting terminology aside, on the Confucian view, the agents in these discrepant cases are not *cheng*. This is because *cheng* has the more demanding requirement that one is not in conflict, that is, one is not in any states that might result in a conflict between internal states or between internal states and actions.

Even if we assume that it is theoretically possible for one to have contradictory beliefs or conflicting motivations, one who is *cheng* does not have contradictory beliefs nor conflicting motivations. Hence, one who is *cheng* will not encounter scenarios where her actions and words match with some of her mental states but not others. This explains why the early Confucians think that one who is *cheng* internally will necessarily manifest this externally. When one who is *cheng* believes that p, she wholeheartedly believes p, meaning there is no other state that conflicts with the state of believing p. Believing not-p, for example, is a state that conflicts with believing p. Believing that one believes not-p is also a state that conflicts with one's believing p. Although the contents of the belief in the second-order state are different from those in the first-order state, it is still a conflict in the sense that both the first-order state and the second-order state could conflict in motivating one's actions. Even if the belief that p does not necessarily turn up in one's consciousness, it is possible that one will still act in a way that is motivated by the belief that p. However, if one *wholeheartedly* believes that p, there will never arise a situation where one's action is motivated by another conflicting state.[18] And if the belief that *p* turns up in one's consciousness, a situation will not arise where there is another conflicting second-order belief nor another conflicting first-order belief that is not intimated.

Cheng is a state that grounds both *xin* and *zhong*. With regard to *xin*, although *xin* does not require one to be self-aware all the time, being self-aware can help one to be more *xin*. Suppose that one likes *x* and one is aware that one likes *x*: one will be able to tell others that one likes *x* in a *xin* manner. However, when there is a discrepancy between one's self-presentation and the way one is, it is difficult to be *xin*. Assuming there is a limit to self-awareness, there might be situations in which we sincerely believe that we are *x* and present ourselves as *x*, but are not *x*. It might be thought that one is normally aware of most of one's own mental states and that it is only in some special domain or cases that we could be self-deceived or wrong about our beliefs. Such situations might be remedied, for example, by accepting what our therapist told us about ourselves. Assuming what the therapist told us is true and we present ourselves as being that way, then we would still be *xin*.

Nonetheless, there are many states that are only accessible from, or at least vividly present to, a first-person standpoint. Our everyday exchanges with people are full of small moments where we present ourselves. For example, when my friend asks me if I would like to go have coffee with her, I do not have the time to consider evidence as to whether I would like to do so. If I have conflicting desires, no matter what my self-presentation is, I will not be *xin*. But if I am *cheng*, even if I am not self-aware, I will still be *xin* in my self-presentation. The limits of self-awareness alone do not prevent one from being *xin*: someone might lack self-knowledge that she is *x* but still be *xin* as long as she is in fact *x*. However, conflicting inner states will prevent one from being *xin*. If someone is not-*y*, even if she consciously believes that she is *y* and presents herself as *y*, she will not be *xin*.

With regard to *zhong*, *cheng* is necessary to ensure the unity of motivation. One who is *zhong* has to offer advice that looks out for the interests of the recipient of that advice. It is possible for a person to misjudge a situation and offer bad advice to others, but at least from her point of view, her advice is what she sincerely believes will improve the advisee's epistemic position. Bad advice alone does not prevent one from being *zhong*, but advice that does not respect the epistemic limitations of advisees will undermine *zhong*. For example, suppose both my friend and I want to apply for the same job and that it is in fact not good for her to apply for this job. I advise my friend not to apply for this job. While my advice in fact benefits her, whether this is a piece of *zhong* advice depends on what motivates me to offer the advice. I would have failed to be *zhong* if my advice is partly motivated by my desire to eliminate her as a potential rival in the pool of applicants. Even if my advice turns out to be actually beneficial to her, and even if no one, including myself, knows that I have factored in my own selfish interests in offering advice to her, I would still have failed to be *zhong*.

In order to be *zhong*, one cannot let the slightest self-interest affect one's way of offering advice. This is particularly challenging in special relationships when the interests of both parties are intertwined. It is both practically and epistemically more difficult to separate considerations of what is good for others from considerations of what is good for oneself. Sometimes considerations creep in without the subject's awareness. A supervisor might offer what is in fact good advice to her student, but it makes a difference to whether the advice is *zhong* if the supervisor, in offering the advice, only has the student's interest in mind or whether she also has her own interest in mind. The interests in special relationships are so tightly connected that it is epistemically challenging to separate and differentiate considerations of the two.

This does not mean that one who is *zhong* has no self-respect or does not take care of herself. It just means that when offering *zhong* advice to others, the focus of one who is *zhong* is on others and not on oneself. For example, when a wife has a job offer and asks for her husband's opinion on whether she should accept the job, the *zhong* husband's focus is on what is good for his wife. And in considering her circumstances, it is inevitable that he will have to consider how accepting this job affects her family and her relationships, all these with him being part of that picture. In considering his wife's circumstances, the husband's own interest is a factor because their interests are bound together in an intimate relationship. Although their interests are bound together, it is still psychologically possible for the husband to offer advice in a way that is motivated by his respect for his wife's epistemic position instead of a concern for what is good for himself.

What grounds the state of *zhong* is not knowledge of what is in fact good for the recipient, for even if one is mistaken, it could still be the case that one is *zhong*, as long as one has done one's due diligence and is sincerely looking out for one's advisees. What grounds *zhong* is being in a state of *cheng*. When one is *cheng*, one is in a state that is devoid of inner conflicts. Even if a person cannot consciously discriminate between her own interests and the recipient's interests when the two are intimately bound, her considerations arise from a psychological stance that respects the epistemic positions of others.

CHARACTERISTICS OF THE CONFUCIAN CONCEPTION OF TRUSTWORTHINESS

Understood together, the early Confucian concepts *xin*, *zhong*, and *cheng* approximate what we nowadays mean by "trustworthiness," broadly construed. In being *xin*, *zhong*, and *cheng*, one is reliable, dependable, and worthy of trust. However, these three concepts alone do not neatly map onto trustworthiness because our discussion has not exhausted other concepts in the cluster, such as *jing* 敬 (reverence) and *shen qi du* 慎其獨 (vigilance). Nonetheless, these three concepts should give us substantial material to work with. In the following, I will highlight three related characteristics of the Confucian conception of trustworthiness.[19]

A Social Stance

Contemporary discussions of trustworthiness tend to center either on the trustor's dependency or expectations, or the trusted person's commitments or responsiveness to the trustor. What is common across these accounts of trustworthiness is that they focus either on the side of the trustor or on the side of the trusted person.[20] We may be able to fit the Confucian account into this framework. We may say that *cheng* focuses on the trusted person's commitments and wholeheartedness and *zhong* and *xin* focus on how the trusted person responds to the trustor's actual or potential dependency. But this way of fitting the Confucian conception into the existing framework risks distorting and overlooking the distinguishing features of the Confucian account.

Confucians are particularly sensitive to the connectedness of people in a society and think that we have to be trustworthy in our words and actions even if a trustor-trusted relationship is not yet formed, for our words and actions will have an impact on other people. Imagine in my first conversation with the barista at a cafe, I present myself as a cat lover. At the point of self-presentation, the barista hardly knows me and is not a trustor yet. But on the basis of that self-presentation, she becomes fond of me because she also likes cats. She becomes always keen to help me and gives me an extra piece of chocolate when I order coffee. The positive way in which she relates to me is in part, even if it is a very small part, due to her seeing me also as a cat lover. Or imagine that an acquaintance posts a question on social media about whether she should travel overseas during the pandemic. The question is not directed to me and there is no obligation for me to answer it. In this situation, she is not yet a trustor asking my advice and I am not a trusted person from whom she is soliciting advice. But if I do want to answer her question in a way that qualifies as what Confucians would regard as trustworthy, I will have to take her circumstances into account and offer advice that I think is good for her. If I think I do not know her circumstances well enough, then I have to be mindful that even if I answer her question, it is not a trustworthy answer. Even though my audience and I are not yet in a trustor-trusted relationship in the above cases, nor in any other special relationship, I still stand in a relation to them in the sense that my actions and advice could have an impact on them given that they are also fellow members of society.

What is characteristic about the Confucian account is that it does not require the presence of a trustor for one to be trustworthy. The state of trustworthiness is not grounded in the subject seeing a relationship between a trustor and a trusted person. One who is trustworthy is not necessarily responding to a specific person who makes certain demands or has certain expectations of, or dependencies on, her. Rather, the state of trustworthiness is grounded in the subject that her actions and words will have an impact on the people she interacts with in her society. It is not merely a transactional or relational perspective in the sense that there is another side demanding something and the trustworthy person's side providing something. The trustworthy person adopts a social perspective in the sense that they see other fellow members of society as having claims to the truth and as deserving to be put into the best epistemic position to make informed decisions about what is good for them. Without a trustor, the trustworthy person will still hold herself responsible, not because she is morally self-indulgent and believes she has to be good for her own sake, but because she has concern or respect for other members of society. I will discuss this point further in the section below. Here, the point worth noting is that being trustworthy is neither merely other-regarding nor merely self-regarding. Rather, it requires the trustworthy person to adopt a social stance.[21] Her being trustworthy is not motivated by considerations such as "I have to respond to my trustor" or "I can't be the kind of person who is not trustworthy." It is in virtue of her being a member of society that she holds herself accountable to her fellow members of society.

The trustworthy person does not necessarily have any specific commitments and obligations. What trustworthiness requires is a proactive stance that is prepared to undertake commitments and obligations. This proactive stance is grounded in the relation we stand to other members of a society. This relation is generic. It includes special relationships but is not limited to these. Although one does not stand in a special relationship to a stranger in the park, one still stands in a relation to them in virtue of being members of a society: whether one is talking too loudly or running too fast will impact the stranger. The specific content of these commitments and obligations that a trustworthy person is prepared to undertake is open-ended and ever-changing, depending on the people one comes into contact with and the relations that one stands in with regard to them.

Epistemic Demandingness and Epistemic Load-Sharing

On the Confucian account, being a trustworthy person is epistemically demanding. Since the trustworthy person is sensitive to her audience's limited epistemic access, she takes on the task of doing some of the epistemic work for them. She has to know her own commitments, abilities, and the background of shared information and expectations so that she can present herself accurately to her audience.[22] This spares the audience some extra epistemic work. In our everyday lives, we are likely to feel offended if someone said they needed to do a background check on us before they befriended us. We do not want to be checked; we want to be trusted. But from the other perspective, if we are a black box, on what basis do they get to know us and trust us? One way to navigate these extremes is for a trustworthy person to provide relevantly true and reliable information about herself for her audience members. It is primarily through what is publicly available—our words, actions, bodily comportment, and so on—that others gather evidence and come to form beliefs about us and decide how they want to relate to us. Thus, the more one's words and actions accurately reflect who one is, including one's values, preferences, concerns, dispositions, motives, desires, and beliefs, the more reliable the information one is providing to others about themselves so that others can make informed judgments and decisions about how they want to relate to her.

The trustworthy person also needs to do her best to understand her audience's circumstances and deliberate about what is good for her. It is not sufficient for her to candidly speak her mind; she has to carefully consider different factors at play, put herself into the other person's shoes, and look out for them. If one is epistemically biased, it will greatly undermine one's ability to be trustworthy in the Confucian sense. For example, suppose a student asks me for advice on what graduate programs she should apply to. I might know the philosophy programs better than the other ones and I personally might want more students to study philosophy, but it will not be trustworthy of me to simply advise her to study philosophy if I just fall back on what I already know about philosophy programs and my desire to see more students studying philosophy without paying attention to her abilities, interests, and circumstances. Rather, I will need to do the work and learn more about her interests and abilities, and the structure of other programs that might suit her.

Since being trustworthy is epistemically demanding, sometimes it requires one not to offer any advice. Being trustworthy does not mean that we have to do unlimited epistemic work for others. There is a reasonable limit somewhere and that limit might be different in different contexts, depending on the context and the commitments we have undertaken. Suppose someone approaches me for legal advice. No matter how much I would like to help her, I would need to decline because I do not believe that I am capable of offering advice that is good for her. The Confucian thinkers seem to agree that we have to share and help reduce others' epistemic workloads, but it does not mean we have to do all the epistemic work for them.

It is also worth noting that it will be very difficult for those who are systemically disadvantaged, such as women in ancient societies, minority groups in systemically oppressive environments, and people who are brainwashed, to be trustworthy in the Confucian sense because they have been subjected to hostile conditions that prevent them from forming reasonable social expectations and learning about relevant facts that can enable them to be good at providing reliable information. The cost for them to communicate accurately might be unreasonably high, or they might lack access to information that enables them to be good information providers. This also suggests the importance of having a society that creates enabling conditions for one to be trustworthy.

Epistemic Empowerment and Epistemic Respect

Another characteristic of the Confucian conception of trustworthiness is that the trustworthy person empowers the epistemic position of her interlocutors. This requires the trustworthy person to proactively show respect for others instead of merely responding to their expectations and dependencies. Before we enter a trustor-trusted relationship, the trustworthy person will do her due diligence to make sure that others' trust is not misplaced. To do so, the trustworthy person has to be sensitive to other people's limited epistemic access to her state of mind, her abilities, and her history. However, sensitivity to others' epistemic limits, without respect and concern, could easily slide into manipulation. One can easily take advantage of others' limited access and use it to benefit oneself. A manipulator withholds what she takes to be crucial information, and in doing so single-handedly steers her relationship with her audience in a direction that she herself welcomes.

Unlike manipulators, the trustworthy person's sensitivity to others' limited epistemic access is tied to her respect and concern for them. She takes active steps to ensure that others are not disadvantaged by the limits of their epistemic position. The trustworthy person empowers the audience by helping them to get in a better epistemic position to make decisions, including decisions about how they want to relate to her. The trustworthy person does not take advantage of others' epistemic limitations to shape their views of her or steer the way they relate to her. Even though she knows quite well that presenting herself accurately might sometimes result in a less favorable view of her, or that sometimes certain advice might upset people, she would still choose being trustworthy over being liked. This psychological state takes effort to sustain and likely runs against our natural inclinations. What motivates the trustworthy person to engage in such an effortful psychological state is her respect for other people's claim to the truth and a concern for others' well-being.

As discussed above, the trustworthy person does not require a trustor to hold her responsible. The trustworthy person holds herself responsible and takes active steps to signal herself accurately, preempting any unwarranted dependency on her. She does not let herself off the hook too easily when there is a misunderstanding on the audience's part. For example, when I tell my colleagues that I am a vegetarian, I am also mindful that in my particular context, people normally assume that one is a vegetarian for ethical reasons and come to form more positive views of the vegetarian. If I were trustworthy, I should quickly correct that possible positive reception and add that I am a vegetarian for health reasons. Suppose I never clarified that I am vegetarian for health reasons and my colleagues were later surprised to find out that I was not a vegetarian for ethical reasons. I could have said something like "I never said I am a vegetarian for ethical reasons." By leaving things vague, I leave some ways to get off the hook. But if I am in a position to reasonably expect that others will assume that I am a vegetarian for ethical reasons, I have to clarify that I am not in order to preempt others relating to me in a way they would not have had they learned my actual reasons.

CHALLENGES TO THE CONFUCIAN CONCEPTION OF TRUSTWORTHINESS

I will close with two potential worries about the Confucian conception of trustworthiness. First, one may question the relevance of the Confucian conception for contemporary societies. Being trustworthy hinges on one's ability to form reasonable expectations about such things as audience uptake of one's self-presentation and when advice would be appropriate. These are largely fixed by social and cultural norms. In a society in which such norms are clear, it is much easier for one to gauge expectations. The early Confucians, for example, were in a society that was governed by a set of well-defined and stable roles, ritual practices, norms, and codes of behavior. In that kind of society, even wearing a certain color could be a clear indication to others of what state one is in. However, such clear norms and expectations are dissolving in contemporary societies. Wearing a maroon outfit to a wedding no longer signals anything significant, and wearing a ring on one's fourth finger does not necessarily signal that one is married. In many of our contemporary societies, our general cultural norms and expectations tend to be more fluid and ambiguous. Compared with the ancient Confucian society, one is now more likely to encounter situations where the relevant norms in a specific domain are ambiguous. One might be more uncertain about others' perspectives or easily mistake their expectations. And in societies that value pluralism and diversity, it is quite likely that the Confucian conception of trustworthiness will lose some of its desirability as a trait, being replaced instead by traits such as tolerance and acceptance.[23]

Still, although we might have relatively fewer well-defined and stable norms and expectations now compared to Confucius's time, there still exist enabling social conditions for trustworthiness. Some implicatures and conventions will still be in place to enable and govern social interactions. One who is trustworthy can also offset uncertainties and potential misunderstanding in some other ways by being more attentive to the particularities of her audience or by relying more on explicit speech acts than behavioral signals in her self-presentation. For example, a mother-in-law can ask her son-in-law whether he needs some advice on taking care of his baby instead of assuming that he needs advice.[24] On the flip side, the Confucian conception of trustworthiness also reminds us of the value of ritual. Ritual can help to facilitate social interactions by marking out to social members general expectations and common ground so that people will not need to engage in excessively explicit signaling, hedging, and guessing.

Second, one might worry that in liberal societies, we value personal freedom and choices, and we should not impose our advice on others and tell others what is good for them. Rather, we should regard others as autonomous individuals capable of making their own decisions and choices. However, the Confucian conception of trustworthiness is compatible with this line of thought. To be trustworthy is not to be paternalistic nor manipulative. The trustworthy person does not make decisions for others nor expect others to follow her advice. Confucius, for example, explicitly says that one should not take any offence if their advice is not taken and that one should know when to stop if their advice is not being listened to. One should observe basic etiquette and behave with decorum when one offers advice, and one should not insist on advising when one is not being listened to (*Analects* 12.23). Confucius does not encourage one to be presumptuous.

The role of the trustworthy person is to provide as much relevant, reliable information as possible to others so that her audience is in a better epistemic position to make informed decisions. As long as we remain epistemically limited, we have to depend on others in order to learn about the world. There are a vast number of things with which we do not have direct acquaintance. We still have to turn to those we trust for advice. They might be more knowledgeable than us in a particular domain; they might be able to see things that are blind spots for us; they might put together things we already know in different ways by drawing different inferences. As long as we have to depend on the point of view of others, the Confucian conception of trustworthiness will still be relevant. It requires the trustworthy person to be sensitive to her audience's limited epistemic access to information. In this way, the trustworthy person empowers her audience by helping them get to what is true and what is good for them.[25]

NOTES

1. These classical texts will be cited by title and section number, in keeping with common practice. Citing by section number will allow readers to find the corresponding passage both in the original Chinese texts and across multiple translations.

2. See *Analects* 1.4, 1.8. 5.28, 7.25, 9.25, 12.10, 15.6.

3. The link between *xin* and *cheng* becomes more conspicuous in the *Liji* and even more so in Zhu Xi's commentaries on the early texts.

4. On the basis of these textual observations, Cecilia Wee, for example, argues that *xin* is primarily concerned with verbal commitments (see Wee 2011).

5. See Sung (2020) for a more detailed analysis of *xin*.

6. Thanks to Ian James Kidd for alerting me to this point. Hagop Sarkissian makes a similar point about how "one's *presence* (including not just one's clothing but one's posture, tone and volume of voice, countenance, demeanor, and other factors that are the focus of others' attention and part of others' perceptual field) is taken to be a source of influence on one's immediate environment, and therefore a site of scrutiny" (Sarkissian 2017, 496–97). In the article, Sarkissian is making a more general point about how one's self-presentation can influence others and may be partly responsible for others' behavior. I agree with Sarkissian on this. Here, I am making a more specific point that one has to be mindful of whether there is a match between one's self-presentation and the way one is.

7. This is like Williams's point that we normally do not demand that a speaker merely tell the truth. If I tell my colleague "Someone's been opening your mail" when in fact it is me who opens her mail, I should reasonably expect that what I said will mislead my colleague to think that I am not the one who opens her mail (see Williams 2002, 96–107).

8. See Olberding (2016, 422–46), for further discussion on the role of etiquette in helping one develop habits that can do away with self-conscious monitoring but remain attentive to others.

9. See Sung (2017) for discussion of early Confucian conception of *zhong*.

10. The character "cheng" is used both as an adjective and sometimes as a verb when discussed in as an ethical state or attribute.

11. In the *Mencius*, the *Xunzi*, and the *Liji*, we see that *cheng* is related to being enlightened about what is good (*ming* 明). It is possible that the early thinkers disagree about the nature of the relation between *cheng* and *ming* and which concept is more fundamental. Here I will bracket the issue about *cheng* and *ming*.

12. Shun (2008) contains a detailed textual analysis of *cheng* and concepts related to *cheng*.

13. See also the "Zhongyong" chapter of the *Liji*.

14. See the "Daxue" chapter of the *Liji*.

15. Shun (2008, 265) notes that *cheng* "involves the absence of any internal division or any discrepancy between one's outward behavior and inner dispositions." I elaborate on this idea and interpret the absence of discrepancy as not limited to that between inner disposition and outward behavior but also to discrepancies within oneself.

16. What I mean by wholehearted here is similar to what Harry Frankfurt (1987) means by "wholeheartedness." While Frankfurt's account is mainly concerned with the absence of the conflict between desires, *cheng* is a broader notion that concerns the absence of conflicting inner states generally and that of conflicting inner and outer states.

17. There can also be cases where there is a discrepancy between what I consciously believe and what I assert but no discrepancy between what I unconsciously believe and what I assert. See, for example, Chan and Kahane (2011) for a variation of Peacocke's example discussed in note 18.

18. For example, Christopher Peacocke's case of someone asserting that overseas and local graduates are equally good but favoring local graduates in making hiring decisions (Peacocke 1998, 90).

19. Note that when I speak of "a trustworthy person," I mean being trustworthy in a particular context.

20. Consider some examples from the contemporary literature. Russell Hardin (1996) argues that the trustworthy person is someone who does what the trustor wants them to do. Paul Faulkner (2011) argues that the trustworthy one is someone who sees the trustor's depending on her φ-ing as a reason to φ and is moved to φ for this reason. Karen Jones (2012) argues that the richly trustworthy person has to take the trustor's counting on her to be a compelling reason for acting as counted on. Stephen Wright (2010) argues that the trustworthy person acknowledges the value of trusting relationships and rationally decides how to act. And Katherine Hawley (2019) argues that to be trustworthy is to have a commitment to act accordingly or to tell the truth.

21. I am not especially committed to the expression "social stance." I use it tentatively to avoid the dichotomy that being trustworthy is exclusively either self-regarding or other-regarding.

22. See also Hawley (2019), Chapter 5, for a discussion of the importance of knowing our commitments and competencies.

23. I am grateful to Ian James Kidd and Graham Parkes for this point.

24. Hawley (2019, 128) makes a similar point that a trustworthy person has to be explicit about her commitments and provides many helpful examples that are also relevant to my point here. Hawley's examples concern communicating one's commitments. My point here is a more general one, which is not restricted to commitments.

25. This project is supported by MOE Tier 1 RG139/19 (NS). I am grateful in particular to Nicolas Bommarito, Youngsun Back, Amber Carpenter, Sin Yee Chan, Chung-yi Cheng, David Collins, Andrew Forcehimes, Ian James Kidd, JeeLoo Liu, Kwong-loi Shun, and Matthew D. Walker.

REFERENCES

Ames, Roger, and Henry Rosemont, Jr. 1998. *The Analects of Confucius: A Philosophical Translation*. New York: Random House.

Chan, Timothy, and Guy Kahane. 2011. "The Trouble with Being Sincere." *Canadian Journal of Philosophy* 41(2): 215–34.
Chan, Wing-Tsit. 1963. *A Source Book in Chinese Philosophy*. Princeton: Princeton University Press.
Faulkner, Paul. 2011. *Knowledge on Trust*. Oxford: Oxford University Press.
Frankfurt, Harry. 1987. "Identification and Wholeheartedness." In *Responsibility, Character, and the Emotions: New Essays in Moral Psychology*, edited by Ferdinand Schoeman, 27–45. New York: Cambridge University Press.
Goffman, Erving. 1971 [1959]. *The Presentation of Self in Everyday Life*. Pelican Books.
Hardin, Russell. 1996. "Trustworthiness." *Ethics* 107(1): 26–42.
Hawley, Katherine. 2019. *How to be Trustworthy*. Oxford: Oxford University Press.
Jones, Karen. 2012. "Trustworthiness." *Ethics* 123(1): 61–85.
Lau, D.C., trans. 2002 [1979]. *Confucius: The Analects*. Hong Kong: The Chinese University Press.
———. 2003 [1970]. *Mencius*. London: Penguin Books.
Lau, D.C., and Chen Fong Ching, eds. 1992. *Liji Zhuzi Suoyin: A Concordance to the Liji* 禮記逐字索引. Taibei: Taiwan shangwu yinshuguan 台灣商務印書館.
Legge, James, trans. 1971. *Confucian Analects, The Great Learning, and The Doctrine of the Mean*. New York: Dover.
Ni, Peimin. 2017. *Understanding the* Analects *of Confucius: A New Translation of* Lunyu *with Annotations*. Albany: SUNY Press.
Olberding, Amy. 2016. "Etiquette: A Confucian Contribution to Moral Philosophy." *Ethics* 126: 422–46.
Peacocke, Christopher. 2000. "Conscious Attitudes, Attention, and Self-Knowledge." In C. Peacocke, *Knowing Our Own Minds*, 63–98. Oxford: Oxford University Press.
Sarkissian, Hagop. 2017. "Situationsim, Manipulation, and Objective Self-Awareness." *Ethical Theory and Moral Practice* 20: 489–503.
Shun, Kwong-loi. 2008. "Wholeness in Confucian Thought: Zhu Xi on Cheng, Zhong, Xin, and Jing." In *The Imperative of Understanding: Chinese Philosophy, Comparative Philosophy, and Onto-Hermeneutics*, edited by On-cho Ng, 261–72. New York: Global Scholarly Publications.
Slingerland, Edward. 2003. *Analects: With Selections from Traditional Commentaries*. Indianapolis: Hackett.
Sung, Winnie. 2017. "*Zhong* in the *Analects*: with Insights into Loyalty." In *Confucianism for a Changing World Cultural Order*, edited by Roger Ames and Peter Hershock, 175–96. Honolulu: University of Hawaii Press.
———. 2020. "*Xin* 信: Being Trustworthy." *International Philosophical Quarterly* 60(3): 271–86.
Waley, Arthur. 1938. *The Analects of Confucius*. London: G. Allen & Unwin Ltd. Reprinted, New York: Book of the Month Club, 1992.
Wee, Cecilia. 2011. "*Xin*, Trust, and Confucius' Ethics." *Philosophy East and West* 61: 516–33.

Williams, Bernard. 2002. *Truth and Truthfulness*. Princeton: Princeton University Press.
Wright, Stephen. 2010. "Trust and Trustworthiness." *Philosophia* 38: 615–27.
Zhu, Xi. 2005. *Sishu Zhangju Jizhu* 四書章句集注. Beijing: Zhonghu Shuju 中華書局.

Chapter 2

Aristotle on Friendship and Trust

Corinne Gartner and Wania Ahmad

Aristotle (384–322 BCE) claims that trust is one of the features required in a complete friendship (*philia*) (*Nicomachean Ethics* VIII 3 1156b27–30, VIII 4 1157a21–26), the sort of friendship that is itself necessary for and partly constitutive of happiness (*eudaimonia*). In this chapter, we explore what it means to trust a friend according to Aristotle. Examining the process by which two nascent friends come to justifiably trust each other sheds light on the sort of character that a trusted friend should possess. Aristotle emphasizes, in *Eudemian Ethics* VII 2, the time and trials involved in coming to know someone else's mental states. If we consider Aristotle's account of friendship more broadly, we might suppose that each friend must come to trust both that her apparent nascent friend has goodwill toward her and returns the genuine goodwill that she herself expresses. However, we argue that trust in complete friendship involves more than wishing the other well for their sake. In complete friendships, each friend should herself be a trustworthy person and should be trusted as such. We look to Aristotle's account of the virtue of truthfulness in *Nicomachean Ethics* IV 7, according to which the truthful person is one who represents herself accurately to others. When a decent agent comes to trust her friend, what she is rightly confident about is that the friend is who he seems to be, where that involves (a) having the loving attitudes he seems to have in relation to her, such as goodwill, and (b) being a generally decent person himself, where that centrally includes the virtue of truthfulness.[1]

In this chapter we also consider two objections to our account. First, once we build virtue into Aristotle's trust conditions, one might worry that the relevant attitude looks less like trust, which requires a degree of risk and the possibility of betrayal, and more like certainty or knowledge. Second, the virtue of truthfulness, which itself includes self-knowledge, seems to be required for complete friendship. Yet one of the valuable contributions that complete friendship makes to happiness seems to be uniquely fostering self-knowledge (*Nicomachean Ethics* IX 9). How, then, can an agent gain the self-knowledge necessary for the virtue of truthfulness without first forming a complete friendship based on their genuinely good features of character? As two decent character friends spend more time together, they come to know both each other and themselves more deeply, gaining more trust in one another, correspondingly becoming better—that is, increasingly trustworthy, virtuous people—from their mutual influence.

BACKGROUND ON ARISTOTELIAN FRIENDSHIP AND TRUST IN *NICOMACHEAN ETHICS*

Aristotle's analysis of friendship (*philia*) in *Nicomachean Ethics* VIII–IX opens with two claims that explain his inclusion of the topic in this treatise on happiness before turning to disputes about the topic. First, he states that friendship is a virtue or involves virtue (1155a3–4). Second, he asserts that it is most necessary for life (1155a5), and then goes on to justify this assertion by showing how one needs friendship at every life stage, in every material circumstance, and in our familial relationships as well as within the broader political community (1155a6–28). This opening line of argument thus demonstrates the breadth of the ancient Greek notion of *philia*; it includes the sorts of chosen relationships that we would classify as friendships but also associations between family members, fellow citizens, and even—if we take seriously Aristotle's opening remarks in *Nicomachean Ethics* VIII 1—between members of the same species (1155a18–20). Relationships of friendship thus permeate and sustain our lives.

Aristotle thinks that our happiness consists in virtuous activity (*NE* I 7 1098a16–17). Thus, to return to the first claim, friendship is a crucial topic of investigation since, if it is a virtue or is closely bound up with virtue, then it will contribute in an important way to happiness. As Aristotle goes on to establish in *Nicomachean Ethics* VIII 2–4, and in *Eudemian Ethics* VII 2, there are three different kinds of friendship, each based on a different psychological source of attraction. We can like others and become friends with them because they are pleasant, useful, or good, where the latter means the source of attraction is our friend's genuinely decent character. In every case, Aristotle emphasizes the reciprocity involved: friendship requires that each agent must share and return the other's friendly feeling, and both parties must be aware of one another's attitudes (*NE* VIII 2 1155b32–1156a5).

One might assume that in all these sorts of associations there will be some degree of trust or confidence in the friend, even if it is attenuated or quite domain restricted (e.g., one friend trusts the other to vote a certain way in a legislative meeting). While Aristotle makes passing remarks about trust in other contexts,[2] his most explicit comments about trust occur in his characterization of the best form of friendship, the complete friendship between two decent individuals, the sort of friendship that is or involves virtue. He explains that these complete friendships are uncommon and take time to develop, for "they cannot accept each other or be friends until each appears lovable to the other and gains the other's trust" (*NE* VIII 3 1156b28–29),[3] which suggests that trust is an essential feature in the highest form of friendship. According to Aristotle, these complete friendships are the only sort that are immune to slander, and in the next clause he maintains that trust is a necessary feature of character-based friendships alone (VIII 4 1157a20–25). In a later passage, he continues to contrast the pleasure- and utility-based forms of friendship with the friendship of virtue, again relying on the point that the latter form is enduring and immune to slander (VIII 6 1158b9–11). The kind of trust with which we are concerned, then, is the abiding, rationally justified trust between decent agents engaged in the best form of friendship, the sort of friendship that is necessary for and partly constitutive of a happy life.

Given the centrality of trust to this valuable type of friendship, one might expect Aristotle to say more about it. To be sure, he considers a puzzle about dissolving friendships in *Nicomachean Ethics* IX 3, to which we will return below. In the context of that puzzle, he countenances the possibility of being deceived by the (supposed) friend who misrepresented her grounds for attraction. But aside from this puzzle, occasional comments about the stability—and thus the enduring trust—that characterizes complete friendships, and a few explicit comments about the necessity and uniqueness of trust in character-based cases of friendship between virtuous agents, trust does not feature prominently in the Nicomachean account. Perhaps this is because there is nothing particularly controversial about the widely endorsed commonsense Greek view—a view that we still share today—that trust is crucial to friendship. Though it is noteworthy that in another ethical treatise, *Eudemian Ethics*, Aristotle shows greater concern with the difficulty of coming to trust a potential or nascent friend.

A THEOGNIS-INSPIRED PUZZLE IN *EUDEMIAN ETHICS*: THE TIME AND TRIALS REQUIRED FOR TRUSTING A FRIEND

We can get clearer on Aristotle's conception of trust in the context of friendship if we turn to *Eudemian Ethics* VII 1, which begins, like the Nicomachean account of friendship, with Aristotle surveying consensus views and introducing puzzles. The content of the two opening chapters diverges at several places, and the Eudemian version contains a more extended discussion of the puzzles, including some that are not in the Nicomachean version. Exactly how these two texts relate is outside the scope of our project to discuss, but drawing on material from both sources will help to provide a fuller picture.[4] In developing and resolving these puzzles, Aristotle's method aims to take into consideration widely held beliefs, commitments that come from his intellectual predecessors, and our observations, ensuring that his own analysis can in some way accommodate all these sources of evidence. He tries to locate the kernel of truth in the seemingly disparate views, hybridizing them where possible, or selecting a middle-ground option and explaining where the other views went astray (*EE* VII 2 1235b13–18).

Our interest is in the set of disputed views with which Aristotle concludes the first chapter. At *Eudemian Ethics* VII 1 1235b6–12, he reports:

> Moreover, some people think that it is easy to acquire a friend, while others think that the opportunity to recognize a friend is very rare and is impossible unless misfortune comes along, on the grounds that everyone wants to appear to be a friend to those who are doing well. And others think we shouldn't even put our trust in those who stand by others amidst misfortunes, on the grounds that they are deceivers who are just pretending: by associating with the unfortunate, they aim to acquire their friendship when they recover their fortunes.[5]

He sketches three positions that one might adopt toward the ease with which one can become a friend, which requires awareness that another is a friend: (1) becoming friends is easy; (2) becoming friends is difficult and misfortune is a revealing test; or (3) even misfortune is not sufficient for discernment, and so, presumably, becoming friends—or, at least the sort of friend who rightly trusts—is impossible. While Aristotle frames the first disputed position in terms of the ease or difficulty of becoming friends, he connects this question with trust in articulating the third stance, indicating that what is at stake in the background is whether the two potential friends trust one other: trust is a potentially limiting factor in forming a friendship. The presentation of this puzzle thus takes it for granted that trust is necessary for friendship. That is, the puzzle concerns whether, how, and how quickly one could come to trust that another is a friend, not whether trust is an important attribute of a good friendship.

Before he proceeds to establish his own position in the second chapter, Aristotle differentiates the three kinds of friendship mentioned in the previous section. He uses this distinction of kinds of friendship between those based on pleasure, those based on utility, and those based on good character in order to address the disputes. Aristotle explains that only the primary sort of character-based friendship is stable (*bebaios*), but stability requires time because establishing trust requires time (*EE* VII 2 1237b9–13). In the friendships of pleasure and utility, stability may be lacking and distrust may arise. As in the Nicomachean account, Aristotle's emphasis on the stability of friendships of the highest kind underscores the necessity of trust in these relationships, and he explains in more detail in the Eudemian version that becoming friends requires time and trials (1237b13–1238a3; 1238a21–30). Later in the Eudemian account, when he discusses the sorts of conflicts that can arise between friends, Aristotle distinguishes between utility friendship based on legal agreement and utility friendship based on character, the latter of which he sets apart because the friends trust one another as decent people (*EE* VII 10 1242b32–1243a2). These mixed transactional cases, in which friends aim at what can be usefully gotten from one another and yet trust that they will get what they expect on account of the other's character, are the ones most likely to generate accusations (1242b37–38). It seems, then, that rationally justified trust in a friend's character is bestowed in the context of a primary friendship, and that disagreements can be avoided if the friends have taken the time to properly assess one another's characters.

The best sort of friendship is immune to slander because the friends have been tested over a long period of time in various circumstances, and so the friends would never trust the word of a slanderer over their own experience of each other (1237b23–27). Interestingly, the Eudemian account makes it even clearer that the concern about slander is not so much that the (supposed) friend might slander the decent person to others, or gossip about her behind her back, but instead about believing negative reports from others. The issue involves determining whether what she hears about the friend from others is accurate: adequate firsthand knowledge of the friend renders the agent impervious to false charges from non-friend sources. Given that friendship requires reciprocity, we can extrapolate that the friend would, similarly, not take the word of those speaking against the agent. The decent person trusts that her friend's confidence in her own good character will not easily be shaken. In *Rhetoric* II 4, enumerating all of the people toward whom we experience friendly feelings, Aristotle does make the more obvious point in passing: we feel friendly toward those who are not themselves slanderers, since, it seems, we assume they would also not slander us (1381b7–9).

In response to the puzzle about the difficulty of recognizing a friend, Aristotle defends a version of the middle option: there is no shortcut to becoming friends. The process is lengthy and difficult, insofar as it involves living with the friend (1237b34–36), testing her, sharing activities and experiences with her. Tellingly, he quotes Theognis at 1237b15–16: "You could not learn the mind of man or woman until you try it out, like a beast of burden" (*Elegies* 125–26). In the surrounding lines of verse, with which Aristotle's audience would have been familiar, Theognis writes that spotting a counterfeit man is both very hard—looks deceive—and very important (115–28). More generally, Theognis's poems display deep pessimism about trusting others and a serious fear of betrayal by a friend, and he often laments the lack of loyal friends, especially in tough circumstances (e.g., 78–80, 209, 415–16, 697–98).[6] We might suppose, then, that Aristotle was drawing on these Theognidean worries in sketching the disputed positions. As Aristotle's resolution of the puzzle proceeds, he agrees that misfortune is indeed more revealing than good fortune, since, he argues, misfortune will separate those who care more about their material resources than about the friend from those who will provide aid to the friend in her hour of need, sharing their possessions (1238a16–20).

Now, one might worry that the requisite knowledge of the other's mind is something one could only come to access once one has become a friend in the first place. The degree of commitment involved in choosing to share activities with someone in a way that "tests" them—that is, that leads to greater insight, disclosure, and intimate awareness of their mental states—might seem to presuppose friendship. Perhaps it is a feature of trust that to sow it one must bestow it. This is surely the case to a point; however, the opening formulation of the puzzle frames the potentially revealing misfortune as being that of more generic others. One might gain some insight into how the potential friend is likely to treat her during a dark time from the way he treats others in similarly tough situations. Furthermore, Aristotle's focus on the *time* involved in the process mitigates this concern. Just because two people are eager to be friends, do things for one another that manifest their attraction, and even take themselves to be friends does not mean that they are already in fact friends (1237b19–21). There is a diachronically extended process of coming to be friends that co-occurs, in the best sort of friendship, with the process of coming to trust the other person, given that the latter is necessary for the former and both come in degrees.

We might also appeal to Aristotle's opening claim from *Nicomachean Ethics* that friendship is a virtue or involves virtue (1155a3–4). Virtue, according to Aristotle, is a state of character, and states are stable and persisting, the product of a lengthy process of ethical habituation. Just as virtue arises from repeatedly performing virtuous actions over a long period of time (*NE* II 1 1103a34–b2, b21–23; II 4 1105b9–10), accompanied by increasing understanding of the right reasons for action, so too friendship, a state of character, comes to be from repeatedly expressing the attitudes and engaging in the actions of being a friend, accompanied by increasing understanding of the potential friend. So too, just as performing a few token virtuous actions is not yet sufficient for being a virtuous person, acting in ways that characterize the behavior of a friend is not yet sufficient for being a friend. Although one might need to be on the road to primary friendship in order to reasonably trust one's potential friend, this is not yet to be friends, properly speaking, and the extent of justified trust between the parties limns the extent of the primary friendship.

As we have seen, Aristotle seems more concerned in *Eudemian Ethics* with the difficulty and necessity of trusting a friend, but, as in *Nicomachean Ethics*, he does not unpack the notion of trust that is at play. Careful consideration of the way he resolves this conflict in conjunction with remarks in other parts of his discussions of friendship can help to shed light on the salient conception of trust. The way that Aristotle formulates and then treats the Theognidean dispute suggests that what matters is getting to know the mind of the friend, where that consists in part in understanding her motivations. The decent person must come to know that the potential friend likes her for her character, rather than for some ulterior motive, and returns the attraction that she herself has for the potential friend. Misfortune can be useful because it can demonstrate that the potential or apparent friend who abandons the decent person when they fall on hard times was in fact motivated to associate with them on the basis of their external goods, for example, wealth or social status. If one truly loves her friend, she will not desert her in times of trouble (*Rhetoric* II 4 1381b27). Misfortune is a test of instrumentality (*EE* VII 2 1238a15–19).

TOWARD AN ACCOUNT OF WHAT IT MEANS TO TRUST A GOOD FRIEND: GOODWILL CONSIDERED AND REJECTED

In *Nicomachean Ethics* VIII 2, Aristotle sketches how two people become friends when they both have goodwill toward one another, where that means wishing goods for the sake of the other, and both being aware of this reciprocal goodwill (1155b31–1156a5). There is considerable controversy over how to interpret these claims, since Aristotle goes on to qualify them in the very next chapter, indicating that in utility- and pleasure-based friendships, the friends wish one another well for the sake of each other's usefulness or pleasantness, respectively (1156a8–16).[7] For our purposes, it is not important to settle the debates about the presence of goodwill, or the extent of wishing goods to the friend, in these subordinate forms of friendship given our concern with the ideal form of friendship, the only form for which justified trust is necessary. In the case of the best friendships, those between decent people based on their good character, goodwill is a central defining characteristic, the one on which Aristotle relies in *Nicomachean Ethics* VIII 2 when offering a shorthand explanation of the attitude of liking or loving directed at another subject. That is, in Aristotelian terms, wishing goods to the friend for her sake is both a formal cause of friendship, since it is part of the account of the attitude of liking another subject, and an aspect of the efficient causal story about coming to be friends in the first place. We might thus be tempted to think that when the decent agent justifiably trusts her friend, what she has confidence in is precisely that the friend has genuine goodwill toward her, that the friend seeks to promote and preserve her well-being.

Trust that the potential friend wishes goods for the agent for her sake, and not for some self-serving ulterior motive, captures what seems to be at stake in the misfortune claim. One needs to know the friend's mind. If one has experienced periods of poverty, for example, she becomes confident that the friend will not only wish her well and desire her company during good times, when she is in a position to, say, pay for a nice dinner together, but also when she cannot cover a meal. The presence of goodwill toward the agent screens out those who are base, the sort of individuals who, according to Aristotle, "choose natural goods instead of their friend" and do not love people more than things (*EE* VII 2 1237b30–32). Goodwill thus seems to set an important minimum character requirement.

However, while mutual and mutually reciprocated wishing of goods for the sake of the other is certainly a necessary part of what one trusts when one rightly trusts a friend, it is not sufficient. First, we saw in the previous section that Aristotle thinks one must live with a nascent friend, engaging in joint activities, in order to get to know her character (1237b35–36). Living together is a technical concept for Aristotle. It does not consist, as it might sound to us, in sharing a household, but instead in spending time together on the sorts of activities, projects, and pursuits that we value, the ones that shape our lives. Like wishing goods for the friend for her sake, sharing activities and spending time together is not only part of the process of becoming friends, it is one of the necessary constitutive attributes of friendship, the one that Aristotle claims is most characteristic of friends (*NE* VIII 5 1157b17–22; IX 10 1171a1–2).

In both *Eudemian Ethics* VII 6 and *Nicomachean Ethics* IX 4, Aristotle details several defining features of friendship. In addition to wishing goods for the sake of the friend and desiring to live together and spend time in one another's company, friends wish for one another to continue to live, they make the same decisions, and they share one another's pleasures and pains (*NE* IX 4 1166a1–9; *EE* VII 6 1240a22–b11). In the Eudemian version, Aristotle repeatedly adds the explicit qualification that each of these formal features of the attitude of love is other-regarding, not for the sake of the one who loves but for the sake of the beloved. Similarly, in *Rhetoric* II 4, the nominal definition of friendly feeling emphasizes that this attitude looks to the good of the other, and not, Aristotle specifies, to one's own good (1380b36–1381a1). Two agents come to be friends, he concludes at *Eudemian Ethics* VII 2 1236a14–15, when they both love the other, reciprocate the other's love, and are both aware of the other's reciprocated love. If the attitude of love consists in this set of characteristics, then we might think that trusting a good friend consists in trusting that she really does love you for who you are, where that means that she manifests all these characteristics and not just goodwill.

A second, related reason for thinking that wishing goods in an unselfinterested way is not sufficient for trust is that one must also *do* the good that one wishes. The potential friend's actions should match her attitudes. Perhaps this point seems obvious, since becoming aware that another person likes you seems to require that they express their good wishes in action. But according to Aristotle's official account of goodwill, what distinguishes it from friendship is that it can arise and persist unnoticed; mere goodwill does not entail activity (*NE* IX 5; *EE* VII 7 1241a10–12).

Two agents must share the same conception of value in order for their well-wishing in relation to one another to yield the right sorts of actions. At *Rhetoric* II 4 1381a8–12, Aristotle claims that the same things should be good and evil to both parties so that they have the same sorts of wishes in relation to one another. If what the agent finds valuable is virtuous activity and what the potential friend finds valuable is wealth, this mismatch can result in conflict and distrust. There may be a circumstance in which, for example, there is an opportunity for a generous action, giving money to a deserving fellow citizen in need. Both the virtuous agent and the potential friend have substantial financial resources and so could readily perform this virtuous action, but let us suppose that the potential friend has significantly more wealth at her disposal. The virtuous agent, looking to promote the potential friend's virtue, defers to her, stepping aside so that the potential friend can attain the good of acting virtuously.[8] However, because the potential friend does not value virtue, but instead money, the virtuous agent's deference and desire to promote the potential friend's genuine good would not be received as such. The potential friend would instead view the virtuous agent's action as self-serving (looking to hold onto the agent's own money) and a harm and would not come to trust the virtuous agent as a friend. The virtuous agent has an accurate conception of value. In the best type of friendship, one's subjective conception of value must correctly track objective value.

There is another sort of interesting epistemic error which also comes to light in examining the requirement that friends who justifiably trust one another must successfully enact their genuinely loving attitudes. It is not sufficient to wish goods to the potential friend, where that means wishing for the friend the same goods that the friend wishes for herself, the goods that are in fact objectively valuable, for the sake of the friend herself. Nor would it be sufficient if we included all the other legitimate expressions of love. Consider a case in which two young decent individuals are in the process of becoming friends, and one of them is headed out of town for a trip. The one who is traveling asks the potential friend if he could take care of her garden in her absence, which involves watering the plants. The potential friend is eager to do a favor for the traveler, who has been treating him well, and so he jumps at the opportunity and assures her that he has it covered. He has the right motivational structure, at least insofar as he wants to benefit and please his friend for her sake, and he attempts to tend her plants in her absence; unfortunately, he has a "black thumb" and has no clue how to garden. The traveler did offer instructions, but they were of the heuristic variety, so, while the potential friend genuinely does his best, he damages several plants. As it turns out, then, she ought not to have trusted him to tend her garden, since he lacked the requisite skill. But he was not deceptive due to malice or some self-serving motive, as his love for his friend is genuine; rather, he overpromised and under-delivered because he was youthfully overconfident. The chief error in this instance is not a lack of goodwill or even a lack of first-order gardening knowledge, but his lack of self-knowledge.

Thus far we have been investigating the mental states of the potential friend as they pertain to the agent herself. After all, we might think, these are the mental states that are salient for the friendship: How do the friends feel about and relate to each other? We have tried to show how wishing the traveler well for her sake is not sufficient for her rational trust in her potential friend. To close this section, we suggest that the presence of goodwill toward a friend is insufficient because the potential friend's attitudes in relation to others matter as well. Consider a case in which, say, a person is out to dinner with a nascent friend who has consistently treated the person well, only to discover that he behaves in an obnoxious and entitled manner toward the wait staff. For one thing, Aristotle thinks that the way someone behaves toward others in general will reveal how they may treat you in the future (*Rhetoric* II 4 1381b6–7). Aristotle does not seem to think that compartmentalizing to this extent reflects human psychology, but, even if it were possible to treat one's close friend in a consistently loving way while treating a server poorly, given that our concern is with trust it is hard to see how the person could be confident in the potential friend's continued good treatment of her after this dinner. For another, Aristotle thinks that friends are particularly receptive to one another's influence. Associating with someone of bad character, even if they are not directing their bad actions at one, may indirectly harm one's own character. Finally, even if it were possible to avoid the direct and indirect harms of associating with the person of base character, the agent of decent character will simply no longer find the formerly nascent friend attractive. She is, as we have seen, attracted to others who share her conception of value, the conception that, according to Aristotle's ethics, is objectively accurate.

TRUSTING A FRIEND: TRUTHFULNESS, SELF-KNOWLEDGE, AND VIRTUE

In the previous section we raised worries for the view that wishing goods to the agent for the agent's sake is sufficient for, and the sole constituent of, trusting a friend. In this section, we argue that a "nameless" virtue of truthfulness is necessary for rationally justified trust and, furthermore, that a decent character more generally is also required. Building virtue into the conception of trust resolves the concerns from the last section, but, as we explore in the next two sections, it generates new difficulties.

Although Aristotle does not, as we explained earlier, devote space to an explicit conceptual analysis of trust as he does with friendship, chapter 7 of *Nicomachean Ethics* IV does investigate in some detail an oft-overlooked "nameless" virtue of importance: truthfulness or trustworthiness (*alêtheia*). One of the five social virtues that Aristotle refers to as "nameless" (these states were not antecedently established virtues), truthfulness, like all of Aristotle's virtues of character, lies in a mean between two vices, one of excess and one of deficiency, in a given domain of feeling and action. As he initially introduces the topic, he refers to "those who are truthful and false, both in words and actions" (*NE* IV 7 1127a19–20). This first-pass way of describing the domain under examination might seem to suggest that being an overall honest and sincere person is what Aristotle has in mind, but it becomes clearer that this domain of virtue more narrowly concerns the way one represents oneself, in particular, to others. The boaster goes to excess in the sense that he presents himself to others as having more than he does, while the self-deprecator is deficient in his self-portrayal, disavowing qualities that he in fact possesses. The truthful person, by contrast, presents herself to others as she actually is.

Being truthful is not the same as merely being honest about oneself, where that means presenting oneself to others as one sees oneself. In order to have the virtue, one must both be sincere and genuinely self-aware. Indeed, in the Eudemian discussion of truthfulness, Aristotle indicates that the self-deprecator and the boaster knowingly misrepresent themselves (*EE* III 7 1233b39–1234a1). While neither of these vicious types may have complete self-knowledge, they have enough awareness about themselves to intentionally deceive others about who they are. We should be cautious, however, in this case to avoid too closely assimilating the Eudemian version to the Nicomachean. Aristotle's Eudemian treatment is significantly briefer and, crucially, he does not treat truthfulness as a virtue in the former; rather, he lists it among the emotional means, which do not involve decision and so fall short of virtue proper. Perhaps, as Gottlieb suggests, this is because he sees truthfulness, along with the other emotional means, as an aspect of one's temperament.⁹ For our purposes, we will assume that the Nicomachean analysis supersedes the Eudemian and will continue to treat truthfulness as a genuine virtue of character, but we take seriously the explicit claim that the misrepresentation of one's own abilities or possessions in the two vicious extremes involves awareness of the falsehood.

As Aristotle's account of this virtue and the corresponding vices continues in *Nicomachean Ethics* IV 7, he differentiates subspecies of the boaster on the basis of their motivations. The person who represents herself as having more than she in fact has because she wants profit is worse and more blameworthy than one seeking honor, though both are vicious boasters (1127b12–14). By contrast, Aristotle says that the person who misrepresents herself without some ulterior motive is foolish but is not actually base (1127b10–12). The self-deprecating person is less bad in part due to her motivations; she is not concerned with profit but with her reputation (1127b25–27). The most vicious sort of person, then, the one who is the opposite of the truthful person, is the boaster motivated by wealth (1127b32–33). This deceptive boaster seems like one of the sorts of people about whom Aristotle, borrowing from Theognis, is concerned, as we saw in the second section. Such a person would hopefully be revealed by misfortune, where time and trials are a way to become confident that the nascent friend possesses the virtue of truthfulness.

Furthermore, because friendship involves reciprocal affection with awareness, we might also suppose that each friend comes to trust the other, rightly, in part because of the other's trust: bestowing trust begets trust. Aristotle explains that we feel friendly toward those who are honest with us, those who make themselves vulnerable with their weaknesses, and we might suppose that this is because their openness demonstrates not only that the potential friend is straightforward and truthful but that he (nascently) trusts the agent (*Rhetoric* II 4 1381b29–30). The agent's awareness of the potential friend's trusting disclosure encourages her to trust him in turn. Moreover, perhaps trusting the potential friend to be a generally decent person also encourages him—as long as he is aware of it—to act in accordance with this standard and not let the agent down.

We are now in a position to revisit the case of the well-meaning but incompetent young garden-tender from the previous section. As we saw, his issue is not that he has self-serving ulterior motives in trying to provide help. He is sincere, presenting himself to his friend as he sees himself, but his self-conception is inaccurate. He does not, however, have the vice of boastfulness. For one thing, he is not knowingly misrepresenting himself. For another, he is not acting for the sake of his own material gain or honor; he genuinely likes the garden-owner for herself. Finally, because he is still young, though he is generally decent and other-regarding, and motivated to pursue full-fledged virtue, he does not yet have a fully settled character. He is in the process of moral development.

In his treatment of the dispute about how easy or hard it is to recognize a friend in *Eudemian Ethics* VII 2, Aristotle claims that good people are more easily deceived than bad people (1237b29–30). The surrounding discussion, however, seems to imply that the virtuous agent will take her time in forming a friendship, testing the nascent friend, to ensure that her judgment is accurate and her trust is justifiably bestowed. She does not seem like the sort who would be readily taken advantage of. But perhaps Aristotle is thinking here of the young person who is decent but has not yet experienced betrayals and so has not had reason to become suspicious of others. In *Rhetoric* II 12, Aristotle sketches a picture of youthfulness in which the young person tends to be optimistic and charitable in their dealings with others because she has not encountered many instances of vice (1389a16–17). He explains that "they trust others readily, because they have not yet often been cheated" (1389a18–19). Aristotle repeats the claim that the young are easily cheated a few lines later before going on to explain that they are fonder of their friends than the old, who tend to associate out of need and for expediency rather than because they enjoy one another's company. The old have become distrustful of others. In *Nicomachean Ethics* he indicates that the young have features of temperament that are characteristic and productive of friendship, such as enjoying their interactions with others (VIII 6 1158a4–5).

The young tend to assume that others are, like them, honest and not deserving of bad treatment (*Rhetoric* II 12 1389b8–9). Decent young people seem worthy of trust insofar as they are sincere and not motivated by material gain, but their tendency to overestimate themselves and to think they know everything (*Rhetoric* II 12 1389b5–6)—their lack of self-knowledge—renders them untrustworthy. Moreover, because their characters are not yet settled, they lack the stability required for reasonable trust, while those in their prime judge people correctly, according trust as befits each person (*Rhetoric* II 14 1390a33–34). As with the process of becoming friends, the process of becoming virtuous involves degrees, such that a given agent's character may more or less consistently exemplify the virtuous activity of truthfulness: an agent may be decent even as she continues to need more practice for fully developed virtue of character.

We have been arguing that the virtue of truthfulness is necessary for, and an important component of, justified trust in friendship. But for Aristotle, individual virtues of character do not occur piecemeal: he endorses some version of the unity of virtue thesis, according to which the virtues of character are mutually inter-entailing. And, in order to have the complete complement of fully fledged character virtues, one must also possess practical wisdom. If an agent is truthful, she will also therefore be just, courageous, moderate, and so on. Of course, it does not follow that these other virtues will be constitutive of trusting a friend. And it seems plausible that the particular virtue of truthfulness matters most in a general account of when one ought to trust another. In a legislative meeting, for example, an agent's awareness of the other's virtue of truthfulness might suffice for rationally justified trust that she will vote as she has said she will in a particular instance. In the case of friendship, however, as we explained in the previous section, trust will encompass more. Friends should have a shared, generally accurate conception of value that which decent and virtuous agents possess. When an agent comes to have justified trust in her friend, what she is rightly confident about is in part that the friend is who he seems to be, which is both, more narrowly, a truthful person and, more broadly, an overall decent person.

There are thus two general sets of components in our account of what, according to Aristotle, explains reasonable trust in a good friend. First, there are the features of the friend qua friend, which consist in her loving attitudes, responses, and actions toward the agent: Does she express and return the defining features of love, including wishing goods for the agent's sake, and desiring to live with her? Second, there are the features of the friend qua good person: her truthfulness, centrally, but also her other virtues. These are not wholly separable, since the friend who is in a position to wish goods for the sake of the agent in an unqualified way, and who will rightly perceive the agent's good wishes, actions, and loving treatment as such, is one with the correct conception of value: that is, is a good person.

Truthfulness and the trust it facilitates are important aspects of the highest kind of friendship, a state of character the activities of which are in turn partly constitutive of happiness. It is worth noting that, in addition to this contribution, truthfulness contributes directly to happiness as well, since it is a virtue of character. Exercising one's truthful character by presenting oneself to others as one knows oneself to be, sincerely and with the right amount of self-disclosure, in appropriate situations, is itself one of the virtuous activities which together constitute happiness.

OBJECTING TO THE ACCOUNT: JUSTIFIED TRUST AND THE POSSIBILITY OF BETRAYAL

We have been arguing that the virtuous agent should trust her friend when she has had the opportunity to interact with him over a long period of time in various contexts, thereby becoming confident that he is the genuinely good person he seems to be. One might worry, however, that an important feature of the structure of trust is that it still allows the possibility of betrayal. Trust is not knowledge; it entails a degree of risk. Yet on the view we have been developing, it looks like the target of the virtuous agent's rationally justified trust simply could never betray her trust.

First, one might think that this represents a difference between the way that Aristotle conceived of the notion of trust (*pistis*) and the way we understand it. Perhaps he thinks of this confidence or conviction as (more) error-proof. But that interpretation would be a mistake. The Greek term has a broad set of uses, and Aristotle (along with Greek thinkers more generally) employs the term in other contexts in a way that is reasonably similar to our use of "trust." For example, in his analysis of *akrasia*, he makes the point that someone with knowledge and someone with belief may both have the same degree of trust or confidence in their own mental states (*NE* VII 3/*EE* VI 3 1146b27–30). Second, the decent agent's aim is knowledge, but it is practical knowledge; that is, the object of knowledge is another person qua complex subject and not, say, a mathematical proof. In the highest sort of friendship, friends make a reciprocal decision to get to know each other (*EE* VII 2 1237a30–31). The agent should trust her friend to the extent that she has come to know the friend.

Third, even the highest degree of reasonable confidence in a virtuous friend leaves some room for the possibility of betrayal. The friend who satisfies the conditions for trustworthiness may still act out of character. As we have mentioned already and explore further in the next section, the development of virtue occurs along a continuum such that a friend may be generally decent, exemplifying the virtues of character to a degree, but still be susceptible to occasional temptations. Of course, the better she is, the less likely this possibility is, and so the more the friend's decent character merits trust.

Fourth, and relatedly, in the course of treating a puzzle about dissolving a friendship in *Nicomachean Ethics* IX 3, Aristotle explores a case in which the agent formed a character friendship with another decent person but then the friend turns vicious (1165b13–22). His stance is that the agent should attempt to rescue her friend's character but, if that does not work, she should distance herself. The setup of this case presupposes that even though virtue is stable, it is nonetheless possible for a virtuous person to undergo character alteration and become worse. Thus, a friend who was formerly virtuous and rightly trusted as such might well betray the friend if he has fallen prey to, for instance, the corrupting influence of others. Indeed, as we have mentioned, friends' receptivity to one another is part of why one should not befriend someone of bad character in the first place (*NE* IX 3 1165b16–17).

Earlier in the same chapter (*NE* IX 3) Aristotle considers an explicit case of deception in which the agent is misled about the grounds of a friend's attraction:

> We might, however, accuse a friend if he really liked us for utility or pleasure, and pretended to like us for our character. For, as we said at the beginning, friends are most at odds when they are not friends in the way they think they are. And so, if we mistakenly suppose we are loved for our character when our friend is doing nothing to suggest this, we must hold ourselves responsible. But if we are deceived by his pretense, we are justified in accusing him—even more justified than in accusing debasers of the currency, to the extent that what is affected by his wrongdoing is more precious. (1165b4–12)

The friend who actively deceives the agent about his intentions has done something seriously wrong. In this case, the agent was duped, her trust was misplaced, and the deception impacted the agent's own character. Of course, she may have had compelling evidence that he liked her for her character because he was going out of his way to provide that evidence. Perhaps he was playing the long game, so that even spending a lot of time with him in myriad contexts did not reveal his true motivations. We might wonder whether her trust was thus rationally justified in this instance. Settling this question definitively would require considerable space on thorny epistemological issues, and Aristotle's emphasis in the passage is on ascribing blame. We might suppose that Aristotle thinks the agent should not have trusted this person as a character friend, and yet, as he states, she is not culpable for the mistake. The blame lies with the deceiver, who again appears to be the sort of person that one should try to suss out through time and trials.

We might start to worry, however, that the virtuous agent is starting to look like an excessively suspicious person, withholding her trust from others, and not the sort of charitable, decent person we encountered in the previous section. But we should recall that we are not talking about either trust in general or localized trust, the sort that one might have in relation to all of one's fellow citizens or in relation to a specific person for a specific purpose, respectively. Nor are we concerned with the merely descriptive phenomenon. Even bad people, Aristotle claims, can form pacts (*EE* VII 5 1239b14–15),[10] though as we saw in the first section they are incapable of participating in the trust that typifies the best sort of friendship. Our concern is with the trust that obtains in the best type of friendship between decent people. Keeping the relevant phenomenon in mind, it seems almost too obvious that one should trust someone as an intimate character friend only if that person is genuinely trustworthy. It is not surprising that the deep and abiding trust which is unique to this sort of relationship effectively minimizes, though does not eliminate, the possibility of betrayal. If anything, this is why, as Aristotle tells us, it is both more unjust and more shocking to steal from a close friend than from a fellow citizen (*NE* VIII 9 1160a3–5). Being a genuinely trustworthy person and friend is hard, and coming to know one's friend as this sort of person is hard. But that is as it should be, given the rarity of these relationships.

OBJECTING TO THE ACCOUNT: A PROBLEM WITH SELF-KNOWLEDGE AND FRIENDSHIP

In our final section, we consider an objection to our view that the virtue of truthfulness makes a core contribution to the set of features which the decent person trusts in her decent friend. *Nicomachean Ethics* IX 9 and *Eudemian Ethics* VII 12 both address a puzzle about why the good person needs friends. There is scholarly consensus that Aristotle's answer to the puzzle speaks to the value of the highest form of friendship or the good attained by friends in a virtuous friendship. According to one prominent line of interpretation, the valuable contribution that complete friendship makes to happiness is facilitating the acquisition of self-knowledge.[11] This reading maintains that the virtuous intimate friend, the friend who is an "other self," serves as a mirror in which the agent can see herself, illuminating aspects of the agent's own character.

As we saw above, the virtue of truthfulness consists in both sincerity and self-knowledge. An agent must first know herself as she is in order to accurately and intentionally present herself that way to others, securing their trust. But if the central valuable contribution of complete friendship is that it yields self-knowledge, how can truthfulness be a precondition for this type of friendship? How can an agent gain the self-knowledge necessary for truthfulness, and in turn necessary for the trust that complete friends have in one another, without first forming a character friendship?

One thing to point out is that this may be a reason to worry about the dominant interpretation—or, at least, we might question whether the particular good of self-knowledge exhausts the story or is the most significant contribution. Without entering too far into the debate over Aristotle's reply to this puzzle, if the main good that an agent gains from her virtuous character friend is her own self-knowledge, even the best form of friendship now starts to look problematically instrumentalizing. It is also worth noting that Aristotle offers other reasons why the virtuous person needs friends, including, for example, that it is difficult to be continuously active by oneself but easier with friends (*NE* IX 9 1170a5–8). Given Aristotle's emphasis on pleasure and our social nature in the surrounding discussion, his point here seems to be that we are less interested and engaged in our activities if we are pursuing them alone; friends amplify our enjoyment, which in turn motivates us to continue our enjoyable virtuous activity.[12]

Even if we accept that self-knowledge is one aspect of the value of virtuous friendships, presumably an agent comes to know herself through many sources and not only her most intimate friend. Much of one's self-awareness may come from interacting with one's other friends (pleasure friends, for instance), family, and other members of one's broader community. Aristotle relies on the claim that one can observe one's neighbors more easily than oneself (*NE* IX 9 1169b34–35), so the relevant observational perspective on virtuous action, the perspective that fosters self-knowledge, may not—or may not only—be the perspective of a friend. Then again, there are certain sorts of things about ourselves to which a friend alone may have privileged epistemic access. Being known by a friend *as a friend*, and so seeing oneself through the friend's eyes qua good "other self," is uniquely actualized in this ideal form of friendship.

Most importantly, as we have been emphasizing throughout, becoming friends and acquiring virtue, including the virtue of truthfulness, and so acquiring self-knowledge, are extended processes. They all come in degrees of development and they are interwoven. There are some virtuous agents who have very settled, stable virtuous characters, for whom there is perhaps less to gain from a virtuous friend with respect to self-knowledge. But it may be that they arrived at this developmental point through intimate friendship. Aristotle again invokes Theognis in his *Nicomachean Ethics* IX 9 argument: "Good people's living together allows the cultivation of virtue" (1170a11–13). And in the conclusion to his Nicomachean account of friendship, he explains that in a friendship between decent people, their characters improve further through engaging in virtuous activity together and from mutual correction (IX 12 1172a11–12). Enjoying virtuous activities together with one's friend over time facilitates, along with other character virtues, the interconnected cultivation of the virtue of truthfulness, including the self-knowledge which partially constitutes it, and the corresponding trust of a friend.

NOTES

1. The decent person (*epieikes*) or good person (*spoudaios*) is not identical to the virtuous person, as an agent may be generally other-regarding and possess natural virtue without yet being a fully virtuous person. Virtue of character proper, which includes the full complement of virtues, also requires possessing practical wisdom. However, Aristotle also includes the virtuous among the good and the decent. As we discuss later in the chapter, younger agents in particular may be on the road to character virtue, and so generally decent, despite not yet meeting the bar for virtue.

2. In *Rhetoric* I 15, for instance, Aristotle discusses the trustworthiness of different kinds of witnesses in a legal context, and at *Rhetoric* II 1 1378a8–20 he describes three qualities of an orator that engender trust in the audience in the absence of proof. In *Politics* V 6, at 1306a14–30, in the context of detailing the causes of revolution in oligarchy, he mentions problems with mutual distrust in the populace. More

generally, in *Politics* V 9, trust plays a role in preserving the established constitution of a polis.

3. Translations throughout are those of Irwin with occasional modifications by Gartner, relying on the Bywater OCT.

4. For a helpful overview of the debate about the relationship between *Eudemian Ethics* and *Nicomachean Ethics*, see Bobonich (2006).

5. We follow the Inwood and Woolf translation of *Eudemian Ethics*.

6. For more on Theognis's bleak view of friendship in the historical context, see Konstan (1997, 49–52).

7. One of us arbitrates this debate in detail elsewhere; see Gartner (2017).

8. Aristotle claims at the end of *Nicomachean Ethics* IX 8 (1169a32–34) that it is possible for a virtuous agent to sacrifice even a virtuous action for her friend, in the cases when it is finer for the friend to perform the action. In the case we sketch here, the friend stands to benefit more from the generous action, since he needs practice acting generously to improve his character.

9. Gottlieb (2009, 47–48). There has been little scholarship on Aristotle's nameless virtue of truthfulness, but Gottlieb's discussion is an exception. We are indebted to her work on the topic. According to her view, truthfulness requires self-knowledge, which in turn informs or constitutes the virtue agent's practical wisdom. It thus helps to connect the practical and intellectual virtues.

10. We follow Inwood and Woolf here, retaining the manuscript reading.

11. The locus classicus and central proponent of the self-knowledge interpretation is Cooper (1999).

12. For an interpretation of Aristotle's response to the puzzle which stresses the hedonic aspect, see Whiting (2006).

REFERENCES

Barnes, Jonathan, ed. 1984. *The Complete Works of Aristotle, Revised Oxford Translation*. Princeton: Princeton University Press.

Bobonich, Christopher. 2006. "Aristotle's Ethical Treatises." In *The Blackwell Guide to Aristotle's Nicomachean Ethics*, edited by Richard Kraut, 12–36. Oxford: Oxford University Press.

Bywater, Ingram, ed. 1894. *Aristotelis Ethica Nicomachea*. Oxford: Oxford University Press.

Cooper, John M. 1999. "Friendship and the Good in Aristotle." In *Reason and Emotion: Essays on Ancient Moral Psychology and Ethical Theory*, 336–55. Princeton: Princeton University Press.

Gartner, Corinne. 2017. "Aristotle on Love and Friendship." In *The Cambridge Companion to Ancient Ethics*, edited by Christopher Bobonich, 143–62. Cambridge: Cambridge University Press.

Gerber, Douglas E., ed. and trans. 1999. *Greek Elegiac Poetry: From the Seventh to the Fifth Centuries B.C.* Loeb Classical Library Series. Cambridge, MA: Harvard University Press.

Gottlieb, Paula. 2009. *The Virtue of Aristotle's Ethics*. Cambridge: Cambridge University Press.

Inwood, Brad, and Raphael Woolf. 2013. *Aristotle: Eudemian Ethics*. Cambridge: Cambridge University Press.

Irwin, Terence. 1999. *Aristotle:* Nicomachean Ethics, *Translated, with Introduction, Notes, and Glossary*, 2nd ed. Indianapolis: Hackett.

Konstan, David. 1997. *Friendship in the Classical World*. Cambridge: Cambridge University Press.

Susemihl, Franz, ed. 1884. *Aristotelis Eudemi Rhodii Ethica*. Leipzig: Teubner, 1884.

Walzer, Richard R., and Jean Mingay, eds. 1991. *Aristotelis Ethica Eudemia*. Oxford: Oxford University Press.

Whiting, Jennifer. 2006. "The Nicomachean Account of *Philia*." In *The Blackwell Guide to Aristotle's Nicomachean Ethics*, edited by Richard Kraut, 276–304. Oxford: Oxford University Press.

Chapter 3

How the Buddha Earns His Disciples' Trust (According to *Some* Pāli Nikāya Texts)

Antoine Panaïoti

Trust in teachers is an important matter, concerning which Buddhist texts have many remarkable things to say. In general terms, Buddhist thought and practice in its various forms is grounded in the conviction that—with the extremely rare exception of the odd "solitary (*paccheka*[1]) Buddha"—it is only with the help and guidance of skillful instructors that human beings can unlock their full intellectual, philosophical, psychological, and ethical potential.[2] For this to happen, however, trust (*saddhā*[3]) in such instructors is essential. So, in that they all agree that Siddhārtha Gautama (c. 490–410 BCE), the historical Buddha, is the supreme teacher, Buddhists widely regard *trust in the Buddha* as a matter of paramount importance.

This chapter proposes to focus on a specific—and rather surprising—way of conceiving of the arising of trust in the Buddha in early Indian Buddhism through the close reading of a selection of texts drawn from the Theravāda or Pāli Canon's Nikāya Section (a body of texts which appears to have reached a stable form by the second century BCE).[4] More specifically, I want to examine some of the Pāli texts which speak to the notion—evidently entertained by at least some early Buddhists—that the Buddha's trustworthiness is closely related to his ability to shun metaphysical disputation and operate a resolute empiricist-cum-pragmatist turn with respect to the closely interrelated questions of authority, knowledge, truth, and language. In other words, on the line of thought I wish to explore, what makes the Buddha worthy of our trust is his ability to guide us away from vain conversations and distracting (at best) beliefs, toward fruitful practice instead.

To be clear, I have no desire to argue that this way of conceiving of the Buddha's trustworthiness as a teacher is closer to some original "pre-dogmatic" or "positivistic" or "strictly practical" early Buddhism which, according to a story often told, later suffered corruption at the hands of more metaphysically or theologically or theoretically inclined Buddhists.[5] Early Pāli texts harbor different strands of thought which, as is the case in all philosophically rich textual corpuses, pull and tug in different directions. And it is, I submit, far from obvious that the impulse to determine which of these strands is the "earliest" or "purest" or "most authentic" is any less deluded than the seemingly cruder urge, widespread among Theravādin traditionalists, to flatten out all the contradictions in this large body of texts to make them all speak with one voice. Steering clear of anything of sort, I simply wish to show that some Pāli texts provide resources for conceiving of trust in the Buddha along empiricist-cum-pragmatist (i.e., resolutely antimetaphysical) lines. I will nevertheless take a moment toward the end of this chapter to reflect on the significance of my philological results for the way we think about the problem of "faith in Buddhism" in the contemporary Western cultural sphere.

HOW THE BUDDHA EARNED THE KĀLĀMA'S TRUST

Our journey begins with a detailed examination of the "Kālāma Sutta" (*AN* I.188–93), a commonly yet often superficially discussed dialogue. This Sutta tells the story of how the Kālāma clanspeople of Kesaputta collectively came to "take refuge" (*saraṇaṃ √gam*) in the Buddha, his teaching (or Dharma), and his community of mendicants.[6] The dialogue begins with the Kālāma gathering around the Buddha, candidly exhibiting various degrees of confidence in the man sitting before them and his claim to be an unsurpassed teacher: introductions range from bowing, through a spectrum of warm, lukewarm, and cool greetings, to polite silence (*AN* I.188). The reason for this quickly becomes obvious, as the Kālāma confess to being plagued by "doubt" (*kaṅkhā*) and "uncertainty" (*vicikicchā*) with respect to religious and philosophical views. Such a wide variety of teachers offering up wildly different doctrines have come to Kesaputta, they tell their honored guest, to "explain their own view" (*sakaṃ . . . vādaṃ dīpenti*) and "undermine their opponents'" (*para-vādaṃ opakkhiṃ karonti*) that the Kālāma are now utterly befuddled and bewildered: "Indeed, who amongst these distinguished renouncers (*samāṇa*[7])," they ask, "tells the truth and who lies?" (*AN* I.188). The breadth and depth of disagreement among people purporting to be wise and learned has turned the Kālāma into painfully unmoored skeptics;[8] they have, in short, no idea whom they should trust.

The Buddha's first response is to validate, as we would now say, the Kālāma's feelings: you indeed have good reasons for doubt and uncertainty, he tells the assembly before him. Then comes his advice, namely, to cease relying on "tradition (*anussavā*), hearsay (*paramparā*), oral transmission (*itikriyā*), texts that are handed down (*piṭaka-sampadāna*), logical (*takka-*) or inferential (*naya-*) reasoning (*-hetu*), the examination of rational grounds (*ākāra-parivitakka*), the consideration of speculative views (*diṭṭhi-nijjhānakkhantī*), estimations of probability (*bhavya-rupatā*), or [deference, having decided:] 'this renouncer is our teacher' (*samāṇa no garū ti*)" when it comes to matters of existential import (*AN* I.189). What the Kālāma should instead do, the Buddha goes on to explain, is focus on the eminently practical matter of which "mental states" (*dhamma*) they ought to "abandon" (*pa+√hā*) and which they ought instead to "cultivate, then dwell in" (*sampajja vi+√har*). And this, he crucially claims, is something the Kālāma must first "determine *for themselves*" (*attanā √jānaya* [causative root of√*jan*, "to know"]; my emphasis), that is, on the basis of their direct—or, as we would now say, "lived"—experience (*AN* I.189–91).

This second-order instruction on what epistemic means to employ (and *not* to employ) to attain true insight is imparted by the Buddha in seamless, performative unity with light-touch first-order psychological instruction: the Kālāma are gently led, by being repeatedly invited to consider their own experience, to agree that it is the mental states of attraction (*lobha*), aversion (*dosa*), and delusion (*moha*) that should first and foremost be abandoned, and their contraries[9] that ought above all to be cultivated and dwelt in. This is, to be clear, fairly boilerplate Indian Buddhist moral psychology, and even the way the Kālāma are repeatedly questioned about what they think, so that the insights the Buddha's seeks to impart are, as it were, drawn out of them, is something that happens over and over again in the Nikāyas. What is distinctive about the "Kālāma Sutta" is that this sort of exchange is prefaced by the Buddha's advice not to rely on authority, "pure" reasoning, or even probabilistic calculations, and instead always to validate ideas for oneself. And what makes the Kālāma Sutta so important is that the Buddha's use of the commonly encountered "question-and-answer method" being prefaced here in this way may plausibly be taken to suggest that the epistemic norms explicitly dictated to the Kālāma are *part of the subtext* in all of those numerous cases where the Buddha engages in dialogical tactics of the kind we see him employing in this Sutta.

Having said this, the second portion of the dialogue, although it is generally ignored, is in my opinion even more significant, if only because it provides the key to fully appreciating the *dénouement* of the Kālāma Sutta's narrative. For, we ought not to forget, this is first and foremost a story about how the suffering and bewilderment that result from overexposure to a plethora of frustratingly equipollent philosophical and religious doctrines can come to cessation and give way to confidence in the Buddha and his teachings.

The second half of the dialogue progresses as follows. First, the Buddha explains how practitioners who have effectively uprooted the three mental states that the Kālāma have now recognized to be pernicious thereby gain increased mental acuity, whence they proceed to engage in the meditative cultivation of boundless goodwill (*metta*), compassion (*karuṇā*), sympathetic joy (*muditā*), and equanimity (*upekhā*) (*AN* I.191). Such reference to the so-called Abode of Brahmā (*brahmā-vihāra*) meditations is, again, fairly boilerplate. The next and final step, however, is rather more original.[10] The Buddha now claims that these same practitioners, their minds purified by the meditative cultivation of boundless goodwill, compassion, sympathetic joy, and equanimity, attain to four "reliefs" (*assāsa*[11]). These four reliefs have the following propositional content: (1) "If life does continue after death and the station one attains through rebirth in *saṃsāra* is determined by the natural laws of karmic justice, then I can rest assured that I have done all I could to ensure a good rebirth"; (2) "If life does not continue after death (i.e., if there is no such thing as rebirth in *saṃsāra*), then I can nevertheless rest assured that I have done all I could to ensure a good life here-and-now"; (3) "If karmic demerit (*pāpa*) does ensue from harmful action, then I can rest assured that further harm will no longer be done by me and consequently, given the natural laws of karmic justice, I will not meet with further suffering (i.e., suffering beyond that which I have already set up for myself through past harmful action)"; and (4) "If karmic demerit does not ensue from harmful action, I can nevertheless rest assured that I am now *doubly* protected against suffering" (*AN* I.192). Setting aside the mysteriousness of the fourth "relief"—a matter orthogonal to our concerns—the takeaway is this: whichever metaphysical theory might be true as regards the nonexistence of life after death (reliefs one and two) and moral accountability (reliefs three and four), the person who has (a) uprooted attraction, aversion, and delusion, (b) cultivated their contraries, and (c) thence gone on to train in the Abode of Brahmā meditations can rest assured that they are better off, where being better off is cashed out as being less exposed to suffering. And *this*, as the conclusion of our Sutta makes clear, is what finally prompts the Kālāma to accept the Buddha as their teacher.

Now, it is of great importance to see that the four metaphysical views that are here described as neutral relative to the beneficial consequences of Buddhist practice are precisely the sorts of things the people who had previously come to Kesaputta to preach to the Kālāma had been teaching about.[12] Thus, there are several closely interrelated layers to the Buddha's teaching regarding the critical examination of a (purported) master's teachings in the "Kālāma Sutta," namely: (1) one ought to rely on one's direct experience alone—as opposed to authority, the "work of reason," and/or probabilistic estimations—to evaluate and validate teachings of existential import; (2) the value of such teachings ought to be determined on the basis of their conduciveness, when implemented, to certain concrete results (viz., in the Kālāma's case, what we may call "peace of mind"); (3) what follows from the practical implementation of teachings that are worth accepting will *render moot* such speculative matters as whether we do or do not survive death and whether karmic demerit does or does not accrue on the basis of action. Beyond depicting the Buddha as the kind of teacher who says, "Don't take my word for it, verify it for yourself!" and insists on *strictly empiricist* standards of verification, what the "Kālāma Sutta" suggests is that the Buddha's trustworthiness is closely tied to his efforts to *change the conversation* by focusing squarely on practical matters by the lights of which the standard questions of religious-cum-philosophical disputation reveal themselves to be, in a word, *irrelevant*.

To conclude this section with a plain and clear statement of my view, I take the story of how the Buddha earns the Kālāma's trust in this text as *paradigmatic* of a certain way—though by no means the only way—of conceiving of the phenomenon of trust in the Buddha in certain—though by no means all—Pāli Nikāya texts. To further support this view, I will now turn to two other types of Nikāya text which strongly resonate with the Buddha's teachings in the "Kālāma Sutta," namely, that Sutta in which the Buddha provides the most detailed description of the process in which *saddhā* (trust/faith/confidence in a teacher) is to be developed, and some of the (far more numerous) Nikāya texts in which metaphysical and/or theoretical views of various kinds are described either as orthogonal to what Buddhist insight is, so to speak, all about—or, more radically yet, as fully transcended when such insight is attained.

THE RECONCEPTUALIZATION OF *SADDHĀ* AND TRUTH IN THE "CAṄKĪ SUTTA"

We will now turn our attention to the "Caṅkī Sutta" (*MN* II.164–76), a text in which the Buddha successfully convinces his interlocutor, the young Brahmin Bharadvāja, to redirect his *saddhā* away from his Brahmin teachers[13] and toward a Buddhist teacher instead. As I will argue, the Buddha achieves this result by convincing Bharadvāja to alter his understanding of *saddhā*'s epistemic role and also to reconsider, by the lights of this, what it is to "know the truth."

To begin, the Buddha presents Bharadvāja with a series of challenging questions that ultimately compel the young priest to acknowledge that one of the principal grounds that Brahmins invoke when they assert "this, verily, is the true [view], other [views are] deluded" (*ida[ṃ] [vādam] eva saccaṃ mogham aññam*), namely, the *saddhā* they place in their teachers, is "groundless" or "rootless" (*amūlika*). For indeed, if neither Bharadvāja's teachers, nor his teachers' teachers, and so on all the way back to the first Brahmins can plausibly claim "I know this, I see this" (*aham etaṃ jānāmi aham etaṃ passāmi*), then such *saddhā* is simply "blind" (*andha*), in the very literal sense that it is rooted in no actual *seeing* (*MN* II.170). *Saddhā* that is not rooted in direct experience (be it one's own or one's teacher's), in short, is baseless (and thus epistemically useless) *saddhā*.

Given the reply that Brahmins have another crucial ground for asserting that theirs is the true view, namely, "orally transmitted tradition" (*anussavā*), the Buddha declares that this is no more reliable than their groundless *saddhā*. Neither *saddhā*, personal inclination (*ruci*), orally transmitted tradition, the examination of rational grounds, nor the consideration of speculative views, he claims, is epistemically sound.[14] The reason the Buddha gives Bharadvāja is that one may fail to hold a correct view though relying on one of these five means, and, conversely, one may hold a false view which appears to be supported by one of these same means. In short, what people normally rely on—respect for teachers, inclination, the authority of tradition, reasoning, and speculation—to "reach the definite determination" (*niṭṭhaṃ √gam*) that a given view is true and others are deluded simply cannot be trusted reliably to deliver the goods (*MN* II.171).

As the rest of the dialogue makes clear, a distinct form of *saddhā* nevertheless has an important—even, as it turns out, a *necessary*[15]—role to play in the arising of true knowledge or insight. A person seeking instruction, the Buddha explains, ought first to examine (*sam+anu+√is*) a potential teacher to determine whether there is any evidence, given his verbal and physical behavior, that his mind might be contaminated by the three pernicious mental states we encountered in our earlier exploration of the "Kālāma Sutta": namely, attraction, aversion, and delusion (*MN* II.171–73). Once it has been determined that this is not the case, she[16] "ought to place *saddhā* in him" (*tamhi saddhaṃ niveseti*), whereupon she will receive instructions that will, after a multilayered process beginning with listening to and memorizing these teachings and ending with their critical examination (*nijjhānaṃ khantī*), give rise to "striving" (*chanda*). It is through such striving, finally, that the Buddhist practitioner may eventually reach the stage where she "directly realizes the highest truth" (*paramasaccaṃ sacchikaroti*) and finally "sees [the highest truth] after penetrating it with insight" (*paññāya . . . taṃ ativijjha passati*) (*MN* II.173).

In the last portion of the "Caṅkī Sutta," accordingly, the Buddha establishes that appropriately grounded *saddhā*—that is, *saddhā* that arises after it has been determined that a teacher is free of pernicious mental states[17]—is essential to the process leading to insight into the so-called highest truth. The reason he gives Bharadvāja is this: "one would not approach [a teacher] without having developed *saddhā* in him" (*no . . . taṃ [satthāraṃ] saddhā jāyetha na-y-idaṃ upasaṃkameyya*), and without approaching a teacher, the process leading up to insight into the highest truth is not set in motion (*MN* II.176).

On the framework the Buddha presents here (and which Bharadvāja ultimately embraces), *saddhā* is not, then, a source of knowledge in and of itself, but rather a precondition for its acquisition.[18] This makes it very different to the *saddhā* which he begins by examining at the beginning of the "Caṅkī Sutta," and thence establishes to be both groundless and unreliable. *Saddhā*, in short, has been reconceptualized.

Going one step further, the Buddha also convinces Bharadvāja to reconceptualize what it is to "know the truth" in this Sutta. For it is far from obvious that the "highest truth" which the Buddhist practitioner eventually comes to "know directly" or "penetrate with insight, then see" (*MN* II.173) is the same kind of "truth" of which Bharadvāja and his teachers, at the beginning of the Sutta, assert: "this, verily, is the true view, others are deluded" (*MN* II.170–71). It is instead—to employ the formula that Bharadvāja admits none of his teachers could sincerely pronounce about any of the purported truths which they taught—precisely the kind of thing of which one says: "I know this, I see this" (*MN* II.171). Genuine knowledge of the truth in the "Caṅkī Sutta," in short, does not appear in a propositional attitude but in something *fully experiential*. As will be made clear in the next section, this Sutta is not the only Nikāya text in which this kind of reconceptualization of the nature of true "knowledge" is envisaged.

THE "POṬṬHAPĀDA SUTTA'S" PRAGMATISM AND THE *AṬṬHAKAVAGGA* POEMS' PRINCIPLED QUIETISM

We shall now turn to those texts in which, in a way reminiscent of the "Kālāma Sutta," metaphysical views of various kinds are described as either orthogonal to what Buddhist insight concerns or, more dismissively, as hurdles to overcome on the progress toward such insight.

Consider, to begin, the "Poṭṭhapāda Sutta" (*DN* I.178–203), which really includes two dialogues, the first between the Buddha and the renouncer Poṭṭhapāda, and the second between the Buddha, on one hand, and both Poṭṭhapāda and the elephant-trainer Citta on the other. The first of these dialogues begins with the Buddha happening upon a large assembly of renunciants busily debating several issues, ranging from the most mundane ("talk of the street and of the well") to abstract matters of ontology, through a vast array of questions philosophical, political, and otherwise (*DN* I.178–79). When he asks what the central debate is about, however, their leader Poṭṭhapāda informs the Buddha that it concerns the question of the "cessation of perception" ((*abhi*)*saññā-nirodha*)[19] and proceeds to list a number of different views on how such cessation takes place (*DN* I.180). Unimpressed, the Buddha quickly redirects the conversation toward the practical question of the desirability of bringing perception to cessation—which he seems to think allows of a clear positive answer (*DN* I.181)—and of the steps leading to this goal—that is, various states of meditative absorption (*jhāna*), all of which are related (positively or negatively) to the phenomenon of perception (*DN* I.181–84).

This is where things get interesting. Poṭṭhapāda observes that the Buddha, in the account of meditative states he has just set out, seems to have alluded both to a single "peak of perception" (*sañña-agga*) and to several such peaks. Acknowledging this, the Buddha explains that he simply talks of the peak of perception in whatever way will happen to be conducive to the cessation thereof (*DN* I.184). What the Buddha seems to be saying, in short, is that theoretical precision is hardly relevant, and that practical considerations should dictate what one teaches and how. Indeed, his attitude seems to be this: whatever way of describing states of affairs contextually "works best" is that which should be opted for, where "working best" is understood in terms of conduciveness to real-world psychological-cum-ethical results.

This echoes very strongly with something that happens toward the end of the "Poṭṭhapāda Sutta." After discussing three prevalent forms or concepts of the "formation of self" (*atta-paṭilābha*) (*DN* I.195–202), the Buddha ends up telling his second interlocutor Citta that all such models are only "common appellations, common ways of speaking, common expressions, common conceptual constructs, by means of which [a teacher] expresses himself, though he does not grasp at them" (*itimā . . . lokasamaññā lokaniruttiyo lokavohārā lokapaññattiyo yāhi [satthā] voharati aparāmasan*) (*DN* I.202). It is surprising, but can hardly be considered accidental, that this last statement is what ends up winning both Citta and Poṭṭhapāda over, whereupon they promptly take refuge in the Buddha, the teaching, and his community. The highly abstract thought here seems to be that theory is thoroughly artificial, and thus that what ought to guide a teacher's choice of concepts and framework are pedagogical, pragmatic considerations, not "factuality." The Buddha's attitude, in short, is one of profound deflationism vis-à-vis theoretical models and, by extension, theoretical language. And *this* is what wins him Citta's and Poṭṭhapāda's trust.

Returning to the more theoretical—or, more precisely, meta-theoretical—matters at hand, note that the Buddha's claim about language in the closing section of the "Poṭṭhapāda Sutta" is highly continuous with his surprising inconclusiveness as he and Poṭṭhapāda reach the end of their exchange on the problem of perception, higher up in the Sutta. Pressed to share his view on whether "a person's self is identical to his perception, or perception and self are distinct" (*saññā purisassa attā ti vā aññā saññā añño attā ti vā*), the

Buddha simply claims that this is "difficult to know" (*dujjāna*) in a context where one is exposed to such a wide variety of contradictory views and teachings (*DN* I.187). This makes it look, on the face of it, like the Buddha has no view or simply does not care to advance one at that precise moment. Within the broader context of the conversations reported in the "Poṭṭhapāda Sutta," however, it begins to seem like the Buddha might have a view after all, albeit one that is second order in character. This second-order view, in a nutshell, would be that the question of the identity/distinctness of perception and self just does not matter.

Such a reading receives strong support from what happens immediately after in our Sutta.[20] (This exchange, I should mention, is without doubt one of the most famous moments in the Nikāya texts, though it is characteristically treated in isolation from the rest of the "Poṭṭhapāda Sutta"[21]—as well as the "Caṅkī" and "Kālāma" Suttas—and thus remains more often than not superficially interpreted.) Seemingly satisfied with the Buddha's noncommittal attitude vis-à-vis the relation of perception to self, Poṭṭhapāda asks the Buddha about ten views, inquiring in each case whether one may say of it "This is the true [view], other [views are] deluded" (*DN* I.188–89; note that this is exactly the same formula we met with in the Caṅkī Sutta, above[22]). These ten views are as follows: that the cosmos is of infinite extension (1)–(2); that it is noneternal (3)–(4); that the life-cum-consciousness-principle (*jīva*) and the body (*sarīra*) are identical/distinct (5)–(6); that a Tathāgata (i.e., someone who has reached highest insight), after dying, exists versus does not exist versus both exists and does not exist versus neither exists nor does not exist (7)–(10). The Buddha provides the same answer to Poṭṭhapāda's ten queries: he has not set out any of these as the true view. He then justifies his refusal to do so by explaining that such matters are in no way conducive to "awakening" or "enlightenment" (*sambodha*) (*DN* I.188–89). In contrast, his teachings about suffering (*dukkha*), its cause (*samudaya*), its cessation, and the path (*mārga*) leading to its cessation *are* conducive to enlightenment, the Buddha continues, and that is why he has set out determinate statements about these topics (*DN* I.189).

Here, the Buddha makes it clear that practical considerations ought to constrain what it is worthwhile—perhaps even *meaningful*—to talk about. Situated within the broader context of the Buddha's claims and interventions in the "Poṭṭhapāda Sutta," the pragmatist bent of this thought shines through even more strongly: even the choices one will make in deciding *how* to talk about those matters that it is worthwhile or meaningful to talk about—that is, what concepts, terms, models, distinctions, and so on a trustworthy teacher may invoke in this context—will be guided *not* by what is "really the case" or "true" from a theoretical, view-from-nowhere stance, but rather by a principle of context-dependent efficacy. On this line of thought, it is not just that certain metaphysical questions are beside the point, but that "factual precision" (a norm grounded in metaphysics if there is any) is not what governs a skillful teacher's choice of discursive framework. And it is in demonstrating his *good judgment* as regards this matter, the "Poṭṭhapāda Sutta" suggests, that the Buddha earns Citta's and Poṭṭhapāda's trust.

Small wonder, then, if we find in the Pāli canon a set of Nikāya texts that unequivocally present the accomplished Buddhist sage as holding no theoretical view whatsoever, and thus as spurning debate and argumentation altogether. Consider the following selection of verses from the "Aṭṭhakavagga" section of the *Suttanipāta* collection of poems:[23]

> *Sn* 787: Only those who are involved with theories (*dhamma*) enter a debate (*vāda*). How and by means of what could an uninvolved (*anūpaya*) person argue? For him, there is nothing that is either "held" (*atta*) nor "rejected" (*niratta*). He has cleansed himself from all views (*diṭṭhi*) here in this world.
>
> *Sn* 796: When a person in this world places something high above, settling in views which he considers to be "supreme" (*uttara*) then he calls all other views "inferior." In this way he fails to go beyond argumentation (*vivāda*).
>
> *Sn* 841, 843: Relying on views and constantly asking questions, you become infatuated with that which you hold on to and thus you do not understand even the smallest idea! You perceive everything through a veil of stupidity (*momuhata*). . . .
>
> Why should the pure one *(brāhmaṇa)* say "this is the truth"? With what should he quarrel, saying "this is a lie"? He for whom there is neither "equal" nor "unequal," with what shall he start a debate?
>
> *Sn* 847: He who is unattached is not tied to what he perceives. He who has been freed by insight (*paññāvimutta*) suffers from no delusions (*moha*). In contrast, those who grasp ideas and views fare in this world attacking each other continuously.
>
> *Sn* 859, 861: He has put greed to an end, he is unselfish (*amaccharin*). The sage does not speak of himself as being among the superior ones, nor amongst the mediocre ones, nor among the inferior ones. He does not adopt a theory (*kappa*), so there is no point in theorizing about him. . . .
>
> He claims to nothing as his own in this world. He does not grieve when something stops existing. He does not thrust himself into doctrines. He, indeed, is the one we called "pacified."[24]

These verses largely speak for themselves. On the ideal of the Buddhist sage they set out, the fully accomplished person entirely ceases to advance and defend any view or doctrine as "the truth." The attainment of the highest

Buddhist insight as described in the "Aṭṭhakavagga" poems implies the relinquishing of all theoretical views and adherence to a principled quietism.[25] Holding theoretical or metaphysical views, here, is regarded as expressive of the malady that Buddhist thought and practice is designed to cure: it is an impediment to self-transformation, even a hurdle which one must overcome. On this line of thought, the only teacher who ought to be trusted is the teacher who, in the manner of the Buddha in the "Kālāma Sutta," points to the way that leads beyond all "teachings."

CONCLUSION

I am aware that in proposing to delineate one of the ways in which the Buddha is understood to earn his disciples' trust (according to *some* Pāli Nikāya texts) I have embarked on a project that bears no resemblance to setting sail on an open expanse of tranquil, uncharted waters aboard a sturdy vessel manned by reliable fellow journeyers. This project is rather akin to quite solitarily parachuting myself down into an overcrowded, energetically fought-over field, victory over which is widely regarded as being very high stakes. For indeed, the problem of "trust in Buddhism" cannot neatly be distinguished from the problem of "faith in Buddhism"—if only because the Pāli term "*saddhā*" (as well as its equivalents in the other major languages of Buddhism, Indic, and otherwise) can denote either trust or faith, depending on context and translators' interpretative choices—and the least that can be said is that the latter problem is very thorny indeed. I shall thus endeavor, in the conclusion of this chapter, to draw the general contours of the fraught terrain of the "faith in Buddhism" debate and to situate my intervention therein.

A broad-stroke map of said terrain brings into relief three major camps, two of which hold very firm positions, while the third maintains a more moderate stance. The first camp is, at the time of writing, by far the most important in size and clout in that its central contention is very broadly circulated (and uncritically accepted by many) in contemporary Western culture, both popular and elite. This camp has it that Buddhism stands alone among so-called world religions in not being faith based. The thought, in its more erudite (and admittedly rather artificial) formulation, goes something like this: while other great religious traditions demand a "leap of faith" of their adherents and conceive of said leap as necessary for personal salvation by and through the intercession of some Higher Being, Buddhists are only expected to place their *trust* in the Buddha, whereupon the path to *self*-salvation (a thoroughly individual affair, at the end of the day) may be tread with tranquil confidence in the soundness of the Great Teacher's mind, method, and teaching. What is more, trust is to be placed in the Buddha only after the practitioner has successfully validated his teachings by the lights of her own life and/or meditative experience(s). Buddhism may thus be described as a *trust* based—rather than a faith based—tradition.[26] Such was the belief of so-called Buddhist Modernists who, in the late nineteenth and early twentieth centuries, set out to revitalize Buddhism by claiming that it is, in essence, an empiricist and even a meditation-based experimentalist tradition.[27] Such is today the belief of those—including many a cognitive neuroscientist and meditation "app" entrepreneur—who wish to portray Buddhism as "mind science,"[28] of psychologists keen to use Buddhist-inspired meditation practices in therapeutic contexts,[29] and of a very large crowd of disenchanted Westerners excited to have discovered a millennia-old, tradition-sanctioned form of so-called nonreligious spirituality.

By the lights of the opposite camp, Buddhism is not just faith based, it is unquestionably *a* Faith. One cannot become a Buddhist without experiencing a "calling" of sorts, whereupon one spontaneously *decides* that the Buddha's teaching contains some sort of Higher Truth which ordinary beings could never dream of "validating for themselves" as long as they have not made significant progress on the Buddhist path. Yes, there might be some preliminary teachings that the Buddha invited his students to confirm in and for themselves in the pedagogic context of early instruction, but "taking refuge" does indeed require a leap of faith. And while Buddhism is indeed ultimately about self-salvation (through the use of various meditation exercises) rather than salvation by an external savior (for even Pure Land Buddhists understand that they will ultimately have to save themselves[30]), such self-transformation would be impossible without the guidance of a master and the sense of security and confidence that only faith in this master can afford. What is more, seeing as (a) just about every Buddhist tradition exported out of or imported from India in the last two millennia has exhibited an astonishing ability to syncretize with the dominant local belief- and practice-systems in the lands in which it spread, and (b) said systems invariably involved faith-based elements of one kind or another, even those strands of Buddhism which may be argued to make little if any room for leaps of faith "on paper" harbor a colorful plethora of devotional and fideistic practices as soon as one turns to the "lived experience" of the overwhelming majority of its real-world adherents. But even when one considers only the elite textual traditions of those Indian Buddhist schools which can most readily be interpreted as promoting trust but *not* faith in the Buddha, the Buddhist Modernists' and their contemporary disciples' story is based on a selective reading of texts that ultimately says more about the desires and fantasies of those in the thrall of the now-dominant naturalism of contemporary Western culture than about Buddhism itself. Such a view will find ample scholarly support in the studies of such early

Buddhologists as Arthur B. Keith (1923) and Louis de la Vallée Poussin (1909). It is also the view held by many Buddhists today who resent being told by more naturalistically inclined Buddhism enthusiasts that their way of being Buddhists is somehow corrupt or naïve, as well as by those, like the philosopher Evan Thompson (2020), who seek to push back against the "Buddhism is mind science" movement (now a major force in both academia and business).

The middling, more moderate position is, predictably, the reserve of scholars with proper philological training and their attentive readers. The focus here is on early Indian Buddhism. A characteristic example of this line of thought is provided by the work of K. N. Jayatilleke on early Indian Buddhist epistemology. In his scrupulously researched and philologically rigorous *Early Buddhist Theory of Knowledge* (1963), Jayatilleke argues there are "two strata" of texts that take up the "evaluation of *saddhā* in the Pāli Canon" (384): the first strata is empiricist in spirit and presents *saddhā* as epistemically earned on the basis of independent critical scrutiny à la Kālāma (385–399); the second is expressive of the "an authoritarian dogmatic attitude" (401) which became more and more common among the Buddhist monastic communities responsible for preserving Pāli texts in the centuries that followed the Buddha's death (399ff.).[31] On this line of thought, "original" early Buddhism was not "faith based," though it quickly became so. It is thus easy to imagine how a more sophisticated proponent of our first camp might wish to seize upon the results of this third, middling camp to promote the "reemergence" of a Buddhism that purports to be at once more modern and closer to its most ancient or "purest" strand.

I have already made it clear in the introduction where I stand relative to the question of what "original Buddhism" might have looked like. I have, in short, no interest in making a case of this kind. I think we should learn to be comfortable with the fact that there are different textual strands in early Pāli texts,[32] strands that will resonate more or less strongly with different people, depending on their temperament and attendant philosophical inclinations. All I have done is to show how one such strand describes the Buddha as earning the trust of his disciples by demonstrating his willingness to operate an empiricist-cum-pragmatist turn with respect to the problems of authority, knowledge, truth, and language by pointing to an eminently practical path that leads beyond all metaphysics, cosmology, and theory.

Though my intention is not to present this strand as speaking for the entire Buddhist tradition, I doubt my results will sit well with most in the "Buddhism is a Faith" camp. It seems obvious to me that, in the strand of Nikāya texts we have been exploring, it is indeed the earning of trust—not the arising of faith—that is at issue. And should one insist on expressing the spirit of these texts in the language of faith, I take it that one would find oneself speaking (seemingly in tongues) of "faith in faithlessness." Having said this, it would take very little effort for members of the faith camp to neutralize, as it were, my results through the kind of creative rereading of the texts at hand for which religious folk have always had a knack.

As regards the first camp, that is, the "Buddhism is not faith-based" crowd, my intervention may seem, prima facie, to align quite neatly with their position. On a closer look, however, it quickly becomes clear that the results of our philologically guided journey are at once far more modest and far more radical than the positions espoused by Buddhist Modernists and their contemporary science-positive heirs. They are more modest in that all I have shown is that there is an arch-empiricist, arch-pragmatist strand in early Pāli Literature, by the lights of which *saddhā* appears to be a matter of trust, not faith. This is in no way a point about all of Buddhism, the "essence" of Buddhism, or anything of the kind. But my results are also more radical in that this strand is at odds with (a) all forms of Buddhism which, like the Buddhist Modernists' form, remain committed to metaphysical doctrinal positions (e.g., rebirth in *saṃsāra*, the existence of the "law of karma," the nonexistence of the self—all of which are precisely the kinds of view which the Buddha bypasses in the "Kālāma Sutta" and the sage spurns in the "Aṭṭhakavagga" poems), and (b) the no-less-metaphysical scientific realism of most contemporary heirs of the Buddhist Modernist movement. To wit, if the Buddha is to be trusted for the reasons I have been exploring in this chapter, it is not only faith that his disciples ought to spurn, but also all and any strongly held belief in what is or is not "really" the case.

NOTES

1. Since I will be drawing from primary source texts originally composed in Pāli, I provide the Pāli forms of Buddhist technical terms and set phrases when relevant. All translations from Pāli in this chapter are my own. I have used the following standard abbreviations: *Aṅguttara Nikāya* = AN; *Dīgha Nikāya* = DN; *Majjhima Nikāya* = MN; *Saṃyutta Nikāya* = SN; and *Suttanipāta* = Sn (volume numbers of Nikāya texts appear in Roman numerals followed by Arabic numerals indicating page number; Arabic numerals in *Sn* references denote the verse number).

2. This is generally taken to involve the attainment of "transformative insight" (*paññā*) or "awakening" (*bodhi/sambodha*), which in turn leads to the "complete cessation of [mental] suffering" (*avisesa [mānasika-]dukkha-nirodha*).

3. Rendering the term *saddhā* as "trust" is the result of the sorts of interpretative choices that a translator of Pāli texts is forced to make, ideally on a case-by-case basis. Indeed, like other Indic languages, Pāli does not distinguish lexically between: (a) *trust* (narrowly) defined as something that can "be earned" or "grow" through a process of independent critical evaluation guided by epistemic norms, and which may

thus be "broken" if/when evidence appears that a person is unreliable or deceitful; (b) *faith* (narrowly) defined as an epistemically unwarrantable "leap" that may thus be "lost" for equally mysterious reasons; and (c) *confidence* (narrowly) defined as a primarily affective sense of security or hope that is causally related to certain doxastic states. It is thus best to allow context to determine how *saddhā*—or *pasāda*, the semantic scope of which broadly overlaps with that of *saddhā*—is to be translated, and even better, in certain contexts, to leave it untranslated, as I do in the section on the "Cankī Sutta," below. The related, much broader, and exceedingly thorny question of "faith in Buddhism" is one that I shall turn to in the conclusion of this chapter. (Let us note in passing that many an ancient language lacks distinct terms for "trust" and "faith": *cf.* Latin: *fides*, *fiducia*; Ancient Greek: πίστις; Ancient Hebrew: אמן, אמונה; Ancient Chinese: 信任.) This, together with the fact that common terms for these two ideas are often used interchangeably in many modern European languages, suggests that the very idea that faith and trust are two firmly distinct concepts might be historically and culturally contingent.

4. What follows is by no means an exhaustive survey of all the Nikāya texts that bear on the points I will be making. To keep this discussion short and crisp, I had to make difficult decisions as to which texts to examine and which to ignore. It is also important to note, before going any further, that the larger body of texts I will be drawing from (viz., the Pāli Nikāya texts of the Theravāda school, which split off as the result of the first schism (c. third century BCE) and represents the dominant form of Buddhism in contemporary South-East Asia and Sri Lanka) do not represent a source for pre-schismatic or "original" early Buddhism (we sadly possess no such sources). Having said this, we can safely assume that the major philosophical problems that arise in the interpretation of Pāli Nikāya texts were also issues of contention in most if not all other early Buddhist traditions. The reason we can safely make this assumption is that no analogues of Pāli Nikāya texts preserved in the extant canonical literature of other, non-Theravāda early Buddhist traditions (mostly in Chinese and Tibetan translation, though some fragmentary texts in other Indic languages have survived) deviate in any significant way from the corresponding Theravāda materials. This being the case, the texts I will be examining in this chapter are as close as any Buddhist text can get to speaking to "universal" early Buddhist attitudes vis-à-vis the question of trust in the Buddha.

5. Characteristic examples of this kind of thinking include Jayatilleke (1963), Steinkellner (2002), and Warder (1998).

6. What I translate as to "take refuge" is a set phrase in many Pāli texts, which—like its analogues in the numerous languages of Buddhism—denotes what may loosely be referred to as "conversion" to Buddhism.

7. The figure of the *samāna* (literally: "wanderer"; by extension: a person who has renounced sedentary life in a city or village, its comforts, social duties, and privileges, etc., to devote themselves to higher philosophic and/or religious pursuits) looms large in early Pāli literature. Many of the various doctrines and teachings reported in Nikāya texts, in particular, are attributed to *samāna* or "renouncer" teachers who, unlike their Brahmin peers, reject the authority Vedic texts. Note that the Buddha consistently classes himself as just such a teacher in these texts.

8. That the term *vicikicchā* (uncertainty) as it is used in the "Kālāma Sutta" denotes a painful condition is corroborated by the not uncommon use of the phrase *vicikicchā-kathaṃkathā-salla* ("the [piercing] arrow of doubt and uncertainty") at various junctures in Pāli texts, Nikāya, and otherwise (see, e.g., *DN* II.283). This also applies to the use of this term in the "Pāṭaliya Sutta" (*SN* IV.340–58), another Nikāya text in which the Buddha's interlocutor confesses to being bewildered by the plethora of contrary teachings he has been exposed to, and a large chunk of which follows the same overall narrative arc as our Sutta's (with one important difference, to which we will return at note 32, below). There is little doubt that this is a very different form of *vicikicchā* to that which forms the fifth so-called impediment (*nīvaraṇa*) to progress on the Buddhist path toward transformative insight, the latter manifesting instead as *inconstancy* in the keeping of vows and application of rules of conduct (see, e.g., *DN* III.49ff.).

9. Although, morphologically speaking, *a-lobha* ("non-attraction"), *a-dosa* ("non-aversion"), and *a-moha* ("non-delusion") are strictly negative, they really denote psychological dispositions that are at least in part if not primarily positive. To wit: *alobha* involves contentment, *adosa* benevolence and compassion, and *amoha* wisdom. Hence the, so to speak, natural transition from the cultivation of these mental states to training in the generation of boundless goodwill, compassion, sympathetic joy, and equanimity a few lines further in the "Kālāma Sutta."

10. Its nearest analogue occurs, again, in the "Pāṭaliya Sutta," which I briefly mentioned above (at note 8).

11. The term *assāsa* is generally used in the literal sense of "breathing out" in Nikāya texts (see, e.g., *DN* II.157). But here its meaning is clearly figurative (I suspect metonymic transfer from "breathing out" to "relief" via "sighing," then "sighing out of relief"). Another use of *assāsa* in the figurative sense intended here may be found in the adjectival compound *assāsappatta* ("having reached relief"), which invariably appears side-by-side with the compound (*tiṇṇavicikiccha*) ("having destroyed uncertainty"), to designate a spiritually advanced person (as at, e.g., *AN* I. 297–98). Such a coupling, if the "Kālāma Sutta" is any guide, is no coincidence at all.

12. This is made all the more obvious by the parallels between the "Kālāma Sutta" and the previously mentioned "Pāṭaliya Sutta," where the metaphysical views of the teachers whose diversity of opinions had initially prompted Pāṭaliya's unhappy uncertainty are, contrary to what happens in the "Kālāma Sutta," first explicitly reported by Pāṭaliya and then repeated verbatim as the sorts of matters Pāṭaliya ceases to be concerned about after receiving the Buddha's instructions. Indeed, these are four in number and correspond very closely to the four views mentioned in the "reliefs" section of the "Kālāma Sutta." Further evidence of the bewilderingly wide variety of metaphysical views taught by rival teachers in the Buddha's day is provided, in particular, by the first discourse of the *DN*, the "Brahmajāla Sutta" (*DN* I.1–46)—where sixty speculative metaphysical and/or cosmological views are listed (and rejected on effectively ad hominem grounds)—by the opening section of the "Sāmaññaphala Sutta" (*DN* I.47–59)—where King Ajātasatta sets out six of the doctrines he has previously been taught, yet failed to be convinced by, and which the Buddha then dismisses

as vain—as well as by the opening section of the "Poṭṭhapāda Sutta" (*DN* I.186–87) and the "Pañcattaya Sutta" (*MN* II.228–38)—two texts which will be discussed below.

13. The figure of the Brahmin (*brāmaṇa*) teacher, like that of the *sāmaṇa* teacher discussed above (note 7), is often met with in early Pāli texts. Such teachers regard the Vedic texts as supreme sources of knowledge and insight, though they are (aptly) portrayed as interpreting these in very different ways. Note, however, that in some Nikāya texts the term *brāmaṇa* is either reconceptualized or simply used (depending on the specific text) as an epithet for a highly accomplished person (viz., a person who is far advanced on the so-called Buddhist path). For exemplary cases of these two types of text, see, in particular, the "Soṇadaṇḍa Sutta" (*DN* I.111–26) and the *Sn*'s "Māgandiya Sutta" poem (*Sn*, 835–47), respectively.

14. This shorter, five-member list significantly overlaps with the longer list of unsound epistemic means produced by the Buddha at the beginning of his conversation with the Kālāma at *AN* I.189 (cited on p. 57, above).

15. This is presumably true of all people save the odd "solitary Buddhas," a type which makes but a few passing appearances in Pāli Nikāya texts (albeit in none of those under study in this chapter).

16. The change in the gender of our hypothetical practitioner is less anachronistic than some may assume. As early Pāli texts make clear, the Buddha regarded women as perfectly capable of attaining the highest forms of insight.

17. In the opening section of the "Vīmaṃsaka Sutta" (*MN* I.317–20), the Buddha provides an account of the development of *saddhā* that is even more stringent, epistemically speaking, than the "Caṅkī Sutta's". Here, an examination of character of same kind as is described in the "Caṅkī Sutta" is presented as an essential prelude to the arising *saddhā* (*MN* I.318–19), but there is now another step: it is only after the student has come to her own independent conclusions on the *content* of the teachings themselves that *saddhā* may be regarded as "established, grounded, supported" (*niviṭṭha mūlajāta patiṭṭhita*) (*MN* I.320). According to this text, then, *saddhā* is not only earned on the force of the teacher's good character, but also by the soundness of his teachings *as validated by the student*. One reason one might take to explain the "Caṅkī" and "Vīmaṃsaka" Suttas' slightly different stories is that the former is concerned with how laypeople develop *saddhā* in Buddhist teachers, while the later describes the process whereby monks develop *saddhā* in the Buddha qua supreme teacher. The underlying thought, here, would be that monks feature as more sophisticated epistemic agents than laypeople in Nikāya texts. This is far from implausible. Note, however, that the assembly that the Buddha addresses in the "Kālāma Sutta" is *not* composed of monastics, but that the Kālāma only take refuge in the Buddha, the Dharma, and so on, after they assess the soundness of the Buddha's teachings (not just the Buddha's character), which suggests the story cannot be quite that simple.

18. The notion that *saddhā* is not, in and of itself, a source of knowledge (let alone a form of knowledge), but rather a prelude for it, is central to the short exchange between the learned Buddhist householder Citta and the Jain teacher Nigarṭha Nāṭaputta recorded at *SN* IV.298–300. First, Citta claims that he does not rely on the *saddhā* he has placed in the Buddha, but on his own direct experience, to determine

the precise character of certain meditative states (*SN* IV.298). Second, he has Nigaṇṭha Nāṭaputta agree that "knowledge is superior to *saddhā*" (*saddhāya kho . . . ñāṇam eva paṇītatara[m]*) (Ibid.), which very clearly entails that *saddhā* neither consists in nor directly yields knowledge. This same Citta, I should mention, is a figure we will shortly encounter in our exploration of the "Poṭṭhapāda Sutta" below. This, I take it, is hardly coincidental.

19. *Saññā* in Theravāda literature, psychology, and philosophy designates a faculty at once sensorial and conceptual. Indeed, it involves both the sensory perception that results from "contact" (*phassa*) between a sense organ and its object and mental "identification" or "labelling" at once. As the "Poṭṭhapāda Sutta" makes clear, the goal of bringing such mentalization to rest—particularly in the context of meditative practices—seems to have been broadly shared among both Brahmin and renouncer teachers.

20. It also receives strong support from the "Pañcattaya Sutta" (*MN* II.228–38). There, the Buddha considers various views about the self that together effectively seem to provide an exhaustive map of logical space, and then rejects all of them as fundamentally misguided. In a way that is reminiscent of what happens in the first segment of the "Poṭṭhapāda Sutta," the approach he promotes is one that is focused on the empirical-practical problem of the "spheres of contact" (*phassa-āyatana*) (i.e., what is responsible for perception or *saññā*) and their cessation.

21. Because of the striking parable the Buddha uses to illustrate his point, the "Cūḷamāluṅkyovāda Sutta's" (*MN* I.426–32) version of the teaching contained in the segment of the "Poṭṭhapāda Sutta" I am about to discuss is more often cited and discussed. Here, Māluṅkyaputta's insistence that the Buddha provide an answer to a number of strictly theoretical matters concerning time, space, the relation of consciousness/life to the body, and the death of maximally accomplished individuals (*tathāgata*-s) is disparagingly compared to a badly wounded man's refusal to receive treatment until he has obtained answers to a number of questions about his aggressor, the precise nature of the bow that was used to shoot the arrow that struck him, and the constitution of said arrow (*MN* I.429–30). The Buddha teaches about suffering and the way to bring it to cessation, period, Māluṅkyaputta is rebukingly told (*MN* I.431). For all the dramatic force of this dialogue, the "Poṭṭhapāda Sutta"—in sandwiching, so to speak, the same teaching (minus Māluṅkyaputta's confrontational attitude, and thus the evocative parable that follows on its heels) between two segments that express a resolutely pragmatist, deflationary attitude toward theory and theoretical language—is in my opinion far more revealing of the broader set of attitudes toward knowledge and truth expressed by the sorts of text we are exploring in this chapter.

22. Cf. the "Cūḷamāluṅkyovāda Sutta," which does not make use of this formula.

23. In the interest of clarity, I have chosen to render these verses in English prose.

24. Other "Aṭṭhakavagga" verses similar in spirit to those I have cited include *Sn*, 760; 799; 823–29; and 846.

25. Cf. Tom Tillemans's incorrect assertion that such *Suttanipāta* verses "seem to be straightforwardly readable as [nothing more than] a prudential caution against *bad* debates" (Tilleman 2017, 112). Indeed, the authors of the "Aṭṭhakavagga" poems

regarded the propensity to engage in philosophical disputation as symptomatic of a mental malady that afflicts us all, not just bad debaters. For a detailed, book-length study of Pāli Nikāya materials which (controversially) argues that the "Aṭṭhakavagga" take on "views" (*diṭṭhi*) faithfully expresses early Theravāda Buddhism's final position on this matter, see Fuller (2005).

26. For a crisp and forceful expression of this view by a celebrated contemporary Theravādin monk-teacher, see Hammalava Saddhātissa's (1978) article, "The Saddhā Concept in Buddhism."

27. On the development, motives, and excesses of Buddhist Modernism, see, in particular, David L. McMahan's *The Making of Buddhist Modernism* (2008). For a critique of the same, see Robert Sharf's (1995) article, "Buddhist Modernism and the Rhetoric of Meditative Experience."

28. For a detailed critical discussion of this development, see Evan Thompson's reflections on what he aptly calls "Buddhist exceptionalism" in his 2020 book *Why I Am Not a Buddhist*, chapter 1.

29. For a critique of this trend, see Sharf (2015).

30. Pure Land Buddhism is a Mahāyānist devotional cult with considerable clout in East Asian Buddhism. Its adherents devote their lives to the worship of the Buddha Amitābha in the hope of being reborn in one of the so-called Pure Lands that Amitābha is believed to emanate through his mental powers. The world we currently inhabit being too corrupt for a person successfully to lend herself to Buddhist practice, it is only in such a realm that self-salvation may, according to Pure Land Buddhists, take place.

31. A similar case is made by Anthony Warder in his widely read *Indian Buddhism* (2000) and *Course in Indian Philosophy* (1998). The more general idea that Indian Buddhism became all-things-considered more "theological" (and thus faith based) over the course of the centuries and millennia is also commonplace in contemporary Buddhist studies scholarship. Note, however, that this is by no means seen as conflicting with the notion that Indian Buddhist philosophy gained considerably in sophistication from roughly the turn of the era onward.

32. This is not to say, of course, that there is no evidence that certain Nikāya texts were reedited by those who had the power and means to impose their arguably more conservative interpretation of what the Buddha's teaching was, so to speak, all about. For example, the "Pāṭaliya Sutta" (*SN* IV.340–58) was clearly tampered with by people hostile to the strand of early Buddhist thought which I have been exploring in this chapter. As mentioned earlier (note 8), the second and third segments of this Sutta follow the same broad narrative arc as the "Kālāma," but when the reader arrives at its equivalent of the "relief" section, she meets with the perfectly incoherent notion that Pāṭaliya may now rest assured that he will have a good rebirth even if those teachers who claim that there is no life after death are correct (*SN* IV.351–52). In short, there *is* evidence of contestation and ideological struggle, and there *is* evidence that more "dogmatic" strands of early Theravāda Buddhism won out and succeeded in making their interpretation of the Buddha's teaching the dominant one. Nevertheless, the notion that such antidogmatic (or radically antimetaphysical) strands as that which I have been exploring were somehow "earlier" or "closer to

the Buddha's actual teaching" is, in my opinion, under-determined by the evidence. We simply do not know what the Buddha taught exactly, and ought to stop worrying about such matters.

REFERENCES

Andersen, Dines, and Helmer Smith, eds. 1990. *Suttanipāta* [*Sn*], Second edition. London: Pāli Text Society.

Carpenter, Joseph E. 2006. *Dīgha Nikāya* [*DN*], vol. III, Second edition. London: Pāli Text Society.

Chalmers, Robert, ed. 2004. *Majjhima Nikāya* [*MN*], vol. II, Second edition. London: Pāli Text Society.

Féer, Léon, ed. 1990. *Saṃyutta Nikāya* [*SN*], vol. IV, Third edition. London: Pāli Text Society.

Fuller, Paul. 2005. *The Notion of Diṭṭhi in Theravāda Buddhism*. London: Routledge Curzon.

Hardy, Edmund, ed. 1994. *Aṅguttara Nikāya* [*AN*], vol. III, Third edition. London: Pāli Text Society.

Jayatilleke, Kulatissa N. 1963. *Early Buddhist Theory of Knowledge*. London: George Allen & Unwin Ltd.

Keith, Arthur B. 1923. *Buddhist Philosophy in India and Ceylon*. Oxford: Clarendon Press.

La Vallée Poussin, Louis de. 1909. *Bouddhisme: Opinions sur l'histoire de la dogmatique*. Paris: George Beauchesne.

MacMahan, David. 2008. *The Making of Buddhist Modernism*. Oxford: Oxford University Press.

Morris, Richard, and Anthony K. Warder, eds. 1989. *Aṅguttara Nikāya* [*AN*], vol. I, Third edition. London: Pāli Text Society.

Rhys Davids, Thomas W., and Joseph E. Carpenter, eds. 1995. *Dīgha Nikāya* [*DN*], vol. II, Third edition. London: Pāli Text Society.

———. 2007. *Dīgha Nikāya* [*DN*], vol. I, Third edition. London: Pāli Text Society.

Saddhātissa, Hammalava. 1978. "The Saddhā Concept in Buddhism." *Eastern Buddhist* 11(2): 137–42.

Sharf, Robert. 1995. "Buddhist Modernism and the Rhetoric of Meditative Experience." *Numen* 43(3): 228–83.

———. 2015. "Is Mindfulness Buddhist? (And Why it Matters)." *Journal of Transcultural Psychiatry* 52(4): 470–84.

Steinkellner, Ernst. 2002. "Zur Lehre vom Nicht-Selbst (anātman) im früher Buddhismus." In *Der Begriff der Seele in der Religionswissenschaft*, edited by Johann Figl and Hans D. Klein, 171–86. Würzburg: Verlag Königshausen & Neumann GmbH.

Thompson, Evan. 2020. *Why I Am Not a Buddhist*. New Haven: Yale University Press.

Tillemans, Tom. 2017. "Philosophical Quietism in Nāgārjuna and the Early Madhyamaka." In *Oxford Handbook of Indian Philosophy*, edited by Jonardon Ganeri, 110–32. Oxford: Oxford University Press.
Trenckner, Vilhelm, ed. 1993. *Majjhima Nikāya [MN]*, vol. I, Second edition. London: Pāli Text Society.
Warder, Anthony K. 1998. *A Course in Indian Philosophy*, Second edition. Delhi: Motilal Banarsidass.
———. 2000. *Indian Buddhism*, Second edition. Delhi: Motilal Banarsidass.

Chapter 4

Mutual Trust and the Foundations of African Communalism

Polycarp Ikuenobe

The dominant cultural traditions, values, modes of being, and ways of life in many sub-Saharan African societies are communalistic. "Communalism" indicates, descriptively, a sense of "commune": people who cooperate, share beliefs, values, and intimate relationships, which are manifested in their attitudes; ways of living; and social, political, moral, and epistemic practices. The idea of "African communalism" is rooted in the traditions of a group of people with common kinship, aspirations, culture, and beliefs, living together proximately in solidarity. Normatively, communalism prescribes that people organize various aspects of their lives cooperatively based on the values of mutual trust, caring, love, and harmonious living. This idea of "communalism" has linguistic expressions in many African languages. It is expressed as *Ubuntu* in Bantu languages, which translates into "a person is a person through other persons." In the Shona language in Zimbabwe, it is *Unhu*, and it is *Botho* in the Tswana language of Botswana. It is captured in Kiswahili by the concept of *Harambee*, which means "everyone pulling together."

This chapter examines the nature of African communalism, which is exemplified in the ethics of duty and the normative conceptions of "personhood" and "elderhood." I argue that the performance or mutual reciprocity of duties, which engenders communal harmony, general welfare, and the attainment of personhood, is grounded in and motivated by mutual trust among people and their trust in communal institutions and processes. With these processes, the community socializes and acculturates people to trust and rely on elders, who act as repositories and custodians of cultural traditions, values, and norms. They perform the duty of imparting cultural traditions to the young in order to perpetuate and promote communal values, mutual trust, and the general welfare. Such trust requires mutual reliance on one another, based on the firm belief that everyone has the goodwill and intention to do what is necessary to maintain communal harmonious living and solidarity. This idea of communalism indicates that my cooperating with and caring about you, accepting requisite norms and values, and performing relevant duties depend on my trust that you *intend* and, most likely, *will* equally care about me, *will* accept these norms and values, and *will* perform requisite duties.

ON THE NATURE OF MUTUAL TRUST AND AFRICAN COMMUNALISM

The African community represents a social cooperation of harmonious relationships based on the moral values and attitudes of goodwill, caring, love, mutuality, friendship, general welfare, and the disposition to rely on and trust others. This African practice of communalism exemplifies the ability of these cooperative values to be manifested substantively in people's lives. It also requires *trusting* others and their willingness to develop and manifest the virtue of *trustworthiness*. This African cooperative idea can be illuminated thus: "Without trust, cooperation never gets off the ground; without trustworthiness, the potential gains from cooperation cannot be realized. Thus, trust and trustworthiness are critical foundations of voluntary cooperation" (Simpson and Harrell 2013, 1531). This indicates that it is difficult to maintain social cooperation without trust because there is always the human tendency for people to exploit others in the community for selfish gain. People perform their communal duties because they trust that others will reciprocate, and this requires the manifestation of trustworthiness.

In Ifeanyi Menkiti's account, an African community involves "a mental commonwealth with others—others whose life histories encompass past, present, and future" (Menkiti 2004, 324). This represents an intimate organic social cooperation that Menkiti refers to as "beingness together" and "beingness-with-others" built on shared memories of the past; beliefs about the present; and desires, hopes, or intentions about the future (Ibid.). The community exemplifies a *collective intentionality*, which reflects mutually shared interests, desires, and the hope of *beingness-together*: of wanting, intending, or accepting together to perform requisite duties and do things to achieve harmonious living, solidarity, and general welfare. In Menkiti's words, "African societies tend to be organized around the requirements of duty . . . *priority* is given to the duties which individuals owe to collectivity, and their rights, whatever these may be, are seen as secondary to their exercise of their duties" (Menkiti 1984, 180). The ideas of collective intentionality and priority of duties that undergird African community of beingness-together can be illuminated by John Rawls's (1971) idea of *overlapping consensus* among citizens in accepting the principles of justice as the basis for the civic life of a well-ordered society.

Lawrence Mitchell's analysis of Rawls's idea of overlapping consensus indicates that "the ability to sustain this civic life itself depends upon the widespread existence of what might be called a civic virtue: trust" (Mitchell 1994, 1920). The practice of mutual dependence, civic virtues, harmonious relationships, caring, and solidarity in the social life of African community involves mutual trust and the confidence that others have the intention and motivation to be trustworthy, reliable, and dependable. The act of trusting involves intentions, where, in Mitchell's view, "trust is centrally about intentions" (Ibid., 1923). "Trust" indicates a kind of *dependence* or *reliance* relationship involving a belief and an assumed or expressed "intention," or a desire to do, accept, and expect something: an "intentionality" or "directedness" at some expectation, action, or commitment. For instance, my trusting John to come to my aid whenever I call is not based on the truth of the statement "John will always come when I call," but on his implied or expressed *intention* to come when I call and my firm belief and confidence in his *intention* and goodwill.

This raises some questions regarding whether "trust," or the belief in the reliability of, or confidence placed in, someone trusted, should be based on truth or adequate justification. In other words, must the belief in the statement regarding what the act of trusting predicts or expects be true, or is trust simply based on hope or faith? It is expected that a person who is trusted will consistently demonstrate trustworthiness in his or her conduct in order to be, or warrant being, trusted. For Mitchell, it is only the acceptance of the intention of the trusted person to follow through on what he or she is trusted to do that matters in understanding the idea of trust and the motivation to trust (Ibid.). Hence, for Annette Baier, the idea (or possibility) of betraying one's trust is an important element of the concept and practice of trusting (see Baier 1986, 234–45). Trust (being trusted and trusting) requires one to accept that others will do what they say they will, or what is expected of them, which one believes they are competent and able to do, for the purpose of achieving some relevant goal.

In the African practice of communalism, achieving harmonious living and general welfare in the community allows everyone to experience well-being and dignity. Such goals become the motivating moral reasons for people to trust, have confidence in others, perform their obligations, and act in relevant ways that will provide for the needs and welfare of everyone. Menkiti captures this African idea of a community as a social cooperation based on trust with the notion of a *collectivist community*, as distinguished from a *constituted community* (Menkiti 1984, 179–80). A *constituted community* is a "non-organic bringing together of atomic individuals into a unit more akin to an association than a community," where it involves "a mere collection of self-interested persons, each with his private set of preferences" (Ibid.). A constituted community is devoid of mutual trust, caring, collective intentionality, interests, and desires because it consists of and is reducible to "the aggregated sum of individuals comprising it" (Ibid., 179).

However, a *collectivist community*, which Menkiti calls "collectivities in the truest sense," has "an organic dimension to the relationship between the component individuals" (Ibid., 180). It is a cohesive group of individuals, based on harmonious relationships, emotional bonds, mutual trust, shared obligations, values, and interests that transcend each individual or their simple collectivity. The organic cohesive nature of the African community is based on the ethical principle of "priority of duty." It requires everyone to act morally to promote harmonious cooperative relationships. In Thaddeus Metz's view, the ethical features that define relationships in African communal traditions can be couched in terms of the notions of "identity," "caring," and "solidarity," which he says are equivalent to "a broad sense of 'love' or 'friendship'" (Metz 2012, 27). In his view, "[a] loving or friendly relationship more or less is one in which the parties think of themselves as a 'we,' engage in common activities, act to benefit one another, and do so consequent to sympathy and for the other's sake" (Ibid.). The affective ethical attitudes and bonds of "love" and "friendship" that bind people together in the community involve mutual trust, concern, and a firm commitment to the good and the welfare of everyone.

The moral attitude that undergirds the social and emotional bond in African communalism is cryptically expressed by John Mbiti's aphorism: "I am because we are, and since we are, therefore I am" (Mbiti 1969, 141). The idea of "we" as a basis for "I" and "I" as a basis for "we" involves mutual trust, which motivates the ethical norms and bonds of human relationships and interactions, individual ethical reasoning, and actions. The African ethical requirements of duty and the bonds of love, friendship, and cooperation are also implicated in Julius Nyerere's idea of *Ujamaa*. He expresses the traditional African communal values of caring, mutuality, and general welfare as principles of social and political cooperation. Nyerere articulates the idea and value of *Ujamaa* as follows: "In traditional African society we were individuals within a community. We took care of the community, and the community took care of us. . . . Nobody starved, either of food or of human dignity, because he lacked personal wealth; he could depend on the wealth possessed by the community of which he was a member" (Nyerere 1968, 165–66).

According to Nyerere, "the organization of traditional African society—its distribution of the wealth it produced—was such that there was hardly any room for parasitism" (Ibid., 163). Usually, everyone believes firmly and trusts that accepting the obligation to contribute to the general welfare, the needs of others, and harmonious communal living will engender a spirit of loving and caring relationships and the attitudes of friendship, solidarity, and mutuality. This idea indicates that the social bond of mutuality in communal cooperation depends on trusting others and the willingness to be trustworthy. This idea is illuminated by Diego Gambetta as follows: "When we say we trust someone or someone is trustworthy, we implicitly mean that the probability that he will perform an action that is beneficial or at least not detrimental to us is high enough for us to consider engaging in some form of cooperation with him" (Gambetta 1988, 217). In African community, people trust that everyone with the requisite capacities will accept communal norms and meet their responsibilities to contribute to the communal welfare in order to ensure that everyone is taken care of. Such contributions provide the material goods, conditions, values, and harmonious context for individuals' well-being. This is based on the acceptance of the norms of priority and reciprocity of duties, mutual commitment, and caring to act to promote the well-being of others based on the trust that others would do likewise.

THE MORAL BASIS FOR TRUST IN AFRICAN COMMUNALISM

This moral stance provides the motivation for the mutual belief and optimism for everyone in the community to expect that others will not abuse or betray each other's trust. Such expectations are based on the norms and values regarding the communally acceptable and expected moral character and virtues that individuals must exemplify, which include trustworthiness, moral integrity, loyalty, and honesty. The act or attitude of trusting exists in social cooperation only when there is mutual commitment to accept the social arrangement and duty of reciprocity. Thus, Carolyn McLeod argues that an important element of trusting others is what we expect the motivation of those we trust to be, which is to be morally motivated to do what we expect and trust them to do (McLeod 2000, 468). In other words, we expect those we trust to be motivated by *moral integrity*, which consists in doing consistently what one has a duty to do, is expected to do morally, and believes one has a moral reason to do.

This requirement of moral integrity in African communalism is consistent with the idea of goodwill, which Baier argues is the motivation for trust: goodwill involves caring about the good of others or having some concern for their welfare (Baier 1986, 234–35). In my view, such caring in the African community is the basis for one's moral integrity—a motivating reason for consistently performing one's duty or acting morally. In addition to moral integrity, the act of "trusting" involves the belief in another person's competence, ability, intentions, and willingness to manifest the virtues or character traits of reliability (i.e., consistency); performing one's obligations; doing what is acceptable or expected (i.e., dependability and loyalty); and being honest, truthful, and abiding by rules, norms, or commitments (i.e., integrity). These moral, epistemic, affective, and behavioral elements of trust are exemplified in African communal ethics of duty, and they find expressions in the attitudes of egalitarianism, reciprocity, mutuality, love, caring, solidarity, and general welfare. These communal moral attitudes are manifested in the cultural practices of fair production and distribution of goods, services, honors, wealth, privileges, responsibilities, and burdens, and in the efforts to achieve general welfare.

What is it that morally motivates mutual trust, commitment, and caring in African community? As Kwame Gyekye indicates, "concern for human welfare constitutes the hub of the Akan axiological wheel" (Gyekye 1997, 143). The moral psychology of mutual trust that undergirds the African practice of communalism and the ethics of duty is exemplified in people's reasoning and considerations about moral concern for others, human flourishing, self-actualization, and general welfare. This idea is expressed in ethical norms that emphasize and prescribe communal mutual interdependence, solidarity, duty, and caring. The concern for human welfare motivates the organization of the community such that the choices that are beneficial to the individual are reciprocally beneficial to the community and vice versa. In Dismas Masolo's view, the ethical motivation for African communalism involves "living a life of mutual concern for the welfare of others, such as in a cooperative creation and distribution of wealth . . . [f]eeling integrated with as well as willing to integrate others into a web of relations free of friction and conflict" (Masolo 2010, 240).

Trusting the community and others to provide social goods, security, caring, and social-psychological conditions for well-being involves the acceptance of the social-moral obligations to promote love, friendship, and mutuality that make human flourishing, self-actualization, and the meaningful choice of a life-plan possible in a community. According to Cohen and Dienhart, "when A trusts B to do something, A invites B to acknowledge and accept an obligation. When—or if—B accepts the invitation, B takes on an obligation, and in that way, trust creates an obligation and forms, or deepens, a trust relationship. When accepted, a trust invitation has a moral effect" (Cohen and Dienhart 2013, 2). People accept that without the community, the material conditions it provides, and trusting relationships with others, one cannot realize one's choice of a good life, or have or experience a sense of self-worth or well-being.

The social-moral element of trust is grounded in certain epistemic states. According to Cohen and Dienhart, trust is characterized as a disposition to act given epistemic states. Trust is said to be an attitude, inclination, or willingness to act and accept certain risks (the disposition), given a set of beliefs or expectation about the trusted party (the epistemic states)—beliefs or expectation that the risks of a trusting action will not materialize and by extension, that the risks are justified by the potential benefit. (Ibid., 1)

In African communalism, trust is understood as a moral disposition based on epistemic attitudes that are manifested consistently in actions involving the performance of requisite duties. Epistemically, trust involves acceptance based on one's belief, evidence, or knowledge of individuals' willingness and abilities to do what they are expected, committed, and trusted to do. Morally, trust involves the goodwill, belief, hope, and optimism that people in a community have the attitudes of concern and integrity, or a sense of duty to do what they are expected, or have committed, to do.

Trust is also an affective attitude, an emotional bond in a relationship between the one trusting and the one trusted, where one has faith or confidence in and depends on the trusted, without any justification for trusting. According to Lewis and Weigert, "[t]his affective component of trust consists in an emotional bond among all those who participate in the relationship. Like the affective bonds of friendship and love, trust creates a social situation in which intense emotional investment may be made, and this is why the betrayal of a personal trust arouses a sense of emotional outrage in the betrayal" (Lewis and Weigert 1985, 971). Such trust creates a sense of emotional comfort with another person to think and hope that they can be relied and depended on to do what is expected of them. Hence, according to Wick, Berman, and Jones, "affect—that is, emotion—is a critical element of trust between persons. Trust occurs because an emotional bond is created between people, enabling them to move beyond rational prediction to take a 'leap of faith' that trust will be honored" (Wick et al. 1999, 100).

The African community as a social cooperation is sustained by the ethical requirement of performing and reciprocating duties, which indicates the behavioral element of trust. This requirement involves efforts to promote the emotional connection implicit in the cooperation and mutual agreement not to betray each other's trust or exploit emotional vulnerability. Such vulnerability is manifested in the disappointment or feeling of betrayal that occurs when one fails to perform one's duties. In the view of Barney and Hansen, trust involves "the mutual confidence that no party to an exchange will exploit another's vulnerabilities" (Barney and Hansen 1994, 176). This implies that one has a right to expect people to do what they are required or have a duty to do. This is the reason why people are morally incensed, offended, or suffer emotional pain when one is betrayed, because trust involves leaving oneself, somehow, emotionally naked, bare, and vulnerable. Thus, trust involves some risks, whereby you expect people to do things that you accept they *may* not do or have a reason not to do, but you have confidence that they will do it anyway. You believe this irrespective of the inability to control what the trusted person will do or ensure that he will do what he says he will do.

The risks that derive from limitations and vulnerabilities in our human nature, which necessitate mutual dependence on others and harmonious living in a community, impose moral imperatives. These imperatives engender moral expectations by others in social-moral relationships that we all perform our relevant duties. In spite of the risk involving the chance that people would not do what we expect of them, Cheshire Calhoun argues that we trust because we morally and socially expect that others have or will manifest moral integrity and so will meet our expectations of them. This involves "standing for something" and consistently doing what "one takes oneself to have the most moral reason to do" (Calhoun 1995, 249). However, Baier argues that we trust others because we believe that everyone has goodwill: that is, there is goodwill on our part to be optimistic that others equally have goodwill to do what is required of them (Baier 1985, 234–35).

The argument from an African communal perspective involving the priority of duties is that everyone in the community ought to take a moral stance or have goodwill. This involves the imperative to perform one's duties based on the firm commitments to the values of caring, harmonious living, relationships, solidarity, and general welfare. African community socializes and acculturates individuals to develop the attitude of trusting, to acquire the virtues of trustworthiness, moral integrity, and the motivation to perform their duties and act on the belief that their own well-being depends on communal welfare. Acquiring and manifesting the attitude of trusting, and the virtues of trustworthiness and moral integrity, provide the basis for participating in communal functions and duties. These virtues are essential for the African normative conception of, and the motivation to attain, personhood, which is a status that is represented by a gradational spectrum of achieved social and moral excellences.

AFRICAN COMMUNALISM AND NORMATIVE PERSONHOOD

Menkiti's idea of the *maximal* conception of "personhood" and the status of an "elder" in African communal traditions can illuminate how trust functions in moral psychology with respect to motivations, reasoning, and actions. One begins the process of attaining personhood by gradually learning norms, acquiring requisite virtues, participating in communal functions, and performing requisite duties. One achieves communal recognition and the status that defines one, socially and morally, as a "person" when one consistently exhibits in one's actions the virtues of caring, love, goodwill, mutuality, trustworthiness, moral integrity, and good moral character. These traits and virtues that engender the ascription of "personhood" are acquired or learned based on the communal processes of integrating, acculturating, and assimilating people into the communal practices. These involve the "rituals of incorporation and the overarching necessity of learning the social rules by which the community lives" (Menkiti 1984, 173).

The processes of learning social rules and acquiring requisite moral character traits, virtues, and values involve trusting the communal processes and institutions to adequately inculcate them. By acquiring and exemplifying these values and virtues, people are able to trust that they will achieve the desired communal conditions that will enhance their well-being, allow them to live meaningful lives, grow up to be mature adults, and become "elders." According to Menkiti, "personhood is the sort of thing which has to be attained, and is attained in direct proportion as one participates in communal life through the discharge of the various obligations defined by one's station" (Ibid., 176). These communal processes and people's trust in them engender the performance of duties and the subsequent attainment personhood. This involves the manifestation of moral excellences, including the virtues of moral integrity and trustworthiness, and the consequent communal recognition.

Discharging one's obligations and participating in communal life are integral for African communalism. According to Menkiti, it is in doing these things that one "attains the full complement of excellencies seen as truly definitive of man" (Ibid., 172). The social and moral status of "personhood" or "elderhood" is earned when an adult has proven himself or herself in the community based on his or her good behavior and moral character. By demonstrating good moral character, practical wisdom, and knowledge of cultural traditions, one is recognized for such excellences as a responsible person of repute and honor. To underscore this, Menkiti argues that social and moral obligations, which are indicator of adulthood, are what transforms someone from "early childhood, [which is] marked by an absence of moral function, into the person-status of later years, marked by a widened maturity of ethical sense—an ethical maturity without which personhood is conceived as eluding one" (Ibid., 176). These communal processes of developing the proper moral attitudes and virtues indicate the African processual and developmental idea of the spectrum of "personhood."

Menkiti describes the gradual processual nature of the spectrum of personhood in African communal traditions as follows: "Through the years of adulthood, there will be other acknowledgements through ceremony, of other important transitions such as marriage, the producing of children, the taking of titles, etc. Finally, there will arrive old age and elderhood and, after elderhood, ancestorhood" (Menkiti 2004, 326–27). "Elderhood" is a stage of adulthood and "personhood" that represents old age and communal recognition that bestows a social and moral status when one demonstrates the moral character, integrity, proper moral functions, insight, and maturity expected of adults in performing their obligations. Old age alone does not make one an elder. The status of "elderhood" represents a normative exemplar of moral virtue, wisdom, knowledge, and life experiences that every individual should aim to attain. In the cultural practices of the community, the idea of an "elder" is instantiated when one exemplifies the relevant moral and epistemic features of "full personhood" and is socially recognized.

"Full personhood" or "elderhood" represents the normative idea of a respectable, trustworthy, dependable, reliable, and responsible older adult who exemplifies good judgment, integrity, significant knowledge, and acts consistently to perform obligations and exemplify moral and epistemic excellence. Thus, Menkiti's *maximal* conception of "personhood" focuses on two aspects of an individual. The first involves the descriptive biological, physical, psychological, and metaphysical features, while the second involves the normative and evaluative features and the social-moral and cultural-ritual processes. These two aspects of the maximal conception of "personhood" indicate that the descriptive features provide the material conditions for the normative. In other words, one cannot satisfy the normative criteria or be called a person in a "true sense" if one has not gone through the communal social, moral, and cultural processes of attaining personhood. But in order to satisfy the normative criteria, one must have the right descriptive physical, biological, psychological, and metaphysical features.

The African conception indicates that "personhood" is a "thick concept" with essential *evaluative* and *descriptive* aspects. The descriptive aspect of personhood involves the natural human metaphysical and physical capacities of autonomy, vitality, soul, and body. The *normative* aspect involves honorific features that are ascribed to or bestowed on humans, based on an evaluation of how properly they use their capacities for the general welfare and for caring in the community. Given this normative connotation of "personhood," the statement "John is not a *person*" is an evaluative judgment. It is not meant to be *descriptive*, that is, it is not meant to deny the descriptive, natural, metaphysical, or psychological features of a person or one's humanity.

The statement, "John is a *person*," is meant to ascribe or bestow a value based on a normative judgment that one has good character or is virtuous; that is, is trustworthy, honest, loyal, dependable, and behaves morally, based on accepted values. As Gyekye indicates:

> The judgment that a human being is "not a person," made on the basis of that individual's consistently morally reprehensible conduct implies that the pursuit

or practice of moral virtue is intrinsic to the conception of a person held in African thought. The position here is, thus, that: for any p, if p is a person, then p ought to display in his conduct the norms and ideals of personhood. For this reason, when a human being fails to conform his behavior to the acceptable moral principles or to exhibit the expected moral virtues in his conduct, he is said to be "not a person." The evaluative statement opposite this is, "he is a person" means, "he has good character," "he is peaceful—not troublesome," "he is kind," "he has respect for others," "he is humble." The statement "he is a person," then, is a clearly moral statement. It is a profound appreciation of the high standards of the morality of an individual's conduct that would draw the judgment "he is truly a person." (Gyekye 1997, 50)

Gyekye argues that this normative conception of personhood in African traditions is essentially correct, and if it is understood as a moral thesis, it is essential for understanding the idea and practice of communalism, that is, communal institutions and processes and their moral foundation. However, as Menkiti indicates, "personhood" is achieved only through the possession of a metaphysical capacity for moral personality and the proper use of such a capacity which engenders admiration, including the willingness of people to trust. Once people see the workings and benefits of the communal institutions and processes, they begin to develop trust and confidence in others and in the social institutions and processes. Trustworthiness, which engenders the attitude of trust, is a virtue that is learned, acquired, and developed by practice and actions in everyday living, guided by communal norms and practices.

The normative aspect of a person underscores Menkiti's idea of the "journey" in the gradational spectrum of personhood, which leads to one's moral and epistemic maturity in adulthood, and then culminates in elderhood. According to him, the fact that "full personhood is not perceived as simply given at the very beginning of one's life, but is attained after one is well along in society, indicates straight away that the older an individual gets the more of a person he becomes" (Menkiti 1984, 173). The status of "elderhood" or "personhood" requires one to demonstrate the highest level of social, moral, and epistemic excellence and competence. Being an "elder" or a "person" requires that those with the requisite metaphysical capacities demonstrate competence, goodwill, and trustworthiness so that others are willing and able to accept and trust their competence, moral integrity, and goodwill. Thus, in the African idea and practice of communalism, "morality is conceived as a fundamental part of what it means [normatively] to be a person" (Ibid., 176).

The normative idea of "personhood" prescribes that individuals should manifest the essential moral values and virtues of caring and love in their actions, in order to promote communal harmonious living, relationships, general welfare, and solidarity with others. However, some adults may not make the requisite efforts or choice to acquire and manifest relevant virtues, in which case they would fail to accept communal normative prescriptions or meet the expected behavior and obligations. These adults would fail to attain "personhood" or "elderhood" and would be treated accordingly without the attendant social recognition, admiration, and privileges. Thus, the status of "elderhood" or "personhood" is an expectation or standard that people could fail to meet. As normative exemplars, "personhood" and "elderhood" represent goals that people should strive to attain and prescriptions of how people ought to act. Hence, in Menkiti's words, "personhood is something at which individuals could fail, at which they could be competent or ineffective, better or worse" (Ibid., 173). This indicates that not all adults or old people achieve personhood or become elders. The honorific judgment about one's character, in virtue of which "personhood" is bestowed, can influence and motivate people positively, to correct bad behavior and maintain good behavior.

The young are motivated to emulate elders in their striving to attain personhood because they trust the integrity of the communal processes in bestowing the honorific status of "elderhood." People trust that when they do what is expected of them, they will be able to live meaningful lives and receive the requisite communal recognition, privileges, and the bestowal of "personhood" and "elderhood." The act or value of trusting which provides the social foundation for bestowing "personhood" is action-guiding, in that it invokes a response that is manifested in one's conduct that meets expectations regarding what one is trusted to do. The communal trust expressed in a judgment about one's character indicates an expectation that a person will continue consistently to demonstrate trustworthiness and responsible behavior. Demonstrating these competencies and virtues engenders admiration due to what the person "stands for" or has achieved, which is essential in the moral psychology of trusting. According to McLeod, "admiration for what people stand for, morally speaking, is an element of our trust in them" (McLeod 2000, 473). Trusting others and the communal institutions, processes, and standards as the bases for attaining and ascribing "personhood" or "elderhood" indicates that trusting is an essential means of motivating and encouraging people to perform requisite duties and empowering them to achieve this honorific status.

TRUSTING AND RELYING ON ELDERS AND COMMUNAL PROCESSES

This idea of trusting African communal processes reflects Menkiti's point that "in the African understanding human community plays a crucial role in the individual's acquisition of full personhood" (Menkiti 1984, 179). The community helps people to acquire the relevant epistemic and moral abilities by nurturing and providing the requisite material conditions and motivations to achieve personhood. Hence, in the process of achieving elderhood or personhood, "the community plays a vital role as a catalyst and as prescriber of norms" (Ibid., 172). These prescribed norms are the standards by which people are evaluated in their behaviors and held accountable. They provide the incentives and reasons for people to perform requisite duties in order to live meaningful and fulfilled lives and enjoy social recognition, respect, communal privileges, and admiration. The trust placed on elders comes from their admired or honored status: namely, the role they play in the community's efforts to acculturate or socialize people into communal practices, impart moral virtues, cultural norms, beliefs, and traditions on the young.

The communal practice of honorifically recognizing and bestowing "personhood" or "elderhood" requires trust in one's capacities and moral integrity. McLeod describes this element of trusting people in terms of believing firmly in "their competence to do what we are trusting them to do and their motivation for doing it" (McLeod 2000, 465). We also trust that the moral adequacy of a person's motivation will be manifested in their moral behaviors. The ascription of "personhood" or "elderhood" assumes that an individual has the metaphysical capacities to acquire and internalize the requisite virtues and values, and that one is competent to use these values as a motivation and basis for reasoning, to make rational autonomous choices, and to act to promote these values.

The normative aspect of personhood reflects human efforts to compensate for our natural limitations and vulnerabilities which motivate the need for cooperation and trust in social relationships. This awareness of human vulnerabilities also motivates the need to manifest certain moral virtues or values, including trustworthiness and caring. These virtues make harmonious living in a community possible, such that one is able to meet the needs that a single individual cannot provide for himself. Trusting implies the belief that some positive outcomes will result from trusting and relying on others in the community. Thus, the act of trusting is an affirmation of our human vulnerabilities, the need to live in a society, and the willingness to trust and depend on others in order to compensate for and address those vulnerabilities. The acceptance of our vulnerabilities is an element of people's moral psychology which motivates their willingness to trust, rely, and depend on others.

The underlying idea is that when I trust and, thus, rely or depend on you as a community member, I expect you to act in a particular way regarding my vulnerabilities and I believe that you have the capacity, intention, and moral disposition to act in response to my expectation. As such, trusting would motivate or activate the disposition to be trustworthy so as not to disappoint the one trusting you, given that such disappointment would be an exploitation of one's vulnerabilities which are affirmed by trusting. This idea makes trust and trustworthiness essential to the social functioning and in the moral psychology of the members of the community. These elements of trust are exemplified in the role of elders in African community who are admired, trusted, and relied on to help the young acquire cultural knowledge, requisite virtues, and moral character by imparting relevant values and beliefs. The place of elders in the community highlights the essential nature of trust in the communal processes of imparting and transmitting traditional beliefs and moral values.

Usually, elders act as custodians, trustees, curators, and repositories of the communal values, norms, and cultural traditions in virtue of which the community promotes and maintains solidarity, cohesiveness, and general well-being so that individuals can achieve personhood. As such, they are trusted to teach and reinforce for the young how to behave in order for everyone to live in peace and harmony within the community. Elders are relied on for their moral and epistemic competencies and their ability to use their life experiences, knowledge, and wisdom to guide and justify prescribed proper conduct. Because most elders are admired and deemed trustworthy, and thus are trusted, they act as mentors and role models. Their actions and words are accepted as exemplifications of the community's values, traditions, and expected and acceptable behavior. By their moral integrity and consistent good behavior, elders are able to model good behavior for others. Thus, the young learn by imitating and following the examples of the elders they admire and trust.

Through practical everyday experience, young people also understand the honorific status, privileges, admiration, and respect accorded to elders, as well as the significance of their duties in the upbringing of the young; the need to trust; and the communal processes of transmitting cultural traditions, norms, and moral values. By understanding the social recognition of elders, their honorific and admired epistemic and moral status, and attached privileges, children get the inspiration and practical incentives to be trustworthy and trusting in order to attain elderhood or personhood. This idea of elders modeling their behaviors as examples that children ought to imitate and rely or depend on can be rationally justified based on the reasonableness of the principles of epistemic trust and reliability, which engender epistemic dependence and deference in the young.

The principles of epistemic trust and dependence indicate that individuals could justify their beliefs based on the epistemic authority of, and the trust placed in, elders as repositories and sources of knowledge. Hardwig illustrates the principle of epistemic dependence thus:

> Suppose that a person A has good reasons—evidence—for believing that p, but a second person B, does not. In *this* sense B has no (or insufficient) reasons

to believe that *p*. However, suppose also that B has good reasons to believe that A has good reasons to believe p. Does B then, *ipso facto*, have good reasons to believe that *p*? If so, B's belief is epistemically grounded in an appeal to the authority of A and A's belief. And if we accept this, we will be able to explain how B's belief can be more than mere belief; how it can indeed, be rational belief; and how B can be rational in his belief that *p*. (Hardwig 1985, 336–37)

This principle indicates that, if people in a community have good reasons to believe that elders—as trusted experts and reliable authorities, sources, custodians, and repositories of knowledge—have good reason, justification, or basis for a certain belief, then the people in the community would also have good reasons to believe justifiably and trust what the elders believe. This is characterized as a *knowledge-based trust* which involves trust in one's competence and an acceptable reliance on one's expertise.

This type of trust raises questions about the adequacy of the commonplace distinction between "reliance" and "trust," which indicates that *reliance* could involve bad or immoral motives, while *trust* must involve good or moral motives. In spite of this distinction, I assume, as Baier does and as McLeod affirms, "that trust is a form of reliance" (McLeod 2000, 474). The African community's reliance or dependence on elders as *reliable* experts or *trusted* authorities assumes that they are morally reliable and motivated by goodwill and duty. And the communal reliance on elders as competent authorities is based on the *principle of epistemic reliabilism*. It states that if we have methods of justification or sources of knowledge that yield true beliefs more often than not, then that source or method is epistemically reliable and adequate as one that we should trust or have confidence in. People in African communities consider their beliefs adequately justified because they consider elders as *reliable*, *competent*, and *trusted* sources of knowledge, as well as adequate methods of acquiring, transmitting, and justifying beliefs. And because of their age, elders have tested and seen the practical adequacy of these beliefs over time.

Kwasi Wiredu underscores the need to rely on elders in African communal cultures by arguing: "In such societies, knowledge is likely to be, on the whole, more a possession of the old than of the young. Prestige and influence, will naturally go along with knowledge, more especially, knowledge of a practical kind" (Wiredu 1996, 67–68). It is important to emphasize the idea of "knowledge of a practical kind," involving how people lead their lives and relate to others on a daily basis. Hence, in Wiredu's view, "the respect accorded to age is not gratuitous" because African communal "societies were of a type in which the elders were rightly considered custodians of knowledge and wisdom" (Wiredu 1980, 68, 29). So, elders are accepted and trusted as reliable because they are truth-conducive sources of beliefs and value-preserving processes of transmitting norms. If these principles are plausible and elders are rightly considered authorities and trusted experts in the community, then Africans can justify the community's reliance on elders as trustworthy or trusted sources and processes of acquiring knowledge of; justifying; and transmitting communal beliefs, traditions, norms, and values.

The trust and confidence by the young in deferring to and relying on elders involve the epistemic and moral correlative of the duty and expectation that elders will be responsible, trustworthy, and reliable sources of knowledge and wisdom for the young regarding how to behave and live a meaningful life. The principle and practice of epistemically trusting, relying on, or deferring to elders are supported by Hardwig's view that the "rational layman recognizes that his own judgment, uninformed by training and inquiry as it is, is *rationally inferior* to that of the expert (and the community of experts for whom the expert usually speaks) and consequently can always be *rationally* overruled" (Hardwig 1985, 342, original emphasis). One intuitive basis for the pragmatic idea of epistemic trust undergirding the principle of epistemic reliance involves the natural limitations of human cognitive abilities, especially those of people who are much younger and who need to sharpen and develop the proper use of their cognitive abilities or judgment. These natural limits indicate human vulnerabilities that undergird the need to trust others in a community and the moral psychology of trusting broadly.

Because *risk* and *vulnerability* are implicit in the act of trusting and the relationship between the ones trusting (young) and the trusted (elders) in African community, the young would be disappointed if their trust is betrayed, and elders would feel a sense of shame for betraying the trust placed in them. This idea is instantiated in the African saying: "it is the obligation of an elder to guide a child, and it is the obligation of the child to heed or follow the guidance of elders." When both fail in their obligations, people cannot achieve communal welfare, solidarity, and harmonious living in the community. Africans have the correlative saying: "it is the fault of the child to refuse to heed or follow the guidance of elders and the fault of the elder to refuse to guide children properly." Thus, elders ought to have moral integrity and have a duty to be trustworthy, responsible, and reliable sources of knowledge, and the young have a duty to be willing and trusting learners. An important element of making the young willing learners involves their obligation to trust and depend on elders and the communal processes for building trust and providing moral guidance. Elders have the responsibility to earn the admiration and trust of the young by being trustworthy and dependable.

CONCLUSION

I argue that the African idea of community involves social cooperation based on mutual trust among people who seek to create the conditions of harmonious and cohesive social living, general welfare, and solidarity. To achieve these conditions, the community stresses the value of trusting; the virtue of trustworthiness; the priority of performing and reciprocating requisite duties; and the need to exemplify in one's behaviors the attitudes of caring, mutuality, love, and friendship. The positive evaluation of one's behaviors and the judgment about the adequacy of one's character engender the bestowal of "personhood" and "elderhood." Elders are accepted and trusted as competent and trustworthy sources; repositories; and custodians of knowledge, cultural traditions, beliefs, and values in the community. The honorific status of "personhood" or "elderhood" indicates a trustworthy, dependable, and reliable individual, and the privilege, respect, and admiration accorded to them will motivate people to trust them and to aspire to be like them. The communal obligations and roles of elders and the admiration and respect accorded to them involve an imperative, which provides the incentive and motivation for everyone to strive to attain "personhood" or "elderhood." The belief that elders would be so motivated to be trustworthy, and have goodwill and moral integrity, motivates and incentivizes the young to trust and rely on them and the communal processes.

REFERENCES

Baier, Annette. 1986. "Trust and Anti-Trust." *Ethics* 96(2): 231–60.
Barney, Jay, and Mark Hansen. 1994. "Trustworthiness as a Source of Competitive Advantage." *Strategic Management Journal* 15(S1): 175–90.
Calhoun, Cheshire. 1995. "Standing for Something." *The Journal of Philosophy* 95(5): 235–60.
Cohen, Marc, and John Dienhart. 2013. "Moral and Amoral Conceptions of Trust, with an Application in Organizational Ethics." *Journal of Business Ethics* 112(1): 1–13.
Gambetta, Diego. 1988. "Can We Trust?" In *Trust: Making and Breaking Cooperative Relation*, edited by Diego Gambetta, 213–35. New York: Basil Blackwell.
Gyekye, Kwame. 1997. *Tradition and Modernity: Philosophical Reflections on the African Experience*. New York: Oxford University Press.
Hardwig, John. 1985. "Epistemic Dependence." *Journal of Philosophy* 82(7): 335–49.
Lewis, David, and Andrew Weigert. 1985. "Trust as a Social Reality." *Social Forces* 63(4): 967–85.
Masolo, Dismas. 2010. *Self and Community in a Changing World*. Indianapolis: Indiana University Press.

Mbiti, John. 1969. *African Religions and Philosophy*. Oxford: Heinemann Publishers.
McLeod, Carolyn. 2000. "Our Attitude towards the Motivation for Those we Trust." *Southern Journal of Philosophy* 38(3): 465–79.
Menkiti, Ifeanyi. 1984. "Person and Community in African Traditional Thought." In *African Philosophy: An Introduction*, edited by Richard A. Wright, 171–81. New York: University Press of America.
———. 2004. "On the Normative Conception of a Person." In *A Companion to African Philosophy*, edited by Kwasi Wiredu, 324–31. Malden: Blackwell.
Metz, Thaddeus. 2012. "African Conceptions of Human Dignity: Vitality and Community as the Ground of Human Rights." *Human Rights Review* 13(1): 19–37.
Mitchell, Lawrence. 1994. "Trust and the Overlapping Consensus." *Columbia Law Review* 94(6): 1918–35.
Nyerere, Julius. 1968. "*Ujaama*–The Basis of African Socialism." In *Freedom and Unity*, 162–71. New York: Oxford University Press.
Rawls, John. 1971. *A Theory of Justice*. Cambridge: Harvard University Press.
Simpson, Brent, and Ashley Harrell. 2013. "Hidden Paths from Morality to Cooperation: Moral Judgments Promote Trust and Trustworthiness." *Social Forces* 91(4): 1529–48.
Wick, Andrew, Shawn Berman, and Thomas Jones. 1999. "The Structure of Optimal Trust: Moral and Strategic Implications." *Academy of Management Review* 24(1): 99–116.
Wiredu, Kwasi. 1980. *Philosophy and an African Culture*. London: Cambridge University Press.
———. 1996. *Cultural Universals and Particulars: An African Perspective*. Bloomington: Indiana University Press.

Chapter 5

Credulity, Diffidence, and Civil Trust in Hobbes

Erfan Xia

The concept of trust is crucial in the philosophy of Thomas Hobbes (1588–1679) as it plays important roles in his epistemology, account of religion, and political theory, being a node where these different areas of his thought interact with each other. For Hobbes, trust is one of the starting points of human reasoning; it is also the foundation of religious and political authority. And yet, as I argue in this chapter, Hobbes also reforms trust: he criticizes the natural credulity of human beings, teaches rational diffidence (i.e., a lack of *fides*, "trust" or "faith"), and rebuilds reasonable trust in and through the civil state. An examination of Hobbes's reformation of trust contributes to our understanding both of his philosophical project as a whole, with its interconnecting parts, and of the problematics of trust in the modern, "enlightened" condition.

Despite its centrality in Hobbes's philosophy, the concept of trust has received little attention in the immense literature on Hobbes. Deborah Baumgold, who pays rare attention to it, complains in a 2013 article that "'trust' is not usually considered a Hobbesian concept, which is odd since it is central to the definition of a covenant" (Baumgold 2013, 838). According to Baumgold's liberal reading, the sovereign is entrusted by the subjects with the contractual obligation of protection, and the subjects' obligation of obedience is conditional upon the latter. However, this liberal theory comes close to the doctrine of the Parliament in *Behemoth*, which Hobbes emphatically refutes.[1] The few other discussions of Hobbesian trust that exist follow in Baumgold's footsteps by focusing almost exclusively on its role in his political theory, as do Peter Schröder (2017) and Eva Odzuck (2017).[2]

Peter Schröder explores the positive political function of trust in Hobbes from a different perspective. Comparing Hobbes's view of trust with that of Locke, he argues that it is Locke who moderates and limits the sovereign's power by making the citizens the judge of whether the government acts in accordance with the trust placed in it; conversely, in Hobbes, trust among citizens is guaranteed by a robust trust in the state. Schröder also challenges the traditional reading of the Hobbesian state as ruled primarily by fear. He points out that trust is essential for civil peace, and fear is not sufficient to create the conditions for mutual trust among citizens. Finally, Schröder highlights the importance of "keeping faith" in Hobbes, whom he contrasts with Machiavelli in this regard, yet he does not clarify the motive for such fidelity or its foundation in human nature.

Eva Odzuck (2017), in contrast to both Baumgold's liberal reading and Schröder's anti-Machiavellian reading of Hobbes's view of trust, presents a Machiavellian Hobbes, whose sovereign prince knows how to use the moral language of the laws of nature and the rhetoric of duty to manipulate ordinary people's trust.[3] While Odzuck is right that in Hobbes trust is sometimes presented as susceptible to manipulation (e.g., in his discussion of religion), the order and peace of the Hobbesian commonwealth are not built upon the gullibility or credulity of the ordinary people. Rather, as Schröder observes, reasonable trust seems to be the foundation for peaceful and fruitful interactions among the citizens in the Hobbesian commonwealth. And yet, these perceptive observations merely raise further questions: What is the relationship between credulity and reasonable trust? And: How can Hobbes criticize trust in the form of credulity while appealing to trust for the sake of civil peace and order? These are the questions I tackle in this chapter.

I agree that Hobbes's concept of trust is politically significant, but I argue that its political significance can only be sufficiently clarified if we also examine its meaning and role in Hobbes's epistemology and his account of religion. We can see how the concept of trust weaves together important themes in Hobbes's philosophy from the following passage in Chapter VII of *Leviathan*:

> When a man's discourse ... beginneth at some saying of another, of whose ability to know the truth, and of whose honesty in not deceiving, he doubteth not; and then the discourse is not so much concerning the thing as the person; And the resolution is called BELIEF, and FAITH: *faith, in* the man; *belief*, both *of* the man, and *of* the truth of what he says. ...
>
> [W]hen we believe any saying, whatsoever it be, to be true, from arguments taken not from the thing itself, or from the principles of natural reason, but from the authority and good opinion we have of him that hath said it; then is the speaker or person we believe in, or trust in, and whose word we take, the object of our faith; and the honour done in believing is done to him only. And consequently, when we believe that the Scriptures are the word of God, having no immediate revelation from God himself, our belief, faith, and trust is in the church, whose word we take, and acquiesce therein. And they that believe

that which a prophet relates unto them in the name of God, take the word of the prophet, do honour to him, and in him trust and believe, touching the truth of what he relateth, whether he be a true or a false prophet. (Hobbes 1994a, VII.5–7)

Trust implies recognition of the authority of the trusted person. It is one of the starting points of human reasoning and is the foundation of both religious and political authority. As I will unpack in this chapter, however, Hobbes criticizes trust in religious authorities and their teachings as an unreliable starting point in reasoning and as dangerously exploitable to the detriment of civil peace. Dismantling such credulity, Hobbes builds a new "political science" starting from the introspective knowledge of human passions. This science teaches diffidence—distrust—in the state of nature, in which people are passion machines rather than political animals. Hobbes shows that as the state of nature is literally unlivable, we should exit it. Inasmuch as diffidence is the ultimate reason why the state of nature is an unlivable state of war, exiting the state of nature means entering a state of confidence or trust. Trust is the defining feature of the Hobbesian state.

Civil trust in Hobbes has two major aspects: on the one hand, the citizens trust their sovereign to punish effectively and equitably and to supervise suitable civic education; on the other hand, the sovereign's fulfillment of these functions constitutes the condition for the citizens to trust one another based on their knowledge of human passions, specifically, their fear of punishment and their cultivated passion for being trustworthy.

NATURAL CREDULITY

For Hobbes, human beings are by nature curious, as they are concerned with finding out what leads to their own good. "It is peculiar to the nature of man to be inquisitive into the causes of the events they see, some more, some less, but all men so much as to be curious in the search of the causes of their own good and evil fortune" (Ibid., XII.2). As it is often not easy to figure out the true causes of good and evil for oneself, people turn to trust others' opinions:

Man observeth how one event hath been produced by another, and remembereth in them antecedence and consequence, and when he cannot assure himself of the true causes of things (for the causes of good and evil fortune for the most part are invisible) he supposes causes of them, either such as his own fancy suggesteth, or trusteth to the authority of other men, such as he thinks to be his friends, and wiser than himself. (Ibid., XII.4)

In other words, "trust is a passion proceeding from belief of him from whom we expect or hope for good." It stands in contrast to "distrust, or diffidence," which "is doubt that maketh him endeavour to provide himself by other means." Moreover, Hobbes observes that people in general are intellectually lazy, as they are more inclined to trust and rely on others' opinions than they are to carry out the scientific investigation into the causes themselves: "a man never provideth himself by a second way [i.e., 'endeavour to provide himself by other means'], but when he mistrusteth that the first [i.e., 'belief of him from whom we expect or hope for good'] will not hold" (Hobbes 1994b, IX.9).

Human beings are concerned with their own good, yet they are so lazy that their first choice is to trust others concerning their own good.[4] In his discussion of religion, Hobbes observes how this inclination to trust is easily exploited: "So easy are men to be drawn to believe anything from such men as have gotten credit with them and can with gentleness and dexterity take hold of their fear and ignorance" (Hobbes 1994a, XII.19).

We may conclude that for Hobbes, human beings are by nature credulous. Their natural concern for their own good makes them curious, and their natural laziness inclines them to soothe their anxious curiosity by trusting in others. Here lies the anthropological explanation of religions: religions satisfy our need to be taught what will bring good or evil to us (Ibid., XII.5). Religion hence enjoys a natural priority over science as the other way to figure out this question.

For Hobbes, trust is an easy but unreliable way to truth: human beings, "by trusting them that reason wrong, fall upon false and absurd general rules" (Ibid., V.19). Or, as he observes in a different context: "All such propositions as are admitted by trust or error, we are not said to know, but think them to be true: and the admittance of them is called opinion" (Hobbes 1994b, VI.6). Furthermore, trust in religious authorities is not only an unreliable guide to the truth about our own good, as it makes people "believe anything"; it is also politically dangerous, as it can be exploited to induce disobedience to the sovereign and civil war. Indeed, the danger to civil peace stemming from Christian authorities' exploitation of credulity is the theme of Hobbes's account in *Behemoth* of the English Civil War running from 1640 to 1660.

In *Behemoth*, Christian authorities disturb the civil peace in two ways. First, diverse interpretations of the Scripture by different sects produce a "diversity of opinion, and consequently (as man's nature is) disputation, breach of charity, disobedience, and at last rebellion" (Hobbes 1990, 52). Second, the Christian authorities compete with the civil authority for the trust of the people. According to "the Church morals," "the principal virtues are, to obey their doctrine, though it be treason, and that is to be religious" (Ibid., 46).[5] Moreover, the pope pretended to "a power of absolving subjects of their duties and their oaths of *fidelity* to their lawful sovereigns, when the Pope should think fit for the extirpation of heresy" (Ibid., 7, my italics). The natural credulity of human beings gives rise to religions, and the Christian religion with its multiplication of sects and otherworldly orientation was particularly disturbing to the civil peace.

In contrast to Christianity, Hobbes sees the pagan religions as civil religions in service to political authority and peace. The purposes of "the first founders and legislators of commonwealths among the Gentiles . . . were only to keep the people in obedience and peace," he writes, and consequently "they have had a care to make it believed that the same things were displeasing to the gods which were forbidden by the laws" (Hobbes 1994a, XII.20). Outside Christendom, "there is no nation in the world, whose religion is not established, and receives not its authority from the laws of that nation" (Hobbes 1990, 46). At the same time, what Hobbes faced was the historical, and one might even say civilizational, challenge to civil authority and peace stemming from religious disturbance in a Christian world. While Hobbes has a Machiavellian understanding of the political nature of pagan religions, he does not counsel the imitation of pagan religions in exploiting ordinary people's credulity for the sake of civil order. Rather, he offers "political science" as the way to civil peace and individual living well. The first step in Hobbesian political science is to dismantle credulity.

ENLIGHTENED DIFFIDENCE

The subject matter of Hobbes's political science is the making of the commonwealth. The reason for contracting into the commonwealth lies in the state of nature: given the character of the state of nature as the state of war, wherein "nature itself is destroyed, and men kill one another," anyone who "desireth to live in such an estate, as is the estate of liberty and right of all to all, contradicteth himself. For every man by natural necessity desireth his own good, to which this estate is contrary" (Hobbes 1994b, XIV.12). Furthermore, as Hobbes expounds in *The Elements of Law*, the reason why the state of nature is the state of war is perpetual diffidence: "Seeing then to the offensiveness of man's nature one to another, there is added a right of every man to every thing, whereby one man invadeth with right, and another with right resisteth; and men live thereby in *perpetual diffidence*, and study how to preoccupate each other" (Ibid., XIV.11, my italics).

Diffidence is the despair of attaining or preserving one's own good; it stems from an individual's expectation that others may come "to dispossess and deprive him, not only of the fruit of his labour, but also of his life or liberty" (Hobbes 1994a, XIII.3). In the famous Chapter XIII of *Leviathan*, diffidence is one of the three "principal causes of quarrel" in the state of nature, the other two being "competition" and "glory." It is notable, however, that competition over the same thing causes only sporadic physical violence; as Hobbes observes, "the nature of war consisteth not in actual fighting, but in the known disposition thereto during all the time there is no assurance to the contrary" (Ibid., XIII.8). Yet if "competition" is one of the causes of war, it is lack of trust—the absence of any "assurance to the contrary"—that perpetuates it, even in the absence of open violence. Moreover, Hobbes recognizes that there are naturally moderate individuals, in contrast to those who are "vainly glorious" (Hobbes 1994b, XIV.3; see also Hobbes 1983, I.4). The reason why "every man," including the moderate ones, has to be in a state of war "against every man" is "not always that a man hopes for a more intensive delight than he has already attained to, or that he cannot be content with a moderate power, but because he *cannot assure* the power and means to live well" (Hobbes 1994a, XI.2, my italics). In sum, then, the crucial reason why the Hobbesian state of nature is a self-contradicting state of constant hostility is perpetual diffidence. The argument for the necessity of contracting into the Hobbesian commonwealth depends on individuals being diffident.

Diffidence is a lack of trust in our fellow human beings and despair of others taking care of our own good. As we have seen in the last section, Hobbes observes that human beings are by nature credulous. They tend to trust and rely on others, especially the clergy, for knowing and attaining their own good. But here we see that in the state of nature, human beings are diffident and guard their own good against that of others. We know that the Hobbesian state of nature is not a state temporally prior to the founding of the commonwealth, but rather a state without a common power: "[D]uring the time men live without a common power to keep them all in awe, they are in that condition which is called war, and such a war as is of every man against every man" (Ibid., XIII.8).

As human beings in the state of nature are diffident and do not trust or recognize any authority as a guide to their own good, we may understand that in the state of nature, not only is there no common power to punish, but the religious authority that commands so much trust among the people in *Behemoth* is absent. Human beings are by nature credulous, and the people of Hobbes's time are superstitious and factious, but the proper material for the Hobbesian commonwealth is people who are diffident. Accordingly, the state of nature, from which the Hobbesian commonwealth arises, already carries normative implications.

Human beings in the state of nature are diffident because they know human thoughts and passions, from which they can infer that others' intentions and actions will not aim at their own good. To be diffident means one has followed the imperative to "read thy self" from the Introduction of *Leviathan* and has thus gained knowledge of human thoughts and passions. Part I of *Leviathan*, devoted to the latter, presents what one would learn from reading oneself. Among other things, one would learn: the unreliability of trust as an approach to knowing and attaining one's own good, the anthropological foundation of religions, and the susceptibility that trust induces to being exploited by others, especially religious authorities, for the sake of the latter's ambition and enrichment and at the cost of one's own good.

Readers of themselves stand in contrast with readers of books in the "Universities" and listeners to preaching from the "pulpit."[6] Obtaining knowledge of human thoughts and passions casts doubt on the motivations and therefore on the credibility of the "Schoolmen" and the clergy, as well as on their specific teachings regarding divine inspiration, the afterlife of the soul, and the natural sociability of human beings. Readers of themselves would know that these are unscientific teachings from untrustworthy people, which encourage unfounded trust both in these particular people and in human beings in general.

In asking his readers to imagine the state of nature—that is, the state without a common authority—Hobbes not only wants us to imagine how we would act without a common power to punish, but also to think again and for ourselves about the world, human nature, and human interaction without assuming the opinions taught by the ideological authorities. Not having "acquiesced in untrue opinions" and not being "tainted with dependence on the potent, or scribbled over with the opinions of their doctors," people's minds would be like the "white paper" or "clean paper" Hobbes hoped people would have (Ibid., XXX.6; Hobbes 1994b, X.8). From the right method of "read[ing] thy self," people would attain knowledge of human thoughts and passions, become diffident, and then learn to trust reasonably.

CIVIL TRUST

The natural credulity of people can be exploited by the religious authorities, which Hobbes identifies as the major cause of the English Civil War. But enlightened diffidence also perpetuates the state of war. So: Should we trust or not?

Diffidence is reasonable in the state of nature, where there is no common power. Hobbes suggests it is no longer reasonable when there is such a power. Without the fear of a common authority with power to coerce, people reasonably fear being the "sucker" (as game theory would have it) in their interactions with each other. They have a "reasonable suspicion" regarding others' intentions and future actions. However, "in a civil estate, where there is a power set up to constrain those that would otherwise violate their faith, that fear is no more reasonable" (Hobbes 1994a, XIV.18–19).[7] It seems, then, that while the state of nature is a state of universal diffidence, the civil state is a state of trust: "either there must be a declared Warre, or a sure and faithfull Peace" (Hobbes 1983, III.2).[8] But questions arise: If my assurance regarding others' faith-keeping depends solely on their fear of punishment, does that count as genuine trust? Is there any other foundation for trust in the civil state than fear of punishment?

For Hobbes, trust that depends on the trustee's fear of punishment is as good as trust can be. As trust proceeds "from belief of him from whom we expect or hope for good" (Hobbes 1994b, IX.9), reasonable trust would be based on anticipation of the trustee's actions, including their speech, in the future—that is, on one's estimation as to whether their actions will conduce to one's own good.[9] According to the fundamental mechanism of human action in Hobbes, all human actions proceed from "endeavour," or "conatus," which is caused by external stimuli, where "endeavour" is the fundamental form of all passions (Hobbes 1994a, VI.1–2).[10] For Hobbes, all human *actions* ultimately proceed from *passions*. Reasonable trust is, accordingly, based on a knowledge of human passions. Trust that depends on the fear of punishment of the trustee has precisely such a solid foundation in the knowledge of human passions.[11] Such trust is therefore much more reasonable than the credulity based on one's ignorance of such passions.

Is there any other foundation for trust in the civil state than fear of punishment? Following our conclusion that reasonable trust is based on anticipation of the trustee's future actions and, therefore, in the context of Hobbes's philosophy, on knowledge of human passions, the question becomes: Are there other passions that motivate faith-keeping in the civil state?

First, it is worth clarifying that fear and the power to punish, while important, are not the exclusive foundations upon which Hobbes establishes civil peace. The promise of the Hobbesian commonwealth is not simply survival based on and under terror, but the secure enjoyment of the pleasures of life. The problem of life in the state of nature is not just that it is "short," but also that it is "poor, nasty, and brutish" (Ibid., XIII.9). The promise of the Hobbesian commonwealth is, accordingly, not a long but terror-stricken and often frustrated life, but rather one in which people live well, commodiously, and contently (Ibid., XIII.14, XV.22, XVII.1). The Hobbesian commonwealth also shapes the citizens' passions through education. Hobbesian civic education makes citizens spontaneously act in a peaceful way, which includes acting in a trustworthy way, so that the coordination of their actions in the civil state need not rely exclusively on the fear of punishment by the sovereign. There are cultivated passions that motivate faith-keeping.

Hobbes's dissatisfaction with the "Universities" and the "pulpits" of his time is well known.[12] He stresses repeatedly the necessity of "the reformation of the Universities" or of "mending the Universitie" (Hobbes 1990, 58, 71). Moreover, he insists that "common people" should be taught "the grounds of their duty" instead of "rebellion" in the "pulpits" (Ibid., 144). Hobbes even boldly counsels the public teaching of his *Leviathan*, presumably in the form of a textbook or catechism.[13]

Scholars have noted that education plays a role in keeping the peace and order of the Hobbesian commonwealth.[14] I argue further that Hobbesian civic education is ultimately the cultivation of the passions. In *Leviathan*, Hobbes states, "*Good* and *evil* are names that signify our appetites and aversions, which in different tempers, customs and doctrines of men are different" (Hobbes 1994a, XV.40). In other words, "customs" and "doctrines of men" can both shape human passions.[15]

I argue that the content of Hobbes's civic education above all consists of the laws of nature, which prescribe the *mores* that should shape the human passions. In the *Elements of Law*, Hobbes says that the laws of nature are "moral laws, because they concern men's manners and conversation one towards another" (Hobbes 1994b, XVIII.1). "Moral" is, of course, an adjective form derived from the Latin *mos/mores*; in seventeenth-century English, it often means what is customary in social interaction.[16] The laws of nature prescribe the "manners" or *mores* of peace. As Hobbes writes:

> By manners I mean . . . those qualities of mankind that concern their living together in peace and unity. (Hobbes 1994a, XI.1)
> Per Mores intelligo hoc loco . . . humani generis qualitates illas, quibus Pax conservator, & Civitatis status confirmatur. (Hobbes 2012, XI.1)

Mores, then, are the human qualities concerning the peace and unity of the civil state. The laws of nature prescribe precisely those human qualities that contribute to these ends.

The quality most relevant to trust is justice. "The fountain and original or JUSTICE" lies in the condition "that men perform their covenants made," and "the definition of INJUSTICE is no other than *the not performance of covenant*. And whatsoever is not unjust, is *just*" (Ibid., XV.2). We may conclude that Hobbesian justice is faith-keeping. How the modification of *conatus* by *mores* works is also clear in Hobbes's explanation of the justice of human beings in the Latin *Leviathan*:

> The names of just and unjust, when they are attributed to men, signify one thing; and when they are attributed to actions, another. When they are attributed to men, they signify a custom or habit [Morem vel Habitum], as a virtue or vice. Thus a man who has a constant will [constans Voluntas] to give to everyone what he has a right to, even if his actions have sometimes been unjust, is still just, provided he loves justice [modo Iustitiam amet], himself condemns what he

has done unjustly, even if he did it secretly [etiamsi clam sit], wishes he had not done it, and if he has done any harm, makes amends as far as he can. (Hobbes 2012, XV.10, fn.)[17]

The quality of justice is "Morem vel Habitum." The just man is one who has the "constans Voluntas" to do just things. We know that in Hobbes's account, "will" is "the last appetite"; it is the one that happens to win the battle of the passions that Hobbes, with evident irony, calls "deliberation." Human beings are naturally inconstant and vacillating.[18] In this passage from the Latin *Leviathan*, however, "will" takes the modifier "constant." The just human beings are so educated or shaped that they always feel pleasure when they do just things. Note that the just human being *loves* justice ("Iustitiam amet"); even if he had the ring of Gyges ("etiamsi clam sit") and could escape punishment, he would not want to be unjust.[19]

Exemplary Hobbesian citizens, then, are educated so that they have a passion for justice, that is, for being trustworthy.[20] Interestingly, Hobbes further calls this passion for justice "nobleness," "gallantness," and "generosity of soul" (animi generositas).

> That which gives to human actions the relish of justice is a certain nobleness or gallantness of courage (rarely found) by which a man scorns to be beholden for the contentment of his life to fraud or breach of promise. (Hobbes 1994a, XV.10)

> Id quod Iustitiam veram & facere, condire solet, est Animi generositas quaedam quicquam fraudi & perfidiae deberi dedignantis. (Hobbes 2012, XV.10)

This noble, gallant, and generous person thinks highly of himself. He scorns "perfidy" and sticks to "fides." His passion for justice seems to be a form of "glory."[21] Hobbes's cultivation of trustworthiness through civic education appeals to the otherwise problematic passion of glory. This Hobbesian insight into the psychology of the trustee anticipates contemporary philosophical discussions on the psychological foundation of trust-responsiveness. For example, Philip Pettit's explanation of trust-responsiveness in terms of the desire to be well considered and the love of regard in the eyes of others could aptly be termed Hobbesian.[22] Karen Jones and Stephen Darwall, meanwhile, each argue that trusting involves a confession of reliance and vulnerability which moves the trustee to be trustworthy.[23] While Hobbes might not agree with Jones's and Darwall's characterizations of such trustworthiness as a benevolent and heartfelt response to trust, he would agree with their observation that trusting involves a confession of reliance and vulnerability, which from his perspective would motivate the trustee to take the opportunity to affirm his superiority by responding with gallant trustworthiness.[24]

To summarize, we can say that within the civil state, trust is reasonable because it has solid foundations in two human passions: the fear of punishment by the sovereign and—in a well-educated Hobbesian commonwealth—the cultivated passion for justice or being trustworthy. So far we have discussed interpersonal trust among citizens in the civil state. But we can see that the condition for the citizens' trust in one another is their trust in the sovereign's effective and equitable execution of punishment and his responsible supervision of suitable civic education. In warning against the danger of "subordinate representatives" arrogating to themselves the people's trust, Hobbes offers "an admonition, for those that are the true, and absolute representative of a people, to instruct men in the nature of that office, and take heed how they admit of any other general representation upon any occasion whatsoever, if they mean to discharge the trust committed to them" (Hobbes 1994a, XIX.3). The citizens trust the sovereign to fulfill his function, and an exclusive trust in the sovereign enables the latter to function well, including effective and equitable execution of punishment and responsible supervision of civic education. Yet what is the basis for the citizens' trust that the sovereign will fulfill his function in the civil state? We may find some clues in the following passage in *Leviathan* Chapter XIX:

> Whosoever beareth the person of the people, or is one of that assembly that bears it, beareth also his own natural person. And though he be careful in his politic person to procure the common interest, yet he is more (or no less) careful to procure the private good of himself, his family, kindred and friends, and for the most part if the public interest chance to cross the private, he prefers the private; for the passions of men are commonly more potent than their reason. From whence it follows that where the public and private interest are most closely united, there is the public most advanced. Now in monarchy the private interest is the same with the public. The riches, power, and honour of a monarch arise only from the riches, strength and reputation of his subjects. (Ibid., XIX.4)

It is clear that, for Hobbes, the basis of the citizens' trust that the sovereign will fulfill his function in the civil state is, again, knowledge of human passions: in this case, the passions of the sovereign. The citizens can trust the sovereign to take care of the public interest because he literally takes the commonwealth as his own, and they can count on his passion for his own good impelling him to fulfill his public function. Drawing on his characteristic understanding of the human passions, Hobbes further argues for the superiority of monarchy as a form of government. Notably, a monarch is more trustworthy: "a monarch cannot disagree with himself out of envy or interest; but an assembly may; and that to such a height as may produce a civil war" (Ibid., XIX.7). Not only do the members of an assembly "envy" one another and stir civil war, but "where the sovereign power is in an assembly," the members of that assembly may also become "one another's flatterers [and] serve one another's covetousness and ambition by turns" (Ibid., XIX.8).[25]

CONCLUSION

Reading Hobbes through the lens of trust, we see the double role of the device of the state of nature in his philosophy, as it is not only the "natural" starting point of his political science but also the product of a critique of traditional trust in religious authorities. It is noteworthy that, on the one hand, Hobbes acknowledges that religious credulity is somewhat *natural*, at least for ordinary people, and on the other hand, that what we find in the state of *nature* is "enlightened" diffidence. In other words, the state of nature is normative in the sense that modern individuals, as material for the civil state, *should* be enlightened skeptics. Then again, in trying to ward off the state of nature and facilitate civil life, Hobbes rebuilds civil trust among the citizens upon the foundation of people's knowledge of others' passions, specifically the fear of punishment and the cultivated passion for being trustworthy. This trust among the citizens, however, is in turn conditioned upon the people's trust that the sovereign will fulfill his function of effective and equitable execution of punishment and responsible supervision of civic education. The people's trust in the sovereign is based on the identification of the public good with the private good of the sovereign, and therefore on the sovereign's passion for his own good.

Hobbes's transformation of trust contributes to the unmaking of traditional sources of religious authority, the clarification of the modern condition for human coexistence, and the establishment of the modern form of trust as civil trust. Moreover, Hobbes's argument for strong trust in the sovereign, though it proved unconvincing to many later thinkers, nevertheless poses the crucial and haunting question of the ground and condition for people's trust in political authority, a problem with which later thinkers continue to wrestle.

Hobbes's clarification of the modern problem of trust—that human beings are by themselves untrustworthy, that trust is necessary for peace and prosperity, and that reasonable trust should be based on knowledge of human passions—also sets the stage for the celebration of two important modern qualities in later ethical and political thought: civility and authenticity. Civility shows that one's passions are in conformity with the social norms of sociability, and authenticity involves transparency about one's passions.

Both qualities facilitate interpersonal trust. The problematics of civility and authenticity, however, call for separate discussions that are beyond the scope of this chapter.

NOTES

1. Hobbes ridicules the following positions of Parliament in *Behemoth*: "That treason cannot be committed against his person, otherwise than as he is entrusted with the kingdom and discharges that trust; and that they have a power to judge whether he have discharged this trust or not"; "Their pretence was this: that neither this nor any other town in England was otherwise the King's, than in trust for the people of England"; "Another said, that his denying of the four bills was the denying protection to his subjects; and that therefore they might deny him subjection" (Hobbes 1990, 104, 120, 145).

2. Schröder (2017, 102) briefly mentions Hobbes's critique of ordinary people's trust in the Christian clergy: "The frontlines for Hobbes were therefore twofold. He attacked the clergy to defend the prerogatives of the sovereign and he had to reckon with the intellectual laziness and gullibility of the ordinary people. Trusting the clergy too carelessly would prove dangerous for the state."

3. Just how "Machiavellian" is Machiavelli's own view on trust is itself an interesting question. For traditional interpretations of Machiavelli as recommending the manipulation of people's trust and belief, see Fleischer (1966) and Tarcov (2013). For an innovative presentation of Machiavelli as recommending the trustworthiness of rulers for the sake of the long-term stability of political authority, see Benner (2017).

4. Machiavelli (1998) has already observed this general tendency to credulity and intellectual "indolence" in human nature. Compare Machiavelli's observation in Chapter XXIV of *The Prince* on the "indolence" of "these princes of ours," who, without defending themselves, found their hope on their people in defending them or calling them back after their loss, on which Machiavelli comments: "one should never fall in the belief you can find someone to pick you up"; see also Chapter IX. One can also see this misplaced trust in others concerning their own good in the people who open the gates to new lords "in the belief that they will fare better" and later find "themselves deceived in their opinion and in that future good they had presumed for themselves" (Chapter III). As astute a prince as Cesare Borgia caused his own "ultimate ruin" by his misplaced trust in Julius II. I read Borgia's credulity as his yielding to the natural indolence in human nature (exploited by a pope!) after such an enterprising career (Chapter VII).

5. See also *De Homine*: "And those who dispute about God desire to win people over not so much to faith in God (in whom all believe already) as to faith in themselves" (Hobbes 2018, XIV.4, my translation).

6. Hobbes's dissatisfaction with the "Universities" and the "pulpit" of his time is well known; see, for example, Hobbes (1990, 23, 58, 64), Hobbes (1994a, XXX.14), and Hobbes (1994b, XXVIII.8).

7. See also *De Cive*, where Hobbes uses "just suspicion" (Hobbes 1983, II.11).

8. As one may note, "reasonable suspicion," or diffidence, poses difficulties regarding how individuals could be united into a civil state based on a set of covenants in the first place. This is an important question, but we are not concerned with it in this chapter.

9. Hobbes would agree with the "evidential constraint on trust" in Thomas Simpson's contemporary philosophical discussion: "it is rational for A to trust B to φ only if, on A's total evidence, it is likely that B will φ" (Simpson 2017, 177).

10. See also Hobbes (1994b, VII.2), Hobbes (1999a, XVV.12), and Hobbes (2018, XI.1–5).

11. Compare Niklas Luhmann's (1979) discussion of trust. Luhmann understands trust as a reduction of a future with open-ended possibilities and great complexity. Moreover, for him, human beings can never attain adequate information for assurance in trusting. I think that underlying his view that the world is extremely complex and the future is unavoidably less than fully predictable is a view of human beings as genuinely free. In my reading, Hobbes is more optimistic regarding the predictability of the future and the level of certainty that trust can achieve, as for him human actions are determined by the passions, which could be inconstant in the state of nature but are much more tractable in the civil state.

12. See, for example, Hobbes (1990, 23, 64), Hobbes (1994a, XXX.14), and Hobbes (1994b, XXVIII.8).

13. See Hobbes (1994a, XXXI.41), A Review & Conclusion.16. In *Behemoth*, Hobbes also seems to imply that his own works contain true political science and should be taught publicly: "The rules of *just* and *unjust* sufficiently demonstrated, and from principles evident to the meanest capacity, have not been wanting; and notwithstanding the obscurity of their author, have shined, not only in this, but also in foreign countries, to men of good education" (Hobbes 1990, 39).

14. For an illuminating discussion of Hobbes's project of reforming education, see Bejan (2010). Gabriella Slomp points out that in *Leviathan*, *De Homine*, and *Behemoth*, Hobbes believes in the effectiveness of education and the plasticity of human beings more than in his earlier works; see Slomp (2000, 108–17).

15. In the following passage from *De Homine*, Hobbes makes clear that the human passions are subject to modification: "Even if first experiences of something be sometimes displeasing, especially when new or rare, by habit they are rendered not displeasing, and afterwards pleasing; that much can habit change the nature of single men" (Hobbes 2018, 11.3). Francis Bacon emphasizes the power of custom in shaping human nature in two of his essays, "Of Nature in Men" and "Of Custom and Education." See Bacon (1985, 177–80). For example, he says, "doctrine and discourse maketh nature less importune; but custom only doth alter and subdue nature" (177) and "Men's thoughts are much according to their inclination; their discourse and speeches according to their learning and infused opinions; but their deeds are after as they have been accustomed" (179). Bacon describes "the predominancy of custom" in a mechanistic metaphor: "as if they were dead images and engines moved only by the wheel of custom" (179).

16. See Abizadeh (2018, 219–23).

17. I have used Curley's translation from a footnote in his edition (Hobbes 1994a, 93).

18. For Hobbes on deliberation and will, see Hobbes (1994a, VI.53), Hobbes (1994b, XII.1–2, 70–71), Hobbes (1999a, XXV.13), and Hobbes (1999b).

19. See also Hobbes (1983, III.5): "But when the words are applyed to Persons, to be just, signifies as much as to be delighted in just dealing."

20. Compare Hume in *A Treatise on Human Nature* on the artificiality of the motive, namely, passion, variously called "sense of duty," "sense of obligation," and "fidelity" (Hume 2007, 3.2.5).

21. Hobbes says that "Vain-glory" is "nourished by the histories or fictions of gallant persons." Hobbes (1994a, VI.41).

22. See Pettit (1995).

23. See Jones (1996) and Darwall (2017).

24. The contemporary scholars discussed here do not pay much attention to the question of to what extent the phenomenon of trust-responsiveness is natural, while, for Hobbes, gallant trustworthiness is a quality cultivated through civic education.

25. Hobbes's argument for a strong trust in the sovereign and his related argument for the superiority of absolute monarchy are among the most criticized aspects of his political theory. From a Lockean perspective, these arguments are as unreasonable as to trust a lion to protect you. See Locke (2010, VII.93).

REFERENCES

Abizadeh, Arash. 2018. *Hobbes and the Two Faces of Ethics*. Cambridge: Cambridge University Press.

Bacon, Francis. 1985. *The Essays*, edited by John Pitcher. New York and London: Penguin Books.

Baumgold, Deborah. 2013. "'Trust' in Hobbes's Political Thought." *Political Theory* 41(6): 838–55.

Bejan, Teresa. 2010. "Teaching the 'Leviathan': Thomas Hobbes on Education." *Oxford Review of Education* 36(5): 607–26.

Benner, Erica. 2017. "Natural Suspicion and Reasonable Trust: Machiavelli on Trust in Politics." *Trust and Happiness in the History of European Political Thought* 11: 53–75.

Darwall, Stephen. 2017. "Trust as a Second-Personal Attitude (of the Heart)." In *The Philosophy of Trust*, edited by Paul Faulkner and Thomas Simpson, 35–50. Oxford: Oxford University Press.

Fleischer, Martin. 1966. "Trust and Deceit in Machiavelli's Comedies." *Journal of the History of Ideas* 27(3): 365–80.

Hobbes, Thomas. 1983. *De Cive*, edited by Howard Warrender. Oxford: Oxford University Press.

———. 1990. *Behemoth*, edited by Ferdinand Tönnies. Chicago and London: University of Chicago Press.

———. 1994a. *Leviathan*, edited by Edwin Curley. Indianapolis: Hackett.
———. 1994b. *The Elements of Law*, edited by G.C.A. Gaskin. Oxford: Oxford University Press.
———. 1999a. *De Corpore*, edited by Karl Schuhmann. Paris: Vrin.
———. 1999b. *Hobbes and Bramhall on Liberty and Necessity*, edited by Vere Chappell. Cambridge: Cambridge University Press.
———. 2012. *Leviathan: The English and Latin Texts*, edited by Noel Malcolm. Oxford: Oxford University Press.
———. 2018. *De Homine*, edited by Josep Monserrat Molas. Paris: Vrin.
Hume, David. 2007. *A Treatise on Human Nature*, edited by David Fate Norton and Mary J. Norton. Oxford: Oxford University Press.
Jones, Karen. 1996. "Trust as an Affective Attitude." *Ethics* 107(1): 4–25.
Locke, John. 2010. *Second Treatise of Government*, edited by C.B. Macpherson. Indianapolis: Hackett.
Luhmann, Niklas. 1979. *Trust and Power*, edited by Christian Morgner and Michael King. Cambridge: Polity Press.
Machiavelli, Niccolò. 1998. *The Prince*, translated by Harvey Mansfield. Chicago and London: University of Chicago Press.
Odzuck, Eva. 2017. "The Concept of Trust in Hobbes's Political Philosophy." *Trust and Happiness in the History of European Political Thought* 11: 118–41.
Pettit, Philip. 1995. "The Cunning of Trust." *Philosophy and Public Affairs* 24(3): 202–25.
Schröder, Peter. 2017. "'Fidem observandam esse'—Trust and Fear in Hobbes and Locke." *Trust and Happiness in the History of European Political Thought* 11: 99–117.
Simpson, Thomas. 2017. "Trust and Evidence." In *The Philosophy of Trust*, edited by Paul Faulkner and Thomas Simpson, 177–94. Oxford: Oxford University Press.
Slomp, Gabriella. 2000. *Thomas Hobbes and the Political Philosophy of Glory*. Basingstoke: Macmillan Press.
Tarcov, Nathan. 2013. "Belief and Opinion in Machiavelli's 'Prince.'" *The Review of Politics* 75(4): 573–86.

Chapter 6

David Hume and Adam Smith on the Nature and Functions of Trust and Trustworthiness

Christel Fricke

David Hume (1711–1776) and Adam Smith (1723–1790) share an interest in the "science of man": both set themselves the task to provide an accurate description of human nature in general and of humans' natural, emotional, and motivational dispositions in particular. They use this description as a starting point for explaining how morality and justice originate in human societies. However, their explanations differ substantially. Underlying these explanations are different views of the emotional and motivational dispositions that humans naturally have. In particular, they provide different accounts of people's trustworthiness and of their dispositions to trust others.

Neither Hume nor Smith makes "trust" an explicit topic of his enquiry. Neither mentions "trust" frequently; the same applies to the related notion of "confidence." Concluding that they have nothing to contribute to the topic would, however, be premature. On the contrary, they agree that trust or confidence, either in other people or in the functioning of political institutions and their representatives, is a central condition for the existence of stable and flourishing societies.

Economists have been particularly interested in Hume's moral theory and his explanation of the emergence of people's trust in others' trustworthiness as found mostly in Book III of his *Treatise of Human Nature* (hereafter, *T*). They share the Humean assumption according to which selfishness is the motive underlying all human choices and actions. And they read Hume's moral theory as an early attempt to reconstruct how originally selfish agents can learn to cooperate and to constitute and follow conventions without first becoming citizens of a state and establishing a ruler and political institutions whose task it is to legislate positive laws, to judge individual actions, and to punish all violations of these laws. For them, Hume's originally selfish agents are forerunners of "economic man," the construct of a rational agent whose rationality consists in his exclusive interest in maximizing his own utility.[1]

Adam Smith's account of human nature does not offer itself as a starting point for economists interested in economic man and his prospects to learn to cooperate with others as straightforwardly as Hume's account does. In his *Inquiry into the Nature and Causes of the Wealth of Nations* (1776, hereafter *WN*), Smith seems to agree with Hume when he claims that agents in economic society aim at accumulating wealth. But in his *Theory of Moral Sentiments* (1759, hereafter *TMS*), Smith had rejected Hume's view of human nature. There, he claims that humans are originally provided with both self-love and sympathy. Their interest in their own well-being does not prevent them from being concerned about others. Indeed, trusting others and being in agreement with them on moral matters is an equally genuine interest and motivational drive as self-love. Smith's accounts of human agents and their most basic interests in *WN* on the one hand and in *TMS* on the other have given rise to the so-called Adam Smith Problem: Are the members of economic society the same as the moral agents Smith describes in his *TMS?* Most scholars now believe that there is no incompatibility: members of economic society do not have to deny their concern for other people. It is quite the contrary. A successful seller of goods must be attentive to the needs and interests of his potential clients, and both must trust each other.

Smith does not reduce the human agent to the construct of economic man, but neither does Hume. While Hume commonly denies that reason guides human choices and actions, Smith denies that human agents' only basic concern is to maximize their utility. One major difference between their accounts of human nature concerns their disposition to trust others and to be trustworthy. As I shall argue in the following, Hume holds the view that humans do not naturally relate to others, whoever they are, as trustworthy people. Nor do they naturally aspire to be trustworthy. On the contrary, all people need to learn to trust each other as reliable cooperators and to become such cooperators themselves. Or rather, they need to learn to trust those others who do not belong to the narrow circles of their family and friends. However, Smith does not follow Hume in his account of the naturally narrow limits of humans' trust in others. According to him, humans are naturally disposed to extend their original trust in their caregivers beyond the confines of their family circles and approach all people as if they were trustworthy. But they need to learn two things, namely, what proper trustworthiness requires of them and whom they are well advised to trust.

In the following, I shall first provide an account of Hume's explanation of the emergence of the conventions of justice, of people's willingness to follow these conventions, and of their acquired disposition to trust in others' trustworthiness. I shall then turn to Smith and his alternative account of justice, and the trust without which the rules of justice could not have any authority. I shall conclude with a short account of the role of trust in Smith's analysis of the dynamics of commercial society.[2]

HUME ON THE CONVENTIONS OF JUSTICE AND THE CHALLENGE TO ACQUIRE TRUST IN OTHERS' TRUSTWORTHINESS

According to Hume, the main factors that influence the human will are "direct passions," namely, "desire and aversion": that is, the desire of pleasure and the aversion of pain (T 2.3.1.1, 257; 2.3.3.3, 266). Without any prospects of feeling pleasure or avoiding pain, there is no motivation or direction of the will. He famously reduces the role of reason in the choices an agent makes to that of a "slave of the passions" (T 2.3.3.4, 266), that is, to a purely instrumental function. Self-love is humans' main motivational source: the pleasure an agent aims to achieve is her or his own pleasure, and the pain she or he desires to avoid is her or his own pain. People's natural disposition to care for others and to share the available—and commonly scarce—resources is limited to the members of a narrow circle of family and friends: "in the original frame of our mind, our strongest attention is confin'd to ourselves; our next is extended to our relations and acquaintance; and 'tis only the weakest which reaches to strangers and indifferent persons" (T 3.2.3.8, 314).

Passions direct human agents toward the enjoyment of pleasure and the avoidance of pain; the success of actions depends on the underlying passions being informed by—or "accompanied with," as Hume puts it (T 2.3.3.6, 267)—truthful judgments about factual causes and effects and the corresponding anticipations.[3] The impact a successful action will have on people outside an agent's narrow social circle does not itself provide a reason for or against choosing it: "Tis not contrary to reason to prefer the destruction of the whole world to the scratching of my finger." And it is no more contrary to reason "to prefer even my own acknowledg'd lesser good to my greater, and have a more ardent affection for the former than the latter" (T 2.3.3.6, 267). Thus, long-term planning and weighing of short-term gains against larger long-term gains is not an essential part of passion-induced choices and actions. Indeed, before according to reason more than the role of a slave, such planning and weighing of expected gains against each other is hardly possible.

Hume is perfectly aware of the fact that an individual human being cannot survive without the help and support of others. Born in a state of fragility and neediness, human children need to rely on others' help for their food, their clothes, and their shelter.[4] As long as this help and support is provided by the members of the respective families, there is no reason to cooperation with those outside these circles. But humans, once they have grown up, commonly move outside these circles. There, they encounter others for whom they do not feel much benevolence; conflicts between them are likely to arise.[5] On the one hand, the resources that people try to possess are scarce. On the other, selfish people tend to be greedy; they are disposed to take more of the available resources than they really need. "This avidity . . . of acquiring goods and possessions for ourselves and our nearest friends, is insatiable, perpetual, universal, and directly destructive of society" (*T* 3.2.2.12, 316).

According to Hume, people have reasons to fear others:[6] what they are afraid of is not so much that others might kill them or physically harm them, or show some other kind of disrespect and thus make them lose their peace of mind and happiness[7]—because, according to Hume, none of these unpleasant actions will provide those who perform them with anything useful.[8] What people do have reason to fear is that others will take away those "possessions as . . . [they] have acquir'd through . . . [their] industry and good fortune" (*T* 3.2.2.7, 313). This is because such goods tend to be useful for anyone who has taken possession of them.

Thus, people's natural interest in avoiding harm can focus on the reduction of the risk to have their possessions taken away. Reducing this risk is the main function of the conventions of justice; accordingly, the rules of justice concern, first and foremost, the stability and protection of people's possessions as well as the assignment of property to owners and the succession of ownership of one and the same object.[9] These rules are "artificial" in the sense of their authority being dependent on humans' willingness to adjust their choices and actions to them and to constitute conventions of justice. But, as Hume himself emphasizes, this does not mean that these rules are "arbitrary" (*T* 3.2.1.19, 311).

Establishing conventions of justice means that "all the members of the society [enter into it and] bestow stability on the possession of those external goods, and leave every one in the peaceable enjoyment of what he may acquire by his fortune and industry" (*T* 3.2.2.9, 314). Establishing such conventions is in the interest of every selfish agent. Since the reasons for submitting to these conventions arise from people's natural selfishness and greed and from the scarcity of goods in their natural environment, one can conclude that there are selfish reasons for limiting people's natural selfishness.[10]

The question is how naturally selfish and passion-driven individuals can successfully constitute a convention. According to Hume, this cannot be achieved by making promises, since the institution of promises is conventional in kind and thus cannot be relied on for constituting a convention in the first place.[11] Nor can this be achieved by a social contract, because such a contract takes the shape of mutual promises of the contracting partners.

Hume's claim is that conventions are established gradually through a process of interaction and the communicative sharing of interests and intentions.[12] One condition for the emergence of a convention among selfish people is that they have an interest in common, an interest for the satisfaction of which they must cooperate. For Hume, the interest all selfish individuals inevitably have is to reduce the risk of losing their possessions to others. The best strategy to reduce this risk is to try and prevent others from taking one's possessions. But how can individual agents prevent other individual agents from trying to take their possessions? Others need to be encouraged not to take their possessions, and the only way an individual can contribute to this encouragement is to start by refraining from taking others' possessions—and to respond to others' taking objects which are not theirs by taking their possessions from them. In the process of this interaction, people can observe an emerging regularity of behavior. They will gradually learn that respecting others' possessions is a successful strategy for reducing the risk of having their own possessions taken away. Once people respond to people's disrespect of others' possessions with disrespect of *their* possessions, this response is more than a mere impact of the passion of selfishness; it acquires an additional function, namely, that of punishing those who fail to control their selfishness and who disrespect others' possessions.[13]

The conventions of justice transform an agent's merely natural possessions into her or his "property." The difference is crucial. Possessions are those external objects which agents have under their actual control but which can be taken from them any time; once these same objects have acquired the status of an agent's property, this agent's possession of these objects "is establish'd by the laws of justice" (*T* 3.2.2.11, 315); others are legally obligated to recognize these objects as her or his property—and they will be punished for failing to do so. Recognizing the right to property is, according to Hume, a virtue. But this virtue is artificial in kind because it depends on the institution of a convention. Conventions are not of natural origin; people need to cooperate in order to bring them into existence: ". . . *those impressions, which give rise to this sense of justice, are not natural to the minds of man, but arise from artifice and human conventions*" (*T* 3.2.2.21, 319, Hume's emphasis).

There is the question of how the "confidence of the future regularity of . . . [others'] conduct" arises. Who makes the first move and refrains from taking others' possessions, even if she or he has the opportunity of doing so and doing so would be in her or his selfish interest? What restrains an agent's natural selfishness? After all, expecting personal advantages from such restraint makes sense only if others follow the agent's example. How can an agent trust that others will indeed do so before the conventions of justice have been established? In the passage quoted above, Hume seems to claim that an agent who makes the first move submits to the rules of justice before the respective conventions have been constituted. How can anyone obey rules which do not yet exist? Hume avoids this absurdity by granting that people rely on their reasoning for spelling out the potentially advantageous consequences for all people to be expected from the conventions of justice. The one who makes the first move allows her or his selfishness to be limited by reasoning.[14] The confidence that others will follow this example derives from the assumption that they pursue their own interest and that they are at the same time capable of reasoning and thus of understanding and anticipating the advantages to be gained from contributing to the constitution of the conventions of justice. This confidence needs to be encouraged by experience, that is, by observing other agents respecting others' property more and more often.[15]

This confidence is not of the same kind as the confidence people have in those who belong to their narrow social circles. The latter confidence or trust is natural and accompanied by goodwill, love, and benevolence in both the trustor and the trustee.[16] By contrast, the confidence in others which agents acquire in the process of gradually constituting the conventions of justice is informed by the belief that others are similar to themselves—equally selfish, equally non-benevolent, and emotionally indifferent, but also equally capable of understanding the advantages to be gained from contributing to the constitution of the conventions of justice and to upholding their authority.[17] To put it in terms of "trust" and "trustworthiness": an agent is motivated to submit to the conventions of justice because she or he trusts that others will do the same. Trustworthy agents share the disposition to respect and uphold the conventions of justice; they do so because they understand that submitting to these conventions is to their own advantage. Trusting that another will submit to the conventions of justice does not imply any attribution of goodwill or benevolence to her or him. Just as the disposition to submit to the conventions of justice is an artificial virtue, the disposition to trust others' disposition to do the same is not natural but artificial. Given Hume's claims about the way the world is and about how humans naturally are, people will acquire this trust sooner rather than later. Large societies cannot exist without convention-based trust. People are sociable beings: they need society for flourishing and, according to Hume, they even develop a taste for living in accordance with social conventions, such that acting in accordance with the conventions of justice becomes a source of "satisfaction" or pleasure.[18] This taste will be shared by the members of a society and thereby will confirm every member's trustworthiness; at the same time, it encourages everyone's disposition to trust others.

Hume makes this explicit in his account of the origin of the convention of promises.[19] Even though, according to Hume, taking an attitude of confidence in others' dispositions to respect the conventions of justice does not imply any attribution of goodwill to them, this does not mean that he reduces an agent's trustworthiness to mere reliability. Trusting an agent not to violate the conventions of justice is not merely anticipating and expecting that she or he will submit to these conventions. In an early stage of the process during which the conventions of justice come into being, people may merely expect and anticipate others not to take their possessions and thus rely on their not doing so, but once these conventions have been authorized and widely accepted, trusting others takes on the shape of a normative expectation. The conventions of justice acquire normative authority and oblige those who share an interest in upholding them. Accordingly, taking an agent to be trustworthy implies the claim that this agent is under the obligation to submit to the conventions of justice. An agent's violation of this obligation does not lead to mere disappointment on the side of those who had trusted in this agent; the trustors rightly feel to have been betrayed by this agent and consider him a rightful target of punishment.[20]

Since Hume claims that an agent's motivation to submit to the rules of justice is ultimately based on her or his informed self-interest, he has to grant that every agent can be tempted to be a "sensible knave,"[21] namely, to violate the conventions of justice whenever this is in their selfish interest. Natural selfish passions may trump an acquired moral taste at any time. Such violations serve an agent's interests under two conditions: she or he will not be found out and punished, and the authority of these conventions is not thereby undermined. Otherwise, the long-term costs for an actual gain might be so high that they would outweigh the actual gain. But once selfish passions reign, there is no time for weighing short-term gains against long-term gains (or costs). Hume cannot exclude the possibility that individual agents might give in to this temptation and choose an action that is "a violation of equity." Everyone's trust in everyone's disposition to submit to the conventions of justice can be betrayed.[22]

With respect to confidence and trust in others' trustworthiness, this means that trusting others always bears the risk of being betrayed; this is all the more regrettable since trust was meant to reduce the risk of losing one's possessions in the first place. Nevertheless, human agents, as Hume describes them, have no reason to be very selective when it comes to trusting other people. Their trust in others is not established by personal interactions with one person after another: "The *general rule* reaches beyond those instances from which it arose" (*T* 3.2.2.24, 320, Hume's emphasis). An agent's trustworthiness is closely connected to her or his natural needs and interests, needs and interests furthermore which all human beings share. Every single agent thus has good reasons to trust that she or he, as well as all others, is obliged by the conventions of justice. Those who choose to be sensible knaves are no exception. Thus, people even have a reason to trust sensible knaves; indeed, the success of the latter depends on the trust of the former. Trust in a sensible knave will inevitably be abused. The risk of finding one's trust abused is a risk with which all people must live. While they constitute conventions for reducing the risk of losing their possessions, they acquire a new kind of risk, namely, the risk of being betrayed by those they trusted.

SMITH ON SYMPATHY, BASIC TRUST, HUMAN WEAKNESSES, AND THE CHALLENGES ARISING WITH COMMERCIAL SOCIETY

At one point in Book III of the *Treatise*, Hume speculates about what would have become of the world if humans were less selfish than he assumed they were, if their benevolence commonly reached beyond their narrow social circles, and if nature's provisions were more abundant: "Encrease to a sufficient degree the benevolence of men, or the bounty of nature, and you render justice useless, by supplying its place with much nobler virtues, and more valuable blessings" (*T* 3.2.2.16, 317–18). Smith's *Theory of Moral Sentiments* proposes a view of the world and of people which seems to be inspired by this speculation, only he does not literally "increase benevolence": instead, he assumes that human selfishness is accompanied by an equally natural capacity, namely, sympathy. Sympathy sets limits both to people's selfishness and to their greed, and it provides the basis for attitudes of trust in other people and for attributions of goodwill to them, whoever they are. Sympathy lies at the foundation of people's learning to be virtuous: people learn this by interacting, guided equally by self-love and sympathy. Among the virtues is a commitment to justice and to trustworthiness. Indeed, Smith's alternative account of human nature does not make all kinds of justice useless: what it does make useless is justice of the conventional kind, along with an account of trustworthiness as an artificial virtue.

The *TMS*

Smith considers Hume's account of human nature to be incomplete, and a source of misleading conclusions about the nature and origin of social and moral norms and the disposition to submit to them. In *TMS*, while not denying our natural selfishness, he claims that humans have an additional, equally natural disposition, namely, "sympathy" (*TMS* I.i.I.1, 9). Smith's "sympathy" is a disposition to empathically share others' feelings, whoever they are. In conjunction with the imagination, it allows people to switch standpoints, look at matters of fact from different angles, and imagine the beneficial or harmful impact these facts have on different people. He assumes that people commonly respond to others' beneficial actions with gratitude and to their malevolent actions with resentment. People in the role of uninvolved spectators seek to sympathize with such feelings of gratitude and resentment. Underlying this is the default assumption that everybody is like everybody else with respect to their capacities to properly detect and approve of beneficial actions, and to properly detect and disapprove of malevolent ones. According to Smith, all sufficiently mentally healthy people share this assumption about each other.

This does not mean that Smith denies the impact of family relations and other kinds of personal attachments on people's attention and responsive sentiments. He is perfectly aware of the fact that people naturally care more about those close to them than about strangers.[23] Also, they are disposed to share their own feelings more easily with loved ones than with strangers. But since the sympathetic sharing of feelings is an important step in the process of achieving mutual sympathy and a shared understanding of the universal demands of morality and justice, personal attachments can become sources of bias which need to be detected and, as far as possible, eliminated.[24] The moral judge is supposed to be impartial.[25] People's partiality for those they love can muddle their moral judgments.[26]

Against the background of Hume's account of natural trust—and of the lack of it beyond the confines of individual agents' narrow social circles—Smith's assumption of the universal similarity of people and their desire to achieve mutual sympathy with others can be taken to imply that people naturally trust (a) that others perceive objects in similar ways, and (b) that they feel similar responses to certain kinds of action. Accordingly, they trust that others will judge the moral worth of people's actions as they do themselves. But people do not only trust others. They naturally trust also in their own perceptual, epistemic, and moral competence. Due to their sympathy, they assume that all people are similar with respect to their commitment to morality and their capacity to tell morally right from wrong actions. This said, he also claims that people need to learn what morality and justice, properly understood, require. This means that they need to learn to be impartial spectators, of others as well as of themselves. His focus is not on either the singular or the general moral judgments which an impartial spectator approves; it is rather on the interactive and sympathy-driven process during which people learn to question sentiment-based moral judgments—both their own and those made by others—and to settle disagreements on moral matters.

For this process to get started, it is important that people naturally trust others whenever they encounter them. They trust that they will tell the truth and that they share an interest in learning how to make proper moral distinctions. This basic trust, the attribution of "goodwill" and trustworthiness to the trustee, is not limited to the members of a narrow circle of family and friends: "Though our effectual good offices can very seldom be extended to any wider society than that of our own country; our good-will is circumscribed by no boundary, but may embrace the immensity of the universe" (*TMS* VI.ii.3.1, 235). This natural, basic, and potentially unlimited trust extends beyond children's disposition to believe what they are told; they believe in their caregivers' goodwill and trustworthiness to help them understand what to eat, what to do, and what to be afraid of.[27] Furthermore, this trust, originally focused on their caregivers, will extend beyond the narrow confines of their families. Once they leave these confines, they will be surprised to find that not everybody is equally trustworthy. Some people tell lies; others flatter in the hope of getting an advantage from the recipients of their false praise. Some people praise those who do not deserve to be praised. Some enjoy others' praise without deserving it.[28] People who praise those who are not praiseworthy are not to be trusted, and the same applies to those who enjoy undeserved praise. Outside their family circles, people need to learn to distinguish between actual praise and proper praiseworthiness.[29] Only the "real man of virtue, the only real and proper object of love, respect, and admiration" is fully praiseworthy (*TMS* VI.iii.18, 245). Because he is virtuous, this man is impartial and trustworthy.[30] Like impartiality, virtue is a state people naturally aspire to achieve.

Due to their sympathy, people morally judge others and care about how others morally judge them. They seek "mutual sympathy," a shared feeling of sympathy based on a shared understanding of what morality and justice require of an agent.[31] Disagreement in moral matters is therefore challenging for people. Questions arise about whose judgment they can trust and whether they can trust their own judgment.[32] Here, I cannot go into the details of Smith's account of the communicative process in which people engage for the purpose of settling their moral disagreements.[33] Smith claims that people are naturally disposed to mutually adjust their ways of feeling about and judging the moral propriety or impropriety of an action, and thus confirm their disposition to trust themselves and others. In the process of doing so, they learn to distinguish between mere praise and real praiseworthiness. Furthermore, they learn to follow a "general rule," namely, "that all such actions are to be avoided, as tending to render us odious, contemptible or punishable, the objects of all those sentiments for which we have the greatest dread and aversion" (*TMS* III.4.7, 159). By following this, the "general rules of morality are formed." These rules "are ultimately founded upon experience of what, in particular instances, our moral faculties, our natural sense of merit and propriety, approve, or disapprove of" (*TMS* III.4.8, 159).

These rules, and the process of their constitution, are not conventional. Rather, the constitution of these rules is like a process of interactive learning of what morality and justice, properly understood, require. During this process, people learn to be impartial spectators and to be virtuous, without ever reaching ideal impartiality or perfect virtue. Implicit is Smith's rejection of Hume's claim that people, who are naturally selfish and distrusting of others, need to learn that cooperation and trust in others' trustworthiness are to their mutual advantage. Smith argues in favor of the view that trust and the disposition to cooperate with others, whoever they are, come to people naturally. This natural disposition to trust makes people more vulnerable to harmful actions committed from "avarice, envy, or unjust resentment" (*TMS* III.4.8, 159) than Hume would have claimed they are. During their lives, they need to learn whom they can trust. Smith makes the following observation: "Frankness and openness conciliate confidence. We trust the man who is willing to trust us" (*TMS* VII.iv.28, 337). Furthermore, trusting others who deserve to be trusted and who rightly trust in one's own trustworthiness is an essential condition for personal happiness: "It is always mortifying not to be believed, and it is doubly so when we suspect that it is because we are supposed to be unworthy of belief and capable of seriously and willfully deceiving" (*TMS* VII.iv.26, 336).

The general rules of morality include what Smith labels the "rules of justice," and, like Hume claimed before him, these rules require the respect for other people's property. Doing so comes as naturally to people as respecting "the general rules which determine what are the offices of prudence, of charity, of generosity, of gratitude, [and] of friendship" (*TMS* III.6.9, 174).[34] I suggest labeling these latter rules the "rules of virtue." There is, according to Smith, one major difference between the rules of virtue and the rules of justice: the latter "are accurate in the highest degree, and admit of no exceptions or modifications" (*TMS* III.6.10, 175); the former, however, are "loose and inaccurate, and . . . admit of ten thousand exceptions" (*TMS* III.6.9, 174).[35] For making the content of the rules of justice accurate, institutions need to be in place, institutions which are authorized to specify, among other things, what counts as someone's property and what counts as stealing it.[36] While there can be a social reality of justice before political institutions are in place, they cannot acquire a sufficiently accurate content without any interference from such institutions. Smith returns to this topic in *WN*.

A man who violates the rules of justice "is no longer to be trusted" (*TMS* III.6.10, 175). Something similar applies to the man who violates the other rules of morality, namely, the rules of virtue. But the question whether someone, by performing an action, did violate the rules of virtue does not always allow for a straightforward answer. There is room for interpretation; this applies especially to the rule that requires people to show gratitude to their benefactors.[37]

In general, in *TMS* Smith presents us with a picture of human nature according to which humans are naturally disposed to trust themselves and others. Social life and cooperation are natural manifestations of this disposition. The social and moral norms which cooperators follow are not conventional in kind, nor do they need to be backed by political and legal institutions. This said, Smith is not blind to social reality where people do not always follow the rules of virtue and justice; they depart from them mostly because they are misled by various biases, including, especially, too much self-love, or the assumption that they are more important than anyone else.[38] This is why people need to learn to be properly trustworthy just as much as they have to learn who is trustworthy and who deserves their trust. But even while they are learning this their default attitude to others remains that of trust, and they hold on to their trust that they are themselves trustworthy.

The *Inquiry into the Nature and Causes of the Wealth of Nations*

In his *Inquiry*, Smith changes his topic. The question is no longer how people, provided with sympathy and self-love as they naturally are, can learn to be impartial and virtuous. Here, Smith explores the evolution, nature, and functioning of commercial society. He famously distinguishes between four stages of civilization, namely, the age of hunter-gatherers, the age of shepherds, the age of agriculture, and that of commercial society (*WN*, V.i.a, 689–708).[39] Since people, naturally provided with both self-love and sympathy, are naturally disposed to trust others and to interact with them peacefully, for long periods of human history there has not been much need for institutions of justice. People have always been disposed to "better . . . [their] condition" (*WN* II.iii.28, 341) and to acquire property.[40] This disposition has driven the history of civilization. But before people could accumulate large amounts of property and engage in trade for further "increasing [their] wealth" (*WN* I.viii.42, 99), institutions of justice were needed only to a limited extent.[41] Only with the emergence of commercial society did this change. In the market, people seek their own advantage. Some of them accumulate large amounts of property. Others fail to do so and end up poor. The gap between rich and poor increases. Smith says explicitly that "wherever there is great property, there is great inequality" (*WN* V.i.b.2, 709–10).

While justice is a concern of every society, institutionalizing it is a central condition for commercial society to evolve and flourish. There are at least two reasons for this. The first derives from the role of wealth: increasing wealth far beyond what anyone needs for their and their families' subsistence is possible only if there are strong and trustworthy institutions of justice to protect private possessions—especially when these possessions are not equally distributed. "The acquisition of valuable and extensive property . . . necessarily requires the establishment of civil government" (*WN* V.i.b.2, 710). The second reason is psychological and concerns people's trustworthiness. The motivation to increase one's wealth diminishes people's goodwill and benevolence: in both the wealthy and the poor the disposition to be trustworthy and to respect other people's property diminishes. "[A]varice and ambition in the rich, in the poor the hatred of labour and the love of present ease and enjoyment, are the passions which prompt to invade property" (*WN* V.i.b.2, 709).

In commercial society, learning to be virtuous is not people's main concern.[42] Rather, their main concern is to become wealthy. Smith famously claims that "it is not from the benevolence of the butcher, the brewer, or the baker, that we expect our dinner, but from their regard to their own interest" (*WN* I.ii.2, 26–27).[43] People's regard for their own interest does not inevitably make them unworthy of trust. It is, however, easier to trust them if there are positive laws in place that regulate people's behavior. Positive laws, including property laws, force people to act as if they were trustworthy. There may still be people who are virtuous enough to be intrinsically trustworthy and to follow the laws of justice for the sake of these laws, but whether someone follows the laws because they are virtuous and trustworthy or because they fear to be punished for violations matters less where the pro-social and cooperative behavior of people is more important than their underlying commitment to virtue. The authority of justice becomes the main and most reliable force for people to be trustworthy: it pushes virtue as the main motivational concern to a lower rank.

Within commercial society, people's trustworthiness is more important than it has ever been in human history. This is because the accumulation of wealth in this kind of society depends on the division of labor, the division of trades, and the making of contracts.[44] The success of the division of labor in a production process depends on everyone involved contributing her or his part, as previously defined (*WN* I.i.1, 13). A tradesman, specializing in something other than food production, depends on food supplies from others (*LJ* ii.40, 86). The institution of contracts cannot persist unless the contracting partners trust in each other's trustworthiness and recognize the authority of a contract (*LJ* ii.50, 89). In order to fill the gap opening within commercial society between the increasing need to trust in others' trustworthiness, and the decreasing intrinsic trustworthiness of people who think of their own wealth more than about others' neediness, political institutions, including institutions of justice, have a key role to play. The laws of justice not only regulate issues related to property; they should make sure that every member of commercial society is free to make her or his own choices without being oppressed by others. As Smith points out, the "second duty of the sovereign" is that "of protecting, as far as possible, every member of the society from the injustice or oppression of every other member of it" and to establish "an exact administration of justice" (*WN* V.i.b.1, 708–09).[45]

As early as *TMS*, Smith rejects Hume's account of the laws of justice as conventional. He provides a psychological reason for even poor people's willingness to submit to these laws, even though it can hardly be in their interest to protect private property independently of how much anyone owns. Poor people "feel ... a peculiar sympathy" with the "satisfaction" of the rich; they imagine the rich to be in a "perfect and happy state," the state they had in their "waking dreams and idle reveries" sketched as "the final object of all ... [their] desires" (*TMS* I.iii.2.2, 51–52).[46] In his *WN*, he adds another reason for rejecting Hume's conventional account of justice: "[c]ivil government, so far as it is instituted for the security of property, is in reality instituted for the defence of the rich against the poor, or of those who have some property against those who have none at all" (*WN* V.i.b.12, 715).

Within commercial societies, the disposition to behave in accordance with the laws of justice as Smith describes them is very different from the disposition to act in accordance with the conventions of justice as Hume describes them. Since the disposition to act in accordance with the law of justice is what makes an agent trustworthy, their accounts of trustworthiness are accordingly very different. According to Smith, in commercial society, trustworthiness is enforced by law; it is not mainly a matter of virtue (as it was in *TMS*) but of fear of punishment. By contrast, according to Hume, trustworthiness arises in all societies in the shape of informed selfishness; once habituated, it is transformed into a kind of artificial virtue, namely, sympathy for the common good and a moral taste for pro-social conventional behavior. As Hume himself put it: "Thus *self-interest* is the original motive to the *establishment* of justice: But a *sympathy* with *public* interest is the source of the *moral* approbation, which attends that virtue" (*T* 3.3.3.24, 320, Hume's emphasis).

Smith avoids the problem Hume has, namely, that of explaining how mutual trust can arise between selfish people. After all, his claim is that trust in others is the default attitude of people, and members of a commercial society are no exception. But within such a society the risk of trusting someone who is not trustworthy increases. The question whom one can trust acquires more importance the more an agent is vulnerable to being betrayed by someone who did not deserve her or his trust. Accordingly, in commercial societies, publicly exemplified trustworthiness becomes a kind of commodity; those who have proved to be trustworthy have access to well-paid jobs and higher status.[47] Indeed, according to Smith, in a commercial society the poor are no more "honestly inclined," that is, trustworthy, than in ancient times, and this further minimizes their prospects of leaving poverty behind: "The poor never own any thing as no one will trust them" (*LJ* iii.144, 197).

In the political realm, citizens need to trust their legislators (as well as judges and the executioners of the law), because this kind of trust is a condition for their willingness to obey the laws legislated for them as well as for the flourishing of the society.[48] Smith, however, is well known for his skepticism as to the general trustworthiness of political rulers.[49] Instead, he underlines the opposite direction of trust: "the law ought always to trust people with the care of their own interest, as in their local situations they must generally be able to judge better of it than the legislator can do" (*WN* IV.v.b.16, 531). Trust, namely, the ruler's trust in the citizens of the state whose ruler he is, is at the core of Smith's political liberalism. Rather than trying to regulate by law many kinds of action, citizens should be left to their own devices as far as possible because they have the expertise to make the best decisions. Beyond their rulers, they should trust the famous "invisible hand" which will coordinate individual agents' various activities in such a way that they contribute to the common good of the respective society, even though none of them meant to promote anything but his own interest.[50] This applies to all dealings with individual agents' capital: no statesman should involve himself in such dealings.[51] By assuming the authority to interfere with the way people invest their capital, a statesman would reveal himself to be unworthy of his citizens' trust.[52]

CONCLUSION

To sum up, Hume claims that people are naturally selfish and their natural disposition to trust others is limited to the members of their narrow social circles. Trust in strangers needs to be acquired. This acquisition is part of the process of constituting the conventions of justice. The trustworthiness which people acquire in this process is the trustworthiness of agents who submit to the laws of justice because they understand that this is the best way for them to prosper, at least if most of the other members of this society do so as well. Hume grants that trustworthiness is a virtue, but, because it needs to be acquired and because its acquisition depends on people joining forces and constituting the conventions of justice, this virtue is artificial.

By contrast, for Smith, the virtue of justice is as natural as all other virtues, including trustworthiness. Underlying this is his claim that people, because they are naturally provided with both self-love and sympathy, are naturally disposed to trust others and themselves. This natural disposition does not, however, guarantee that they hold a proper understanding of what virtues—mainly morality and justice—require. In *TMS*, he explains in detail how people can learn to properly understand what these requirements are. Their need to learn this does not, however, transform the virtue of justice—or any other virtue—into an artificial virtue.

Smith rejects the Humean claim according to which all justice is conventional, a claim that is closely tied to the claim that the virtue of justice is artificial. It is this disagreement on the nature and origin of the laws of justice that leads to their different accounts of people's dispositions to trust others and to be trustworthy. For Hume, informed self-interest underlies trustworthiness: people trust in others' trustworthiness because they attribute to them a kind of informed self-interest that is like their own. Smith's account of trustworthiness is twofold. On the one hand, it is a natural virtue. People naturally trust in themselves and others, and learning what trustworthiness requires is part of learning to be impartial and virtuous. Like impartiality and virtue in general, the virtue of trustworthiness is an ideal. People are naturally disposed to move toward this ideal, but they have a long way to go and many obstacles are awaiting them on this path. This is the topic of *TMS*. In *WN*, Smith presents a somewhat different account of people's trustworthiness, or rather, of the trustworthiness of the members of a commercial society. The development and flourishing of a commercial society depends to a very large degree on the trustworthiness of its members. At the same time, and due to the economic structure of this kind of society, these members are much more concerned to accumulate wealth than to learn to be virtuous and trustworthy. Within such a society, the laws of justice need to be institutionalized. For the functioning of a commercial society, it is of no importance whether its citizens follow the laws of justice because they are trustworthy and virtuous, or because they fear the punishment for all law violations.

NOTES

1. Indeed, economists read Hume's explanation of how the conventions of justice arise within human societies as an early—and informal—example of rational choice theory and of the methodological tool of trust-games. Peter Vanderschraaf provides a very helpful overview of Hume's game-theoretic arguments; see Vanderschraaf (1998). On the same topic, see Skyrms (2008). But economists, when looking for early examples of rational choice theory and trust-games, have not exclusively looked at Hume's theory of justice. Bruni and Sugden read Hume and Smith—and Genovesi—as forerunners of rational choice theory (see Bruni and Sugden 2000), and Vernon Smith has suggested a reading of Smith's main works from the point of view of experimental economics (see V. Smith 2016).

2. McGeer has pointed out the difference between trust as a naturally acquired basic attitude and trust as based on reasons to limit distrust, but she does not refer these respective accounts of the function of trust in interpersonal relations to either Hume or Smith. See McGeer (2002).

3. Hume does indeed admit that reason can have an indirect impact on humans' choices and actions, namely, by providing correct information about those matters of fact on which the success of the chosen action depends. See *T* 3.1.1.16, 297–98.

4. See *T* 3.2.2.2–3, 311–12.

5. Hume speaks of humans' "selfishness and limited generosity" (*T* 3.22.216, 317).

6. On the fear to which the natural human dispositions of selfishness and greed give rise, see *T* 3.2.2.12, 316.

7. This is how I understand Hume when he mentions a person's "internal satisfaction of . . . [her or his] mind" along with this person's "external advantages of . . . [her or his] body." See *T* 3.2.2.7, 313.

8. See *T* 3.2.2.7, 313. There is the question how plausible this claim is, but for now I leave this question aside. See Pack and Schliesser (2006, 58).

9. Hume discusses the content of the conventions of property in *T* 3.2.3–4, 322–30.

10. See *T* 3.2.2.13, 316.

11. Hume discusses the institutional or conventional nature of promises in *T* 3.2.5, 331–37.

12. See *WN* I.x.b.17–19, 122.

13. See *T* 3.2.2.22, 320.

14. This is where Pack and Schliesser see a violation of the methodological procedure which Hume had imposed on himself; see Pack and Schliesser (2006).

15. It has already been pointed out that Hume's explanation of how conventions arise within a society resembles to a large extent David Lewis's account of the origins of social conventions and their self-enforcing nature (see Skyrms 2008, 232). What Lewis adds to the Humean account is not only the reconstruction of the emergence of conventions with the formal means of game theory; he also points out that, for the constitution of a convention, people do not inevitably have to communicate; they do not even need to share a language. It is sufficient that they can observe each other. This argument allows Lewis to defend the claim that natural languages are conventional in kind. See Lewis (1969).

16. See *T* 3.2.5.10, 335. While the confines of these circles are permeable, learning to trust people outside these circles is, according to Hume, not just a matter of extending the circle. On this point I disagree with Annette Baier's reading of Hume's account of the emergence of widespread trust within a society (see Baier 1991, chapter 10). While she does not compare Hume's account of the emergence of widespread trust within a society to that of Smith, her reading of Hume lets his account appear to be much more like that of Smith than it really is.

17. Annette Baier challenges this distinction, but she can hardly refer to Hume as her key witness. See Baier (1992, 141–43).

18. See *T* 3.2.2.24, 320–21. Hume even attributes a "moral sense" to people (*T* 3.3.1.25, 375; see also *T* 3.1.2.1, 302). However, this is an acquired sense: people must rely on reasoning for setting limits to their natural selfish passions before they can acquire a sensitivity to actions which are in accordance with the conventions of justice.

19. See *T* 3.2.5.9, 334–35.

20. In *T* 3.2.5, 331–37, Hume explains in some detail how conventions give rise to obligations with a particular focus on the convention of promises. He grants that there remains something "mysterious" in the transition from desiring that another performs a certain action and anticipating it, to making it a normative expectation which implies that the other is obligated to perform this action; he even speaks of it, maybe

with some tone of irony, in biblical terms, namely in terms of a "transubstantiation" (*T* 3.2.5.14, 336).

In contrast to Hume, David Lewis denies that conventions are intrinsically tied to norms and the obligations to follow them (see Lewis 1969, III.3, 97ff.). That Hume thinks otherwise may be explicable in terms of the needs and interests he ascribes to people which motivate them to engage in convention building. These needs and interests are not entirely contingent. Satisfying them or failing to do so is a matter of a society's flourishing or of its falling apart; thus, it is ultimately a matter of living a flourishing life or merely surviving in a savage condition: "'tis utterly impossible for men to remain any considerable time in that savage condition, which precedes society [and the existence of conventions]; but that his very first state and situation may justly be[?] esteem'd social" (*T* 3.2.2.14, 316). People do not choose to embrace these needs and interests as they might choose or not choose to nourish an interest to meet with all their neighbors on the village green on a Sunday morning. According to Lewis, merely contingent interests that people jointly endorse provide sufficient reasons for their constituting a convention; the only conditions which need to be fulfilled are that all people share these interests and that they cannot satisfy them without the cooperation of other people.

21. Hume uses the notion of the "sensible knave" not in his *Treatise*, but in his *Enquiry Concerning the Principles of Morals* (Hume 1748, 9.22, 282–83).

22. See *T* 3.2.7.4, 343.

23. See *TMS* VI.ii.I, 219–27. According to Sam Fleischacker, there is also room for a moderate kind of cultural relativism in Smith: it is easier for people to empathize with those of their own culture than with those from other cultures. See Fleischacker (2011). However, as he argues elsewhere, the boundaries of a culture do not set limits to Smith's universalism. See Fleischacker (2004, 72–80).

24. See *TMS* I.i.4, 19–23.

25. See *TMS* II.i.2.1–3, 69–70.

26. As Maria Carrasco has argued, one distinction that people need to learn to make is the distinction between morally acceptable and morally unacceptable or misleading partialities. Examples of the latter are the special attachments which emotionally bind parents to their children. See Carrasco (2015).

27. According to Smith, a child's disposition to trust others continues into adulthood; it persists even after the adult has encountered more than one liar. See *TMS* VII.iv, 26, 336–37. On children's natural disposition to trust other people, including their caregivers, and to hold on to this trust when they grow up, see Erikson (1959).

28. Smith speaks of a "coxcomb"; see *TMS* III.2.4, 115.

29. See *TMS* III2., 113–34, especially 129.

30. On trustworthiness as a virtue in Adam Smith, see Griswold (1999, 298–99).

31. Hume also attributes a faculty of "sympathy" to humans, but it is very different from Smith's sympathy. For Hume, sympathy is an acquired faculty rather than a natural disposition. On the difference between Hume's and Smith's accounts of sympathy, see Fleischacker (2012).

32. See *TMS* III.2.15, 122.

33. For such details, see Carrasco (2011) and Fricke (2013).

34. I agree with Eric Schliesser, who has pointed out that, for Smith, property is possible before institutions of justice have come in place in order to protect it (see Schliesser 2017, 177). Schliesser rightly emphasizes that Smith rejects Hume's explanation of the origin of the rules of justice and of people's disposition to submit to them in terms of the utility of these rules (see Schliesser 2017, 26–39).

35. On Smith's account of the laws of justice and their content, see Hanley (2009, 62–67).

36. The distinction between "rules of virtue" and "rules of justice" is not meant to imply any denial that justice is a virtue. Among the virtues, justice has a special place: it allows for a level of precision of content that the other virtues lack. It is for this reason that justice can be institutionalized and take the shape of positive laws.

37. See *TMS* III.6.9, 174.

38. According to Smith, "self-deceit . . . is the source of half the disorders of human life" (*TMS* III.4.6, 158). On the role of self-bias and self-deceit in Smith's moral theory, see Fricke (2013) and Debes (2012, 115).

39. See also Smith's *Lectures on Jurisprudence* (hereafter, *LJ*) I, 14ff.

40. Note that Smith, contrary to Hume, does not distinguish between "possessions" and "property."

41. See Smith's line of thought in *WN* V.i.b, 708–23.

42. As Griswold has pointed out, there is nevertheless room for improving one's virtues even in commercial society. See Griswold (1999, 298).

43. For a very helpful comment on this passage, see Fleischacker (2004, 90–94).

44. This has already been pointed out by Jerry Evensky (2011).

45. The "first duty of the sovereign" is, according to Smith, that of "defending the society from the violence and injustice of other independent societies" (*WN* V.i.a.42, 707). The "third and last duty" is that of "erecting and maintaining" various public institutions and works (*WN* V.i.c.1, 723).

46. Smith returns to the topic in *LJ* 401ff.

47. See *WN* I.x.b.17–19, 122. See also *WN* I.x.b.1, 116–17; *WN* I.x.b.35, 128–29; *WN* V.i.g.14, 796. In pre-commercial societies, trust became an issue mostly during times of war. Where people, when going to war, cannot take their possessions along, there is the question of to whom they can entrust it. On this issue, see *WN* V.i.a, 689–708.

48. See *WN* V.iii.7, 910.

49. The main evidence for this skepticism is to be found in *TMS*, where Smith criticizes "the man of system." See *TMS* VI.ii.2.16–17, 233–34.

50. See *WN* IV.ii.9, 456.

51. See *WN* IV.ii.10, 456.

52. Here, Smith anticipates an aspect of what it means to be trustworthy which Katherine Hawley has recently pointed out, namely, that being trustworthy includes a certain kind of modesty concerning the tasks one promises to deliver. Those who promise more than they can deliver reveal themselves to be untrustworthy. This untrustworthiness is compatible with an attitude of benevolence. See Hawley (2019).

REFERENCES

Baier, Annette. 1991. *A Progress of Sentiments*. Cambridge: Harvard University Press.
Ballestrem, Karl Graf. 2001. *Adam Smith*. München: C.H. Beck Verlag.
Bruni, Luigino, and Robert Sugden. 2000. "Moral Canals: Trust and Social Capital in the Work of Hume, Smith and Genovesi." *Economics and Philosophy* 16: 21–45.
Carrasco, Maria. 2011. "From Psychology to Moral Normativity." In *The Adam Smith Review*, vol. 6, edited by Fonna Forman-Barzilai, 9–29. London: Routledge.
———. 2015. "Morality, Impartiality and Due Partialities." *The Journal of Value Inquiry* 49: 667–89.
Debes, Remy. 2012. "Adam Smith on Dignity and Equality." *British Journal for the History of Philosophy* 20(1): 109–40.
Erikson, Erik H. 1959. *Childhood and Society*. New York: Norton.
Evensky, Jerry. 2011. "Adam Smith's Essentials: On Trust, Faith, and Free Markets." *Journal of the History of Economic Thought* 33(2): 249–67.
Fleischacker, Samuel. 2004. *On Adam Smith's Wealth of Nations*. Princeton: Princeton University Press.
———. 2011. "Smith und der Kulturrelativismus." In *Adam Smith als Moralphilosoph*, edited by Christel Fricke, 100–27. Berlin: De Gruyter.
———. 2012. "Empathy in Hume and Smith: A Contrast, Critique, and Reconstruction." In *Intersubjectivity and Objectivity in Adam Smith and Edmund Husserl*, edited by Christel Fricke and Dagfinn Føllesdal, 273–312. Frankfurt: Ontos Vertag.
Fricke, Christel. 2013. "Adam Smith: The Sympathetic Process and the Origin and Function of Conscience." In *The Oxford Handbook of Adam Smith*, edited by Christopher J. Berry, Maria Pia Paganelli, and Craig Smith, 177–200. Oxford: Oxford University Press.
Griswold, Charles. 1999. *Adam Smith and the Virtues of Enlightenment*. Cambridge: Cambridge University Press.
Hanley, Ryan Patrick. 2009. *Adam Smith and the Character of Virtue*. Cambridge: Cambridge University Press.
Hawley, Katherine. 2019. *How to Be Trustworthy*. Oxford: Oxford University Press.
Hume, David. 1975 [1748]. *Enquiry Concerning Human Understanding and the Principles of Morals*, edited by L.A. Selby-Bigge and P.H. Nidditch. Oxford: Oxford University Press.
———. 2007 [1739–40]. *A Treatise of Human Nature*, edited by David Fate Norton and Mary J. Norton. Oxford: Oxford University Press. [*T*]
Lerner, Melvin J. 1980. *The Belief in a Just World. A Fundamental Delusion*. New York: Plenum Press.
Lewis, David. 1969. *Convention: A Philosophical Study*. London: Blackwell.
McGeer, Victoria. 2002. "Developing Trust." *Philosophical Explorations* 5(1): 21–38.
Pack, Spencer J., and Eric Schliesser. 2006. "Smith's Humeean Criticism of Hume's Account of the Origin of Justice." *Journal of the History of Philosophy* 44(1): 47–63.

Raekstad, Paul. 2016. "Human Development and Social Stratification in Adam Smith." *The Adam Smith Review* 9: 275–94.

Schliesser, Eric. 2017. *Adam Smith: Systematic Philosopher and Public Thinker*. Oxford: Oxford University Press.

Skyrms, Brian. 2008. "Trust, Risk, and the Social Contract." *Synthese* 160(1): 21–25.

Smith, Adam. 1981 [1776]. *An Inquiry in to the Nature and Causes of the Wealth of Nations. Vols. I and II*, edited by R.H. Campbell and A.S. Skinner in cooperation with W.B. Todd. Indianapolis: Liberty Fund. [*WN*]

———. 1982 [1759]. *The Theory of Moral Sentiments*, edited by D.D. Raphael and A.L. Macfie. Indianapolis: Liberty Fund. [*TMS*]

———. 1982 [1763]. *Lectures on Jurisprudence*, edited by R.L. Meek, D.D. Raphael, and P.G. Stein. Indianapolis: Liberty Fund. [*LJ*]

Smith, Vernon. 2016. "Adam Smith and Experimental Economics: *Sentiments* to *Wealth*." In *Adam Smith. His Life, Thought and Legacy*, edited by Ryan Patrick Hanley, 262–80. Princeton: Princeton University Press.

Vanderschraaf, Peter. 1998. "The Informal Game Theory in Hume's Account of Convention." *Economics and Philosophy* 14: 215–47.

Chapter 7

The Obligation to be Trustworthy and the Ability to Trust

An Investigation into Kant's Scattered Remarks on Trust

Esther Oluffa Pedersen

Immanuel Kant (1724–1804) did not make trust an explicit focus in his philosophical works. After publishing *Critique of Pure Reason* and instigating transcendental philosophy in 1781, Kant published extensively on questions of practical philosophy. Here we find Kant's scattered remarks on trust. It is, however, an open question for interpreters whether Kant thought of these remarks as a coherent whole which would allow us to interpret them as a proto-theory of trust. Sussman (2002) ties the interpretation of trust within Kant's works tightly to the question of religious faith. Similarly, Longworth (2017) explores a conception of moral faith within Kant's moral philosophy and argues that it can be rationally reconstructed to give an argument for the reasonableness of trusting. Focusing on how a duty to be trustworthy can be backed by a sanctioning authority, Schröder (2010) argues that trust between citizens in a civil state is upheld by coercive laws, with trust being pertinent in relations between states, with a minimal trust between states being necessary to create peace in international politics.

While Sussman's, Logworth's, and Schröder's discussions are interesting, they do not take account of the full scope of Kant's remarks on trust. Other interpreters have taken Kant's practical philosophy as a starting point to produce a functional theory of trust. For instance, O'Neill (2002) argues that principled autonomy, which she views as a consistent interpretation of the categorical imperative, can be applied to comprehend and solve questions of trust, specifically in bioethics. Pedersen (2012) has argued that it is possible to develop a Kantian conception of trust as a supplement to modern theories of trust. Such constructions of Kantian answers to modern questions expand

and fill the gaps in Kant's scattered remarks to form a full-blown theory of trust. In 2010, Rice et al. even published an empirical study which presumably showed that people invest more trust in what Kant called perfect duties (such as the duty not to lie), and that violations of perfect duties lead to a higher decrease in trust than any other types of violation of trust.

This short overview of the discussions of trust in Kant's philosophy highlights a diversity of interest within this limited set of interpretations. The following exposition aims to reconstruct Kant's remarks on trust as they unfold over different books: *Groundwork of the Metaphysics of Morals*, *Critique of Practical Reason*, *Metaphysics of Morals*, *Religion within the Boundaries of Mere Reason*, *Anthropology from a Pragmatic Point of View*, and *Toward Perpetual Peace*. The main suggestion is that, with Kant's comprehension of the human cognitive faculties, a differentiated understanding of various forms of trust emerges. Therefore, we will commence with a short recapitulation of Kant's transcendental philosophy.

THE DOUBLE PERSPECTIVE OF COGNIZING NATURE AND THINKING FREEDOM

The metaphysical distinction between the human as a noumenal person and as a phenomenal being is crucial to the discussion of trust in Kant's philosophy. The distinction entails a double perspective for examining ourselves and others. On one hand, we should *think* of our noumenal character as a person who is free to choose her own actions. On the other, we may *observe* ourselves and everybody else as appearances who take part in sensible nature and thus are determined by natural laws. Kant launches this double perspective in the *Critique of Pure Reason* as he argues for a fundamental difference within human intellectual capacities between understanding and reason, and an ensuing split between the ability of the understanding to *cognize* objects as appearances and the ability of reason to *think* things in themselves.

Understanding and sensible intuition let us cognize appearances in space and time as parts of the mechanism of nature. As sensible beings we—like all appearances—are determined by causality. The understanding together with sensibility makes up the boundaries of possible experience, and as such, Kant proclaims these to be "the land of truth" (Kant 1781/87, B 294).[1] It is only through the concepts of the understanding and the sensibility of pure intuition that we may establish what and how there is "agreement of our cognition with objects" (Ibid., B 295). The pure principles for such theoretical explanations are accounted for in the doctrine of nature.

Reason construes its own intelligible concepts either as speculative reason or as practical reason. As speculative reason, it should "never . . .

venture . . . beyond the boundaries of experience" (Ibid., B xxiv). Consequently, Kant limits the cognitive powers of speculative reason. Traditional metaphysical concepts such as God, cosmos, and the soul are ideas that reach beyond any possible sensible experience and thus beyond any empirical evidence that would either affirm or reject them. As transcendent concepts they cannot contribute cognitive content to the comprehension of possible experience. One role Kant designates to the intelligible concepts of speculative metaphysics is that of regulative ideas which provide empirical research and practical thinking with a "focus imaginarius" (Ibid., B 672).

The critical examination of speculative metaphysics has a "negative" conclusion, as it "teaches us never to venture with speculative reason beyond the boundaries of experience" (Ibid., B xxiv).[2] However, it has a related positive outcome, as it points to the "absolute necessary practical use of reason" (Ibid., B xxv). Kant clears a space for our moral use of reason in which practical reason extends "itself beyond the boundaries of sensibility, without needing any assistance from speculative reason" (Ibid., B xxv). Understanding moral reasoning as a particular use of reason which resides outside of the cognition of nature, Kant argues that the principles of pure practical philosophy are a self-determining domain. Practical reason construes its own intelligible concepts that demonstrate the possibility to think of ourselves as noumenal persons. The intelligible concepts of practical reason point out how we "at least must be able to *think* [objects] as things in themselves" (Ibid., B xxvi). To think of myself as a thing in itself implies that I, without contradiction, can think of myself as free, as an autonomous and self-governing person. Freedom is not part of the causally determined objects of nature: "I cannot *cognize* freedom as a property of any being to which I ascribe effects in the world of senses, because then I would have to cognize such an existence as determined and yet not as determined in time . . . nevertheless, I can *think* freedom to myself" (Ibid., B xxviii).

The concept of freedom that Kant rescues from the universal causality of nature, and thus from the laws of nature, is an intelligible concept. Practical reason enables us to think of ourselves as noumenal persons independent of all empirical conditions. Such personhood implies that we who can determine ourselves by practical reason are free insofar as we follow the law which we give ourselves. This law originates in practical reason and is the moral law we oblige ourselves to follow. Thus, Kant explains morality as practical reason giving itself a law, namely, the self-governing moral law, the categorical imperative. The foundation of morality in pure practical reason without any recourse to empirical facts gives Kant's practical philosophy its unique and complicated form.

PRUDENT TRUST

The double perspective from which Kant argues we should view ourselves as well as other humans, namely, as things in ourselves *and* as appearances in experience, entails that we must also approach trust from this double perspective. While Kant is primarily interested in the concept of trust that concerns the moral character of the person, the contours of a conception of trust informed by experience—that is, prudent trust—can be discerned. It includes reference to the hypothetical imperatives which Kant, in *Groundwork of the Metaphysics of Morals*, defines as "imperatives of *skill*" (Kant 1785, 4:415). Such imperatives declare that "whoever wills the end also wills (insofar as reason has decisive influence on his actions) the indispensably necessary means to it that are within his power" (Ibid., 4:417). The simplicity of the imperative of skill announces that to commit ourselves to rational actions we must commit ourselves to the known means necessary for such actions.

The imperative of skill is basically a definition of human rationality.[3] Thus, if an agent rationally assumes that to achieve some end it is necessary to trust another agent to cooperate in bringing it about, it will be rational to trust the other *given that* the agent calculates that the end is best attained by trusting the other. This kind of prudent trust is basically (a) strategically goal-oriented action, which includes the cooperation of others to succeed, and, as such, (b) an estimation of whether the risk of failure is greater by trusting another agent to cooperate or by pursuing the action without the cooperation of the other agent. Furthermore, the desired end is empirical, as is the principle to act upon that the agent establishes.

Kant was aware of how human beings strategically use (and abuse) one another as means to obtain ends in society. In *Anthropology from a Pragmatic Point of View*, Kant's point of departure is experiential observation of how humans live together in societies. He underscores how experientially developed customs in different cultures create habits on which we can depend when interacting prudentially with each other. At a dinner party in Königsberg, one can expect "even without [the participants] making a special agreement about it, . . . a certain holiness and a duty of secrecy [concerning the said] . . . with respect to what could later cause inconveniency . . . for without this trust [Vertrauen], the healthy enjoyment of moral culture within a social gathering and the enjoyment of this social gathering itself would be denied" (Kant 1798, 7:279). This shows in an analogous way in the

> ancient customs in the trust [Vertrauen] between human beings who eat together at the same table; for example, those of the Arab with whom a stranger can feel safe as soon as he has merely been able to coax a refreshment from him (a drink of water) in his tent; or when the deputies coming from Moscow to meet the

Russian Tsarina offered her *salt* and *bread*, and by the enjoyment of them she could regard herself as safe from all snares by the right of hospitality. – Eating together at one table is regarded as the formality of such a covenant of safety. (Ibid.)

Kant seems to suggest that it is prudent to trust other agents if we know their cultural etiquette. Habitual norms govern much human intercourse and assist us in daily evaluations of who and when it is prudent to trust, as we need agents to cooperate with us to achieve our ends.

An example of how humans abuse culturally learned behavior concerns reading the intentions of others from facial expressions. Kant remarks that those who can control their face's expressions in a manner that conceals their affections and thoughts may deceive others: "those who are masters in this art are not exactly regarded as the best human beings with whom one can deal in confidence [im Vertrauen Handeln kann], especially if they are practiced in affecting expression that contradict what they do" (Ibid., 7:300). Because we ordinarily judge each other's trustworthiness by presuming that an individual's facial "play of expressions" to some degree "expose[s] his interior" (Ibid., 7:300), humans can control their facial expressions strategically. Those who can put on a poker face and display expressions that mislead are not trustworthy in interactions. It would therefore be prudent not to trust them to cooperate in bringing about an action.

The fascinating insight into decorum and habits we can gain from studying pragmatic anthropology, social psychology, and pedagogics, and which enables human beings to interact with each other and prudentially trust one another to cooperate in realizing rational ends, forms the background to Kant's discussion of trust as a moral concept. Against this pragmatic observation of humans in their customary interactions, Kant highlights the demands of pure practical reason.

In *Critique of Practical Reason*, Kant draws attention to how we are aware of "the boundaries of morality and self-love," that is, the difference between morality and our egoistic ends. We seldom "fail to distinguish whether something belongs to the one or the other" (Kant 1788, 5:36) when agents act strategically and abuse everyday trust between people. Kant emphasizes how we do not trust someone who gives false testimony and especially not if he pleads that it was the "sacred duty of his own happiness" which obliged him, "pointing out the prudence he had observed in order to be secure from discovery even by yourself, to whom he reveals the secret only because he can deny it at any time" (Ibid., 5:35). In a similar manner, we would not take seriously

> someone [who] recommends to you as steward a man to whom you could blindly trust [anvertrauen] all your affairs and, in order to inspire you with confidence [Zutrauen], extols him as a prudent human being with masterly understanding

of his own advantage . . . and is ready to use other people's money and goods for his end as if they were his own, provided he knows that he can do so without being discovered or thwarted. (Ibid., 5:35–36)

Kant employs these examples to argue *ex negativo* that all humans—because we are beings endowed with reason—have an inherent comprehension of morality. According to Kant, such insight is deeply rooted in "common human reason . . . and . . . there is, accordingly, no need of science and philosophy to know what one has to do in order to be honest and good, and even wise and virtuous" (Kant 1785, 4:404). In line with this, Kant comprehends the purpose of pure practical philosophy to be the articulation of the sources and principles of pure morality within human reason.

HUMAN NATURE AND SOCIETY

To grasp Kant's conception of the role trust plays in pure practical reason, we will start by focusing in greater detail on how he comprehends the human being. In the first part of *Religion within the Boundaries of Mere Reason*, Kant famously claims that the human being, endowed with the capacity to choose freely, inherently contains the roots of evil. Taking as his point of departure that every human being chooses to act from self-love, Kant argues that "when [self-love is] adopted as the principle of our maxims, [it] is precisely the source of all evil" (Kant 1793, 6:45). This definition differs from the typical everyday understanding of evil as deeds that harm others. Kant underscores that all strategically motivated actions—all actions guided by imperatives of skill—as far as these are instigated by self-love are, as such, morally evil. Actions motived by self-love stem from "a free power of choice" that constitutes a "deviation of the maxims from the moral law" (Ibid., 6:29). With this definition, Kant can delimitate the source of evil to the free choice of the human being. Every individual human being with the propensity [Hang][4] to act in accordance with maxims of self-love also has a propensity for evil. By freely choosing to act from maxims of self-love, the individual also carries full responsibility for her maxims and the morally evil motivation.

Every one of us is accountable for choosing maxims of self-love. We cannot excuse ourselves with our sensible nature and its appetites. On the contrary, Kant emphasizes that human nature in and of itself is not evil. Human nature consists of three natural predispositions [Anlagen], namely, the predispositions "1) to the *animality* of the human being, as a *living being*; 2) to the *humanity* in him, as a living and at the same time *rational* being; 3) to his *personality*, as a rational and at the same time *responsible* being" (Ibid., 6:26). The human propensity for evil is not part of our natural predispositions.

It arises from the free choice [freie Willkür] of the individual who chooses a maxim of self-love and thereby uses her naturally good predispositions for what is morally evil.

If the human being only had the predisposition to *animality* she would be neither good nor evil—she would simply be an instinctual animal. If the human being, on the other hand, only had the predisposition to *personality* she would in and of herself be good, a sort of holy creature who always acted in accordance with the moral law. Now, as the human being contains the predisposition to *humanity* and therefore also the free choice of her motivation to act—the ability to establish maxims as principles for action—she freely chooses to act out of self-love and consequently also freely chooses evil. Radical evil, in Kant's contention, is the inherent corrupting principle of free choice to act for the sake of self-love instead of acting out of respect for the moral law. Therefore, *all* humans who use their ability for rational choice become evil—not in the sense that they thereby do evil deeds but in the sense that their incentive to act is corrupted by self-love.

The predispositions, instincts, and human feelings are good and only turned evil by human choice. Kant indicates that the individual tends to assure himself that this predicament and its causes

> do not come his way from his own raw nature, so far as he exists in isolation, but rather from the human beings to whom he stands in relation or association. It is not the instigation of nature that arouses what should properly be called the *passions* which wreak such great devastation in his originally good predisposition. His needs are but limited, and his state of mind in providing for them moderate and tranquil. He is poor (or considers himself so) only to the extent that he is anxious that other human beings will consider him poor and will despise him for it. Envy [Neid], ambition [Herrschsucht], avarice [Habsucht], and the malignant inclinations associated with these, assail his nature, which on its own is undemanding, *as soon as he is among human beings.* Nor is it necessary to assume that these are sunk into evil and are examples that lead him astray: it suffices that they are there, that they surround him, and that they are human beings, and they will mutually corrupt each other's moral disposition and make one another evil. (Ibid., 6:93)

While the individual may attempt to accuse others of corrupting her, Kant underscores how everyone is personally responsible for choosing self-love as the source of their motivations in social interactions. Engaging with others in any societal form, however primitive, instigates the passions of envy, ambition, and avarice (see also Kant 1784a, 8:17, 1793, 6:97). These passions make humans compete, thereby developing human talents and cultural forms while envy, ambition, and avarice eat away our good intentions and induce each human being to act even more profoundly out of maxims of self-love. Thus, Kant depicts human society as a breeding ground for egoistic and evil choices.[5] The predisposition to humanity including the rational capacity of free choice of maxims is the condition of the possibility of human culture *and* of corrupt human motivations.

Human cohabitation in society is, according to Kant in *Metaphysics of Morals*, a "*state of nature*" so long as there is "no *civil* society (which secures what is mine or yours by public laws)" (Ibid., 6:242). A society only ruled by custom is a state of nature because the members of that society do not have access to a public, stable, and common institution that can settle their disputes. In a society in the state of nature, such disputes are subject to coincidental rulings and settlements reached through custom and arbitrary power relations. In a state of nature, the conditions for culpability are not public and transparent; the establishment of public laws lifts human society out of the state of nature and "into . . . civil right [ins . . . bürgerliche Recht]" (Ibid.). This is a necessary condition for developing reciprocal freedom because public laws direct the actions of individuals and make them predictable. As we shall discuss later, public laws are also important for reciprocal trust.

FREE CHOICE IS NOT FREEDOM

In *Metaphysics of Morals*, Kant also underscores how "experience shows the human being as a *sensible being* is able to choose in *opposition to* as well as *in conformity with* the law" (Ibid., 6:226), and, as such, he reiterates that the human being has the propensity for evil as well as the possibility to choose to act out of respect for the moral law. Our experiential acquaintance with human culture seems to be evidence of the free choices of humans. Within the framework of Kant's practical philosophy, free choice is not freedom; instead, and in opposition to defining freedom as the mere ability to choose, Kant defines freedom as the act of self-governing in which we produce the moral law as our own incentive: we "act on a maxim which can also hold as a universal law" (Ibid.). When acting in freedom, our maxim is completely void of self-love and empirical incentives. Freedom is the ability of the "lawgiving of reason" and amounts to the ability to act in accordance with the categorical imperative which "binds us a priori and unconditionally by our own reason" (Ibid., 6:227). The obligation and binding force of the categorical imperative is a voluntary self-binding of reason and is exempt from external force and constraint.

We come to know freedom "as a *negative* property in us, namely that of not being *necessitated* to act through any sensible determining grounds" (Ibid., 6:226). To assume that the free choice of maxims—that is, the rational ability to choose maxims of self-love as incentives for action—is freedom amounts to the contradictory assumption that freedom should be "located in a rational subject's being able to choose in opposition to his (lawgiving) reason" (Ibid., 6:227). Thus, the free choice of maxims may work in harmony with the lawgiving of reason if all maxims are compatible with the categorical imperative. If the individual's free choice opposes the categorical imperative, freedom is not the determining ground exactly because the individual lets sensible determining grounds necessitate his maxims. The empirical ends of attaining some culturally valued goal necessitate the free choice, and it turns conceptions of sensibility and calculations of the possibility to interfere in the causal chains of events into its governing principle.

Universal lawgiving is the most fundamental trait of the will and thereby of the human being as an intelligible being. Seen from this perspective, it is evident that free choice "for or against the law (*libertas indifferentiae*), even though choice as a *phenomenon* provides frequent examples of this in experience" (Ibid., 6:226), cannot be equated with freedom. Prudent trust in all its guises, as either a vehicle for egoistic advantages or cultural decorum, is a subsample of the free choice of maxims of self-love and, as such, part of what Kant has defined as radical evil. According to Kant, the foremost task of every human being, and humanity in its totality, is to acquire a moral disposition [Gesinnung] which enables the person to act in accordance with the moral law. Different forms of trust are crucial to accomplish this most difficult life task. Consequently, the roles that trust plays in the endeavor of humans to become moral persons will be our focus going forward.

SELF-TRUST

The most fundamental and recurring mode of trust in relation to the moral character of the person is trust in oneself. We must trust ourselves to be assured that we have decided on and continue to uphold a moral disposition. While we have a moral duty to cultivate maxims in accordance with the moral law, we cannot obtain definite empirical confirmation of our efforts. The noumenal character of the human being is not part of any possible experience. The self, as well as our dispositions, is fundamentally opaque to ourselves as well as to others. Thus, reference to the *legality of the action* does not confirm the *morality of the disposition*:

> For a human being cannot see into the depths of his own heart so as to be quite certain, in even a *single* action, of the purity of his moral intention and the sincerity of his disposition, even when he has no doubt about the legality of the action.... In the case of any deed it remains hidden from the agent himself how much pure moral content there has been in his disposition. (Ibid., 6:392–93)

There are no means to confirm whether one's maxim for action was motivated by self-love. Once an action has been performed, the legality of the action becomes transparent for everyone and can be evaluated as its effects are visible in the world of experience. The agent's disposition, however, is part of the noumenal character of which we cannot have knowledge. We think our motivation, but we cannot confirm that we really did act from a maxim that corresponds with the moral law, nor can we reaffirm to ourselves that our disposition is stable and consistent. This fundamental opacity of the self and our dispositions calls for trust and hope for us not to lose self-confidence. In *Religion within the Boundaries of Mere Reason*, Kant emphasizes that in order "to hope to become pleasing to God," the agent must be "conscious of such a moral disposition in himself as enables him to *believe* [*glauben*] and self-assuredly trust [auf sich gegründetes Vertrauen] that he . . . would steadfastly cling to the prototype of humanity [the Son of God] and follow this prototype's example in loyal emulation" (Ibid., 6:62).

Belief [Glaube], hope, and trust in interconnection are the only remedies the individual can reach for to affirm to herself that she strives after a "moral disposition in all its purity" (Ibid., 6:61). Neither of these can be upheld with any certainty. But there is a crucial difference between belief [Glaube] and hope on one side and trust in oneself on the other. Belief [Glaube] concerns the agent's conviction that the cultivation of a pure moral disposition will make her pleasing to God, and the agent can hold on to this conviction even if she fails in cultivating a moral disposition. The attitude of hope alludes to a state in which the agent truly is pleasing to God, and this hope is directed toward the judgment of the believed-in transcendent God. As such, belief [Glaube] and hope both aim at a power outside the individual (and outside the world of experience), namely, the transcendent God. Trust in oneself is different as it relates to the agent's self-assurance. Kant emphasizes that the human ability of self-assessment is contested, as "one is never more easily deceived than in what promotes a good opinion of oneself" (Ibid., 6:68).

To trust oneself to have a moral character entails setting one's mind at rest with persuasion that one's disposition really is moral. Since there is no possible evidence for this persuasion, self-trust always involves uncertainty and the risk of being mistaken. Therefore, it "seems never advisable to be encouraged to such a state of trust [Vertrauen] but much more beneficial (for morality) to 'work out one's salvation with *fear* and *trembling*'" (Ibid.). However, such constant distrust of oneself, "if misunderstood, can drive one to the darkest enthusiasm" (Ibid.). Aware of this imbalance between the moral duty to cultivate a moral disposition and the impossibility of reassuring oneself of the perseverance of one's moral disposition, Kant argues that a balanced trust in oneself is required. Self-trust is an act of balance, as the agent should not trust himself too much, while "without *any* trust [Vertrauen] in the disposition once acquired, perseverance in it would hardly be possible" (Ibid.).

Kant's comprehension of self-trust is closely related to truthfully estimating oneself. In the *Doctrine of Virtue*, Kant emphasizes that "the greatest violation of a human being's duty to himself regarded merely as a moral being (the humanity in his own person) is the contrary of truthfulness, *lying*" (Kant 1797, 6:429). Lying to oneself is not only a corruption of one's personality but "from such a rotten spot [faulen Stelle] (falsity, which seems to be rooted in human nature itself) the ill of untruthfulness spreads into his relations with other human beings" (Ibid., 6:431). Striving to become a truthful and, as such, a trustworthy (noumenal) person is the most fundamental perfect duty of the human being to himself. As beings endowed with reason, we have an obligation to be trustworthy.

To be able to strike a balance between setting one's mind at rest in self-trust and continually truthfully searching one's disposition for corrupting maxims of self-love requires that the agent has some measuring stick. The only evidence available for the agent is the effects of his moral disposition in the world of experience. Thus, Kant argues that the balance between too much self-trust and continuous distrust is reached "by comparing our life conduct so far pursued with the resolution we once embraced" (Kant 1793, 6:68). Adopting the "principles of the good" and perceiving "the efficacy of these principles . . . on the conduct of his life as it steadily improves" (Ibid.), the agent gains some confidence that the decision to cultivate a moral disposition has had effects on his actions. The agent may assume this to indicate some accuracy in his self-trust and therefore he "can also reasonably hope that in this life he will no longer forsake his present course . . . for, on the basis of what he has perceived in himself so far, he can legitimately assume that his disposition is fundamentally improved" (Ibid.). The assurance of self-trust is a reasonable hope that the effects of one's actions are reliable indications of one's moral disposition.

LAZY TRUST

Self-trust in its pure practical form involves, as a sine qua non, the agent's choice to work to create a "moral conversion" in his disposition which "is an exit from evil and an entry into goodness" (Ibid., 6:73). This "abandonment of evil is only possible through the good disposition that effects the entrance into goodness" (Ibid., 6:74). Having chosen the moral conversion, the individual needs self-trust to reassure himself that his moral disposition has perseverance. The only possible means for assessing the moral disposition is his life conduct. However, this opens the door for the individual to deceive himself that his disposition is better than it really is.

Kant underscores that other humans and the institutions of religion offer no assistance in the individual's assessment of his moral conversion, "for that ideal must be adopted in our disposition before it can stand in place of the deed" (Ibid., 6:76). Social rituals as "expiations, be they of the penitential or the ceremonial sort, . . . invocations or exaltations (even those of the vicarious ideal of God's Son)" (Ibid.), and so on, cannot be used as signs of the betterment of the agent's moral disposition. Social endorsement of one's behavior is no confirmation of the purity of one's heart. On the contrary, if the agent focuses on sanction and support from social institutions, Kant suggests the agent is really deceiving himself and falling into a form of trust which is not supported by practical reason. Knowing that only the moral goodness of his disposition is relevant for the agent to assess his inner worth, and can make him pleasing to God,

> the sensuous human being still searches for an escape route by which to circumvent that arduous condition; namely that if only he observes *the custom* (the formalities), God will surely accept that for the act itself, and this would of course have to be called an instance of God's superabundant [überschwengliche] grace, were it not rather a grace dreamed up in lazy trust [faulen Vertrauen], or itself perhaps an instance of hypocritical trust [erheucheltes Vertrauen]. (Ibid., 6:193)

Deceiving oneself in lazy trust entails putting on a display in the world of appearances of eager observance of custom, as though such a display could amount to evidence of one's morally good noumenal character. The agent hypocritically trusts that observing custom will make any further efforts to cultivate a morally good disposition unnecessary. As such, lazy trust is a deliberate deceiving of oneself. Lazy trust is furthermore a kind of blind trust in the social order of things.

Trusting that the conformity of one's outer appearances and actions with the rules of the community can make up for the inner worth of a moral disposition amounts to a disregard of the predisposition to *"personality,* as a rational and at the same time *responsible* being" (Ibid., 6:26). The agent renounces his personal responsibility for his moral disposition and assigns responsibility to the custom of, say, the church. Lazy trust makes up the "escape route" of social adaptation—that is, "going along to get along"—which allows the agent to passively rely on custom rather than actively scrutinizing his own disposition for maxims of self-love. In this manner, the agent delivers himself to the socially given.

MINORITY AND ENLIGHTENMENT

The critique of lazy trust as a passive conformity to custom has a parallel in Kant's critique of most people of his time for willingly submitting themselves to the guardianship of authorities. In the short text *What Is Enlightenment*, Kant zealously declares:

> It is because of laziness [Faulheit] and cowardice [Feigheit] that so great a part of humankind, after nature has long since emancipated them from other people's direction (*naturaliter maiorennes*), nevertheless gladly remains minors [unmündig] for life, and that it becomes so easy for others to set themselves up as their guardians. It is so comfortable to be a minor! If I have a book that understands for me, a spiritual advisor who has conscience for me, a doctor who decides upon a regimen for me, and so forth, I need not trouble myself at all. (Kant 1784b, 8:35)

Being lazy or cowardly by relying on instruction from others seems to be traits pertaining to the individual. Answers to questions of how to lead one's life are ready-at-hand, and the individual does not have to bother to think for herself. According to Kant, "the far greatest part of humankind (including the entire fair sex)"[6] voluntarily submit themselves to the ruling of guardians who depict "the step toward majority [Mündigkeit] to be not only troublesome but also highly dangerous" (Ibid.). The individuals are responsible for their minority, while the state of minority is beneficial to and encouraged by the authorities. According to Kant, the dialectic between voluntarily submitting oneself to one's guardians and reinforcing the state of minority describes a dynamic of social life which will continue if left undisturbed.

Being accustomed to following the guidance of authorities makes it almost impossible for the individual to break out of minority: "it is difficult for any individual to extricate himself from the minority that has become almost nature to him. He . . . is really unable for the time being to make use of his own understanding, because he was never allowed to make the attempt" (Ibid., 8: 36). It is easier to passively accommodate one's actions and beliefs to the guidance of social authorities than to "have courage to make use of your *own* understanding" (Ibid., 8:35). What the individual cannot achieve alone, Kant argues, can be accomplished by the interactions between various individuals if they meet as a public [Publikum]. Kant claims that the public will

> almost inevitably [enlighten itself] if only it is left its freedom. For there will always be a few independent thinkers, even among the established guardians of the great masses, who, after having themselves cast off the yoke of minority will

disseminate the spirit of a rational valuing of one's own worth and of the calling of each individual to think for himself. (Ibid., 8:36)

Kant suggests that a reciprocal cultivation of reflective thinking will take place as individuals interact by means of writing and publishing arguments *pro et contra* in questions of politics, life, and science. This argumentation should be completely free for everyone given that they speak for themselves. Kant differentiates what he calls the public use of one's reason from private use. The public use designates the argumentation that an individual puts forth as an independent scholar who has considered an issue. "The *public [öffentlichen]* use of one's freedom must always be free, and it alone can bring about enlightenment among human beings" (Ibid., 8:37). The private use of one's reason, on the other hand, should be "very narrowly restricted," as it involves possible situations where official representatives of, say, a church, argue against the statutory rules of the church they have been appointed to represent.

By restricting the private use of reason, Kant sets limits to the critique an individual may express while carrying out the official role of representing an institution. The individual may, as an independent scholar, make public use of his or her reason and criticize any institution in public writings. But as an official representative executing the authority of an institution, the individual must keep within the limits of that office and is thus restricted in making use of his or her private reason. At the same time, the free public use of one's reason can only take place within the limitations of state laws. Kant articulates and endorses the ideal of the Prussian king Frederic II as "*Argue* as much as you will and about whatever you will, *but obey!*" (Ibid.). The civil laws put necessary public restrictions on behavior by delineating which actions are legal and illegal and, as such, subject to penalties. Within the space of publicly known legal behavior created by civil laws, participants are free to discuss and criticize all subject matters by publishing their views in public journals. This implies that free public argumentation inter alia may criticize and discuss the reasonableness of civil laws.

Kant's contention is that, through rational argument, the enlightened public will be able to move the government in the direction of more just and legitimate laws. The "propensity and calling to *think* freely . . . works back upon the mentality of the people (which thereby gradually becomes capable of *freedom* in acting) and eventually even upon the principles of *government*, which finds it profitable to itself to treat the human being, *who is now more than a machine* in keeping with his dignity" (Ibid., 8:41–42). As such, the aim of enlightenment is to produce a state in which people can think freely and, by means of their free thinking, influence the institutions of government.

Kant took a special interest in *"matters of religion* because . . . that minority, being the most harmful, is also the most disgraceful of all" (Ibid., 8:41). He made a strong case for free thinking in questions of religion. The subjection to forced statutory religion "would be a crime against human nature" (Ibid., 8:39) because one's conscience and inner moral disposition may only be ruled by the freedom of practical reason. In religious matters, as a subspecies of morality, Kant vehemently argued for the abandonment of all outer force: "it is absolutely impermissible to agree, even for a single lifetime, to a permanent religious constitution not to be doubted publicly by anyone and thereby, as it were, to nullify a period of time in the progress of humanity toward improvement" (Ibid.). His own present Kant deemed "an *age of enlightenment*" that, however, was lacking much to be called "an *enlightened age*," since the bulk of people were not "able to be put in the position of using their own understanding confidently and well in religious matters without another's guidance" (Ibid., 8:40).

The ability to actively reflect on one's life conduct and its possible agreement with the demand for purity of the heart is—as we have seen above—a question of being able to trust oneself. Such self-trust requires a general cultivation of the active, reflective use of one's intellectual capacities. Kant depicts the progress toward greater majority [Mündigkeit], casting off the yoke of lazy trust in authorities, as a slow development evolving from group participation in public argumentation. Thus, enlightenment is a social emancipatory development taking place while the people are under more or less voluntary guidance by authorities.

Kant believed that formulating the ideal of enlightenment set a guiding *focus imaginarius* to aim at in the course of history. The progress to an enlightened age would imply that minority [Ünmündigkeit] only occurs as result of the individual's self-imposed lazy trust in authorities and voluntary submission under their guidance. In such an enlightened age, a process of reciprocal cultivation of reflective thinking would ensure that everybody was educated to have a propensity and calling to think freely, and therefore it would truly be the responsibility of the individual to choose a morally good disposition.

LEAVING BEHIND THE ETHICAL STATE OF NATURE

The process of enlightenment is a social development that can only take place in a society. Given that the ability to think freely is a requisite for the individual to have a moral disposition, the trust in one's morally good character also depends on the enlightenment of one's society. Even though Kant underscores that one's noumenal character and moral disposition cannot be judged by social measures, he equally emphasizes the necessary interconnection between humans in the process of cultivating their noumenal characters.

Kant's central point in the discussion of enlightenment is to argue for the establishment of a free public within the framework of a nation state, and ideally in a cosmopolitan international governance of the individual nation states. The purpose hereof is the reciprocal cultivation of the "propensity and calling to *think* freely," which makes up an important condition for self-trust in relation to one's moral disposition. In a similar discussion in his book on religion, Kant expands the scope of the argument, claiming:

> If no means could be found to establish a union which has for its end the prevention of this evil [namely, that societies seem to be breeding grounds for egoistic and evil choices cultivating envy [Neid], ambition [Herrschsucht], avarice [Habsucht] and other malignant inclinations] and the promotion of the good in the human being—an enduring and ever expanding society, solely designed for the preservation of morality by counteracting evil with united forces—however much the individual human being might do to escape from the dominion of this evil, he would still be held in incessant danger of relapsing into it. Inasmuch as we can see, therefore, the dominion of the good principle is not otherwise attainable so far as human beings can work toward it, than through the setting up and the diffusion of a society in accordance with, and for the sake of, the laws of virtues—a society which reason makes it a task and a duty of the entire human race to establish in its full scope. (Kant 1793, 6:94)

Even if the individual can commit herself to moral conversion and strive to cultivate a morally good disposition, this will not suffice to overcome evil. The social environment poses a risk to the individual who is in danger of relapsing into evil simply because human beings have a propensity to mutually corrupt one another's moral dispositions (see above, 10–11; Kant 1793, 6:93). Furthermore, evil as such can only be overcome in "a *kingdom* of virtue" (Ibid., 6:95).[7] According to Kant, the establishment of such a kingdom is necessary, because "even with the good will of each individual . . . the lack of a principle which unites them . . . [makes them] deviate through their dissensions from the common goal of goodness, as though they were *instruments of evil*" (Ibid., 6:97).

The establishment of a kingdom of virtue would entail that humankind could leave the ethical state of nature behind. The ethical state of nature is "one in which the good principle, which resides in each human being, is incessantly attacked by the evil principle which is found in him and every other as well" (Ibid.). The ethical state of nature is analogous to the *juridical state of nature* in the sense that "there is no external law to which he [the individual], along with others, acknowledges himself to be subject . . . and there is no effective *public* [*öffentlichen*] authority with power to determine legitimately, according to laws, what is in given cases the duty of each individual, and to bring about the universal execution of those laws" (Ibid., 6:95). It differs, however, by the fact that, according to Kant, humanity has not yet left the ethical state of nature. Many nations have long ago left the juridical state of nature behind and entered the *"juridical-civil* (political) *state* . . . the relation of human beings to each other inasmuch as they stand jointly under *public juridical laws* (which are coercive laws)" (Ibid.). The development from a juridical state of nature to a political state is a progress of prudent trust, as citizens can rely on each other to comply with the laws. As such, it can also be a support for moral trust, given that reliable conduct assists moral dispositions.

A major difference between the political state and the ideal of a kingdom of virtue (the *"ethico-civil* state" (Ibid.)) relates to the fact that while a political state is established with coercive laws and the right to punish infringement, the ethical state "is one in which they [human beings] are united under laws without being coerced, that is, under *laws of virtue* alone" (Ibid.). Furthermore, there is a difference in scope between the political and the ethico-civil state. Various political states have governments with jurisdiction over a limited group of individuals who are recognized as citizens. The kingdom of virtue, on the other hand, is assumed to be governed by God and, as such, would "concern the entire human race . . . [and] the concept of an ethical community always refers to the ideal of a totality of human beings" (Ibid., 6:96). This leads Kant to underscore that even though the establishment of an ethico-civil state is a task set by human reason, and as such also has "objective reality in human reason," we "cannot subjectively ever hope" that actual human beings will succeed in taking this task upon themselves (Ibid., 6:95). The kingdom of virtue is a moral ideal that we cannot force into being because virtue conceptually entails freedom from coercion. Everyone is "totally free" to choose whether he wants to enter the kingdom of virtue. The noncoercive and intelligible character of such a kingdom entails that everyone must voluntarily necessitate their maxims to be in accordance with the common goal of goodness in humankind.

To approach the realization of the kingdom of virtue, Kant points to the community of the church. The ideal of such an ethical community is an intelligible idea and as such is "not [the] object of a possible experience," and Kant calls it the *"church invisible* (the mere idea of the union of all upright human beings under direct yet moral divine world-governance . . .)" (Ibid., 6:101). Its possible human realization follows from the *"church visible* . . . [as] the actual union of human beings into a whole that accords with this ideal" (Ibid.). This human enterprise of uniting without any coercive means requires both trust and free thinking. Moreover, only the free and noncoercive interaction of the community can make the members mutually trustworthy.

The intelligible ideal of a "religion of reason" has to be interpreted "for a given people at a given time" (Ibid., 6:114). The interpretational effort faces the challenge that it "ultimately becomes just a faith [Glaube] in scholars and in their insight" (Ibid.). The danger is that the interpretations function as substitutes for the individual's active self-trust in her efforts at cultivating a moral disposition. There is a persistent danger of the visible church simply turning into a doctrinal and behavioral set of rules to follow. According to Kant, the remedy and only possible means of ensuring that each member understands that she must oblige herself to the ideals of the religion of reason, and thus to the moral conversion of her whole disposition, is the "public freedom of thought" (Ibid.). All scholars who take it upon themselves to offer interpretations of the religion of reason must therefore be prepared to publicly debate these interpretations: "only if scholars submit their interpretations to public scrutiny, and themselves remain always open and receptive to better insight, can they count on the community's trust [Zutrauen] in their decisions" (Ibid.).

Mutual trust in the righteousness of the interpreters of the religion of reason is necessary for the members of the visible church to strive to be a morally good community. Such trust cannot be given any empirical evidence while the members must actively endorse the interpretations for these to form the common goal of their cultivation of a moral disposition. The members' trust in the goodwill of the interpreters makes up a necessary condition for them to strive to realize the kingdom of virtue by uniting under the common goal of goodness. As there are no means of ascertaining that the interpreters are trustworthy, Kant believes the best route to avoid unwarranted trust in the scholars of the church is the public's freedom of thought. Interpretations should be freely discussed, and only if they can be approved in mutual deliberation as interpretations of the religion of reason by all who think freely can they function as principles that unite the church members in their effort to strive after the kingdom of virtue.

The church members may mutually trust one another to actively reflect upon the moral value of the interpretations of the religion of reason put forth in their visible church. As such, the members will mutually aid each other in striving to cultivate a morally good disposition, with their common efforts coming closer to the ideal than would be possible if each were to work in isolation. Such mutual trust in the moral dispositions of the members of the community ought to be promoted by the public freedom of thought. Such free public deliberations function as a procedure to meta-reflectively assess whether a community truly works toward the ideal of an *ethico-civil* state.

SOME KIND OF TRUST MUST REMAIN

The *juridical-civil* (political) *state* constitutes the basic conditions for prudent trust between citizens regardless of their moral dispositions because it is ruled by public coercive laws that make the behavior of individuals within the state predictable. Within a well-functioning political state, we can reasonably assume that other citizens will obey rules of traffic, contracts, and more generally are not criminals. Public laws and the reinforcement of them function as a force to mold human behavior and thus make everybody more reliable. Consequently, it is rational for an agent to prudently trust his fellow citizens to comply with the laws if transgressions are punished.

In the juridical state of nature and in the communication and interaction between states, there is no public authority to aid in making individuals and agents reliable. With no authority that can ensure transgressive behavior is punished, an authority to settle disputes about unjust behavior is also missing. The question is therefore whether it is rational to prudently trust one's fellow human beings in the state of nature and, analogously, whether states prudently ought to trust one another in international politics. As we have seen, Kant argues that the conditions for some prudent trust are present in the state of nature, namely, in societies with a social structure but no political state apparatus. Insight into habits and cultural decorum will make it possible to predict, to some degree, the behavior of one's fellow human beings.

Regarding trust between states, Kant emphasizes that even during wartime "no state . . . shall allow itself such acts of hostility as would have to make mutual trust impossible during a future peace" (Kant 1793, 8:346). Kant's contention is that in wars between states, as well as in "a state of nature (where there is no court that could judge with rightful force) . . . neither of the two parties can be declared an unjust enemy" (Ibid.). With no highest authority to decide on the legality of the behavior it becomes necessary for both parties to retain some path to common decisions. Therefore, "some trust in the enemy's way of thinking [Denkungsart] must still remain even in the midst of war" (Ibid.).

To trust in the enemy's way of thinking is to trust that the enemy acts in ways similar to oneself. Such trust will be rational—even if it is abused—because it enables durable peace. To end a war between enemies by one party subduing the other is not peace between the parties but merely the subjugation of one by the other. The only means to create peace is to trust the other side to be trustworthy in the minimal sense that they will not carry out a "war of extermination" (Ibid., 8:347). Thus, prudent trust is a requisite for international politics. By analogy, in a juridical state of nature some prudent trust between humans must also obtain for habits and cultural decorum to arise and for humans to cooperate. Prudent trust in a state of nature and in international politics involves more risk and uncertainty than in the political state because there is no ruling and sanctioning authority. In both, prudent trust is estimated as an imperative of skill in which the agent (or political state) deems reaching out in trust to be strategically beneficial.

FRIENDSHIP

Everyday interactions of humans are permeated by prudent trust, in which each assesses whether the other carries out the duty which is explicitly or implicitly required for the interaction to be successful. These estimations pertain to the relations between neighbors who seek "to average out [auszumitteln] whether the *equality* of exactly that part of the requisite and identical duty (for example mutual benevolence) is present in the precise equivalent disposition in the duties of one [neighbor] to the other" (Kant 1797, 6:469, translation altered). This is fundamentally the riddle of prudent trust. Kant assumes that the existence of prudent trust in everyday relations between neighbors is obvious and well documented by empirical studies of human behavior. This minimal requirement for all interactions also makes up the foundation of friendship, but the stakes are higher in friendship since the requirements of reciprocity are greater and the vulnerability of the interacting agents becomes even greater because friendship "(considered in its perfection) is the union of two persons through mutual love and respect" (Ibid.).

Kant distinguishes moral from aesthetic friendship. The basic difference is whether reciprocal love and respect are acquired as duties which are "set by reason" and are "honorable" (Ibid.), or stem from feelings. Friendships based on feelings "are common among the uncultivated people" (Ibid., 6:471) and tend to be turbulent due to the feelings flaming up. In these friendships "people cannot part with each other, and yet they cannot be at one with each other since they need quarrels in order to savor the sweetness of being united in reconciliation" (Ibid.). Such friendships are often "a union aimed at mutual advantage" (Ibid., 6:470) which inevitably leads to loss of respect:

> If one of them accepts a favor from the other, then he may well be able to count on equality in love, but not in respect; for he sees himself obviously a step lower in being under obligation without being able to impose obligation in turn.— Although it is sweet to feel in possession of each other that approaches fusion into one person, friendship is something so delicate (*teneritas amicitiae*) that it is never for a moment safe from interruptions if it is allowed to rest on feelings,

and if this mutual sympathy and self-surrender are not subjected to principles or rules preventing excessive familiarity and limiting mutual love by requirements of respect. (Ibid., 6:471)

Kant's scorn of friendship based on feelings has a metaphysical explanation in the split between pure practical reason, on the one hand, and self-love, inclinations from feelings, and radical evil on the other. However, the way Kant explains this effective delimitation of true friendship to moral friendship based on *duties* rather than *feelings* of love and respect is to appeal to trust: "*Moral friendship* (as distinguished from friendship based on feelings [der ästhetischen]) is the complete trust [das völlige Vertrauen] of two persons in revealing their secret judgments and feelings to each other, as far as such disclosures are consistent with mutual respect" (Ibid.). Reciprocal trust makes it possible for friends to overcome the antagonistic dynamic of society in which the individual "feels strongly the need to *reveal* himself to others (even with no ulterior purpose). But on the other hand, hemmed in and cautioned by fear of the misuse others may make of his disclosing thoughts, he finds himself constrained *to lock up* in himself a good part of his judgments" (Ibid., 6:472). The risks posed by exposure in friendship can be bridged in moral friendship by trust because reciprocal trust in the morally good noumenal character of one another amounts to trusting that both parties, as friends, balance love and respect: "For love can be regarded as attraction and respect as repulsion" (Ibid., 6:470).

Moral friendship is, of course, not the actualization of the kingdom of virtue on earth, but moral friendships and reciprocal moral trust in the good disposition of the friend are the closest Kant comes to arguing that the endeavor to cultivate a moral disposition can produce effects in the world of appearances which do more than make the human being "deserving of happiness" (Ibid., 6:469). The reciprocal trust between friends allows them to have a social relationship in which they do not have to apply the imperatives of skill and incessantly estimate risks. Taking part in moral friendship, the friend "is not completely alone with his thoughts, as in a prison, but enjoys a freedom" (Ibid., 6:472). He trusts when disclosing his inner thoughts that they will be safe with the friend, who also discloses his thoughts in trust that the friend will handle these confidentially. Kant emphasizes that moral friendship "is not just an ideal but (like black swans) actually exists here and there in its perfection" (Ibid.). It is a relation between two independent human beings in which each "with complete trust [völligem Vertrauen] can reveal himself" (Ibid., v). As such, the ability to trust is the most valuable ability human beings possess. It is requisite in the personal and societal cultivation of the human being from maxims of self-love to moral friendship, and in maintaining the ideal of a kingdom of virtue as the *focus imaginarius* of humankind.

NOTES

1. References to the works of Immanuel Kant are given using the official standard pagination of the Prussian *Akademieausgabe*—annotated by reference to year, volume: page number—for example, Kant (1785, 4:28). The official references to the *Critique of Pure Reason*, however, are to the pagination of either the 1781 or the 1787 edition, as either A or B, followed by page number. Employing the official standard reference system for Kant's works makes it possible to find the quotation in the German original as well as in English (and other language) translations. As the standard English translation, the *Cambridge Edition of the Works of Immanuel Kant* is used. The list of references includes both the German and English editions.

2. Unless otherwise noted, italicized words in quotations will indicate an emphasis in the original.

3. *Groundwork of the Metaphysics of Morals* is Kant's first treatise on practical philosophy, and its terminology varies from Kant's subsequent discussions of practical philosophy by not differentiating between the *will* [Wille] as expression of the moral law and *choice* [Willkür] as the ability to choose maxims that one expects will bring about a desired end. Choice [Willkür] is similar to the imperatives of skill. In *Critique of Practical Reason*, Kant defines *choice* [Willkür] as the "representation of an object and that relation of the representation to the subject by which the faculty of desire is determined to realize the object" (Kant 1788, 5:21). In *Groundwork*, Kant understands both imperatives of skill and the categorical imperative as expressions of the will. In subsequent treatises on practical philosophy, Kant associates imperatives of skill, and thus all hypothetical imperatives, with the human ability of choice [Willkür] while designating the categorical imperative to express the determining ground of the will [Wille].

4. Kant defines a propensity to act as follows: "the subjective ground of the possibility of an inclination (habitual desire, *concupiscentia*), insofar as this possibility is contingent for humanity in general" (Kant 1793, 6:29). Further, he underscores that the propensity for evil "is only possible as the determination of a free power of choice and this power for its part can be judged good or evil only on the basis of its maxims [which] must reside in the subjective ground of the possibility of the deviation of the maxims from the moral law" (Kant 1793, 6:29).

5. The antagonism in human society between two opposing forces, namely, the urge for social concord and the disharmonious social inclination and passions such as envy, ambition, and avarice, is what Kant terms "the *unsociable sociability* of human beings, i.e. their propensity to enter into society, which, however, is combined with a thoroughgoing resistance that constantly threatens to break up this society" (Kant 1784a, 8:20). According to Kant, this antagonism is a powerful driver in human culture as each individual tries "to obtain for himself a rank among his fellows, whom he cannot *stand*, but also cannot *leave alone*" (Ibid., 8:21).

6. It is an open question whether Kant really lamented that women, "the entire fair sex," were subjugated under minority as he did not argue for granting women equal rights. In the *Doctrine of Right*, Kant posed and answered the question

> "whether it is also in conflict with the equality of the partners for the law to say of the husband's relation to the wife, he is to be your master (he is the party to direct, she to obey): this cannot be regarded as conflicting with the natural equality of the couple if this dominance is based only on the natural superiority of the husband to the wife in his capacity to promote the common interest of the household, and the right to direct that is based on this can be derived from the very duty of unity and equality with respect to the *end*" (Kant 1788, 6:279).

The argumentation for universal worth of all humankind is distorted by Kant's acceptance of the traditional misogynic assumption of "the natural superiority of the husband." The argument for breaking free from minority by means of free thinking is in principal universal, and the hindsight of history documents women (children and servants) rising to demand equality under the law and to resist being defined as the "rightful possession" of a man and "included in the subject's belongings (his wife, child, servant)" (Ibid., 6:254).

7. Kant's concept of a kingdom of virtue in *Religion within the Boundaries of Mere Reason* is analogous to the kingdom of ends found in Kant's writings on morality, the primary difference being that the kingdom of virtue is the practical exemplification of the good. Striving to become virtuous, according to Kant, implies combatting the enemy of the good (see Kant 1793, 6:57). A kingdom of virtue thus entails the attempt at a realization of an *"ethico-civil* state" (Ibid., 6:95).

REFERENCES

Kant, Immanuel. 1781/87. *Kritik der reinen Vernunft*, vol. 1–2. Berlin: Preussische Akademie der Wissenschaften.

———. 1781/87 [1998]. *Critique of Pure Reason*. Translated by Paul Guyer and Allan Wood. Cambridge: Cambridge University Press.

———. 1784a. *Idee zu einer allgemeinen Geschichte in weltbürgerlicher Absicht*, vol. 8. Berlin: Preussische Akademie der Wissenschaften.

———. 1784a [2009]. *Idea for a Universal History with a Cosmopolitan Aim*. Translated by Allan Wood. In *Kant's Idea for a Universal History with a Cosmopolitan Aim: A Critical Guide*, edited by Amelia O. Rorty and James Schmidt, 9–23. Cambridge: Cambridge University Press.

———. 1784b. *Beantwortung der Frage: Was ist Aufklärung?* vol. 8. Berlin: Preussische Akademie der Wissenschaften.

———. 1784b [1996]. *An Answer to the Question: What Is Enlightenment?* Translated by Mary Gregor. In Kant, *Practical Philosophy*, edited by Mary Gregor, 11–22. Cambridge: Cambridge University Press.

———. 1785. *Grundlegung zur Metaphysik der Sitten*, vol. 4. Berlin: Preussische Akademie der Wissenschaften.

———. 1785 [1998]. *Groundwork of the Metaphysics of Morals*. Translated by Mary Gregor. Cambridge: Cambridge University Press.
———. 1788. *Kritik der praktischen Vernunft*, vol. 5. Berlin: Preussische Akademie der Wissenschaften.
———. 1788 [1997]. *Critique of Practical Reason*. Translated by Mary Gregor. Cambridge: Cambridge University Press.
———. 1793. *Religion innerhalb der Grenzen der Bloßen Vernunft*, vol. 6. Berlin: Preussische Akademie der Wissenschaften.
———. 1793 [2018]. *Religion within the Boundaries of Mere Reason*. Translated by Alen Wood and George di Giovanni. Cambridge: Cambridge University Press.
———. 1795. *Zum ewigen Frieden*, vol. 8. Berlin: Preussische Akademie der Wissenschaften.
———. 1795 [1996]. *Toward Perpetual Peace*. Translated by Mary Gregor. In Kant, *Practical Philosophy*, edited by Mary Gregor, 311–52. Cambridge: Cambridge University Press.
———. 1797. *Metaphysik der Sitten*, vol. 6. Berlin: Preussische Akademie der Wissenschaften.
———. 1797 [1996]. *The Metaphysics of Morals*. Translated by Mary Gregor. Cambridge: Cambridge University Press.
———. 1798. *Anthropologie in pragmatischer Hinsicht*, vol. 7. Berlin: Preussische Akademie der Wissenschaften.
———. 1798 [2006]. *Anthropology from a Pragmatic Point of View*. Translated by Robert Louden. Cambridge: Cambridge University Press.
Longworth, Guy. 2017. "Faith in Kant." In *The Philosophy of Trust*, edited by Paul Faulkner and Thomas Simpson, 251–71. Oxford: Oxford University Press.
O'Neill, Onora. 2002. *Autonomy and Trust in Bioethics*. Cambridge: Cambridge University Press.
Pedersen, Esther Oluffa. 2012. "A Kantian Conception of Trust." *Sats: Northern European Journal of Philosophy* 13(2): 147–69.
Rice, Stephen, David Trafimow, Gayle Hunt, and Joshua Sandry. 2009. "Generalizing Kant's Distinction between Perfect and Imperfect Duties to Trust in Different Situations." *The Journal of General Psychology* 137(1): 20–36.
Schröder, Peter. 2010. "'Irgend ein Vertrauen . . . muss . . . übrig bleiben': The Idea of Trust in Kant's Moral and Political Philosophy." In *Cultivating Personhood: Kant and Asian Philosophy*, edited by Stephen Palmquist, 391–98. Berlin: De Gruyter.
Sussman, David. 2002. *The Idea of Humanity: Anthropology and Anthroponomy in Kant's Ethics*. London: Routledge.

Chapter 8

Nietzsche on Trust and Mistrust

Mark Alfano

Friedrich Nietzsche (1844–1900) talks about trust [*vertraue**] and mistrust [*misstrau**] in all his published and authorized works, from *The Birth of Tragedy* (1872) to *Ecce Homo* (1888).[1] He refers to trust in 90 passages and mistrust in 101, approximately ten times as often as he refers to resentment/*ressentiment*. Yet the scholarly literature on Nietzsche and trust includes just a handful of publications (Dannenberg 2015, 2017; McKiernan 2016; Risse 2003). Worse still, I have been unable to find a single publication devoted to Nietzsche and mistrust. Dannenberg's engagement with Nietzsche draws almost solely from a few remarks about the "right to make promises" in *GM* 2; his philosophical goals are less interpretive and more about how we contemporary philosophers should understand the act of promising. McKiernan focuses only on the prefaces that Nietzsche added to several of his works in 1887; her interpretation points out that in these prefaces, Nietzsche aims to induce self-trust in his readers—a point with which I agree. But there is much more to Nietzsche on trust and mistrust than is found in the prefaces. Finally, Risse interprets Nietzsche as recommending "a joyous and trusting fatalism" (what Nietzsche elsewhere calls *amor fati*) rather than resentment; there is certainly something to this idea, but again it leaves out the vast majority of what Nietzsche has to say about trust and mistrust.

Arguably, this disproportionate scholarly engagement with trust, mistrust, and resentment has been driven by the fact that English translations of Nietzsche's writings systematically italicize and transliterate "ressentiment" rather than treating it as the normal word it is,[2] while translating *Misstrauen* and cognates sometimes as "mistrust," sometimes as "distrust," and sometimes as "suspicion." In any case, this chapter aims to fill the gap in the secondary literature by using digital humanities methods to systematically investigate the functions of trust and mistrust in Nietzsche's writings.[3]

Substantively, I argue that Nietzsche offers three main insights into trust and an additional two into mistrust. When it comes to trust, in his "free spirit" works, he reflects on the development of interpersonal trust with an eye to situations in which trust is or is not reciprocated. He also criticizes some of the heuristics people use to identify trustworthy partners, especially the notion that all and only people with stable characters are trustworthy. Perhaps Nietzsche's most interesting thoughts about trust relate to self-trust, which he thinks is often unjustifiably undermined. When it comes to mistrust, although he regards generalized mistrust as a sign of bad character, he also thinks that harnessing mistrust can be valuable in at least two domains. One is morality, where we are disposed to accept traditional pieties and would benefit from turning a suspicious eye toward these pieties. The other is science, which systematizes both trust and mistrust in pursuit of the truth.

METHODOLOGY

I first use hierarchical clustering to compare the language used in Nietzsche's published and authorized manuscripts, as shown in figure .8.1.

As figure 8.1 shows, starting in 1880, Nietzsche's writings developed a distinctive style, with the "free spirit" works (*HH, D, GS*) clustering together, while the mature works (*BGE, GM*) and the late works (*EH, TI*, though not *A* or *CW*) also cluster together. The analysis in this chapter covers Nietzsche's entire philosophical career, but I will primarily concentrate on these works.

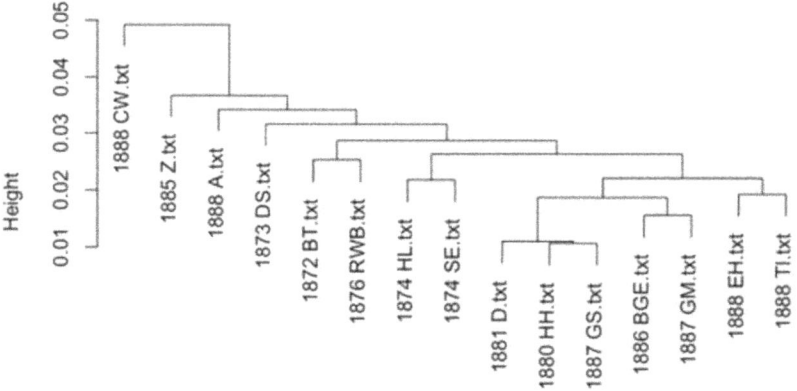

Figure 8.1 Results of Hierarchical Clustering of Nietzsche's Word Usage. *Source*: Created by author.

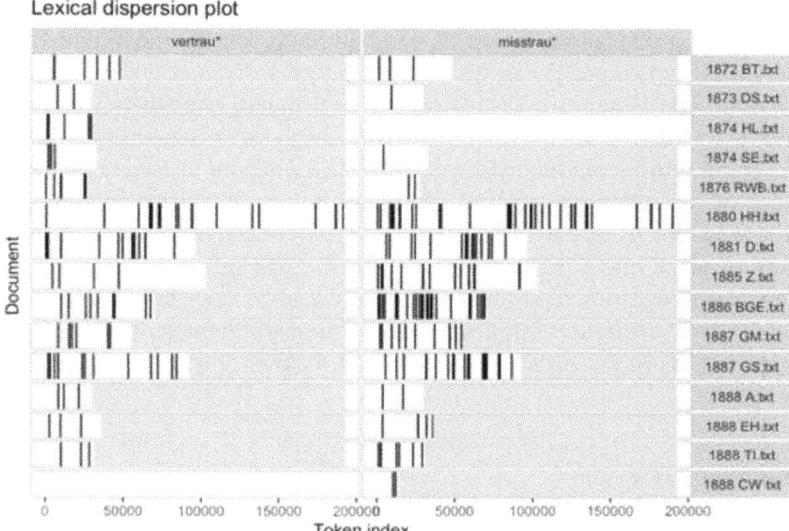

Figure 8.2 Lexical Dispersion of Trust-Related Word Stems. *Source*: Created by author.

Next, figure 8.2 displays the lexical dispersion of the German word stems that Nietzsche uses to talk about trust [*vertraue**] and mistrust [*misstrau**]. Each vertical line represents a usage of the relevant term, and the width of the bars represents the total word count of each book. For instance, *Human, All-too-human* is Nietzsche's longest book, which is why the bar representing it is the widest. As figure 8.2 shows, Nietzsche's interest in trust waned over the course of his philosophical career. It crops up sporadically in the early and middle works, but there are just a handful of attestations in the works of 1888. By contrast, mistrust is almost entirely absent from *The Birth of Tragedy* and the *Untimely Meditations*, but becomes much more an object of concern in the 1880s.

These figures provide some context and demonstrate Nietzsche's ongoing concern with the moral psychology of trust and mistrust. Delving deeper, I next examine all passages in which the relevant terms occur and organize them around the functions that Nietzsche assigns to trust and mistrust.[4]

THE FUNCTIONS OF TRUST

For Nietzsche, as for many contemporary philosophers, trust is an affective attitude. You trust someone when you feel optimistic that they will prove trustworthy—that is, when you feel positively about their disposition to act as you are counting on them to act, and to take into account the fact that you are counting on them as a reason for so acting.⁵ Trustworthiness, in turn, is an underlying disposition to act as counted upon, should the situation arise. Conversely, trustingness can be understood as a disposition to place one's trust in others. When this disposition is well tuned, one trusts wisely. That could mean trusting all and only those who are in fact trustworthy, or perhaps even being more generous with one's trust in order to show respect or high regard, or to enable one to learn firsthand how trustworthy another person really is. Starting in his "free spirit" works, Nietzsche reflects on what it means to place one's trust in others, how to coax others to trust one, what observable properties tend to inspire trust (even if they are not necessarily good evidence of trustworthiness), the relationship between trust and governance, and the value of self-trust. In what follows, I explore each of these themes.

Interpersonal Trust

Nietzsche's thoughts on the nature and cultivation of interpersonal trust are mostly restricted to *Human, All-too-human*, though they are dispersed throughout the original monograph and the two books that he later appended to it (*Assorted Opinions and Maxims* and *The Wanderer and His Shadow*). For instance, in *HH* 296, Nietzsche remarks: "Lack of intimacy or trustingness [*Vertraulichkeit*] among friends is a fault that cannot be reprimanded without becoming incurable." This observation relates to the affective dimension of trust: if I point out that you are not treating me as a trusted friend, this is likely to lead you to react with resentment, not the warm optimism inherent in trust. A few passages later, in a section titled "*Trust and intimacy* [Vertrauen und Vertraulichkeit]" (*HH* 304), Nietzsche says: "He who deliberately seeks to establish an intimacy with another person is usually in doubt as to whether he possesses his trust." Precisely the anxiety associated with lack of trust is what leads people to seek to bind others to them via intimacy. But that anxiety, when detected, may undermine the effort to establish a trusting relationship because it gives off a whiff of desperation. Nietzsche returns to this theme in a later passage titled "*Against the trusting* [Vertraulichen]" (*HH* 311), where he says: "People who give us their complete trust believe that they have thus acquired a right to ours. This is a false conclusion; gifts procure no rights." The assumption he criticizes here is that trust must be reciprocated. Contrary to this assumption, Nietzsche conceptualizes the act of entrusting another person as a gift. Of course, in most gift-giving cultures, failing to reciprocate is considered at best tacky and at worst offensive. But Nietzsche is nevertheless right that reciprocation is not morally required. Why think of trust as a gift, though? He does not explicitly say, but presumably the answer is that in trusting someone we demonstrate a high regard for their competence in the domain of trust (e.g., trusting someone to fly you somewhere in an airplane), as well as esteem for them as (moral) agents.[6]

In *AOM* 254, Nietzsche returns to the presumptuousness of trying to induce a relationship of bidirectional trust by recklessly placing one's trust in another person: "What we have previously kept silent about we sometimes first reveal to our most recent acquaintances: we foolishly believe that this demonstration of our trust [*Vertrauens-Beweis*] is the strongest chain by which we could fetter them to us." But, he goes on, this tactic is not likely to work because "they do not know enough of us to appreciate the sacrifice we are making." If someone does not understand that he is being trusted with a secret, he is not likely to appreciate the regard and esteem expressed by the act of entrusting. Nietzsche also remarks on the relationship between intimacy and trust in *WS* 288, saying: "Those to whom a warm and noble intimacy [*Vertraulichkeit*] is impossible try to display the nobility of their nature through reserve and severity . . . as though their feeling of trust [*Vertrauen*] were so strong it was ashamed to show itself." Here Nietzsche suggests that nobility is associated with the capacity to trust at least some others, echoing his claim in *WS* 190 that "nothing is so beneficial to the soul and body of man" as a sense of "trust [*Vertrauen*] in the future." This passage in turn echoes *HH* 98: "To feel sensations of pleasure on the basis of human relations on the whole makes men better; joy, pleasure, is enhanced when it is enjoyed together with others, it gives the individual security, makes him good-natured, banishes mistrust [*Misstrauen*] and envy." Nietzsche expresses the same sentiment in *HH* 493, saying: "Nobility of mind consists to a great degree in good-naturedness and absence of mistrust [*Misstrauen*]."

Finally, in *EH* Wise.2, Nietzsche asks how one can "know that someone has *turned out well*," and answers by saying (among other things), "He only has a taste for what agrees with him; his enjoyment, his desires stop at the boundary of what is agreeable to him . . . he is a principle of selection, he lets many things fall by the wayside . . . he honors by *choosing*, by *permitting*, by *trusting* [vertraut]."[7] Here, Nietzsche explicitly associates trusting with esteem or honor. In particular, he thinks that being trusted *by the honorable or noble* is what confers honor. In other words, he affirms a sort of principle of affinity, whereby good people recognize themselves in other good people, leading them to honor and esteem those people with their trust. If this is right, noble people's dispositions to trust can be seen as a sort of touchstone or divining rod: those they do or would honor with their trust are also noble, while those they do or would mistrust are not.

(Perceived) Trustworthiness

Not everyone's disposition to trust is as reliable as that of the person who has "turned out well" in *EH* Wise.2. In earlier writings, Nietzsche talks about other ways in which people end up attributing trustworthiness to others, emphasizing the unreliability of these heuristics. The most relevant remarks are to be found in *Human, All-too-human* and *Genealogy*. For instance, in *HH* 604, Nietzsche suggests that one indicator of trustworthiness is stability of character and affect, saying: "People who catch fire quickly, quickly grow cold and are thus on the whole unreliable." However, the opposite inference is not, according to Nietzsche, valid: "all those who are always cold, or pretend to be, have in their favor the prejudice that they are particularly trustworthy [*vertrauenswerthe*] and reliable: people confuse them with those who catch fire slowly and retain it a long time." The relationship between stability of character and trustworthiness also crops up in *HH* 608, where Nietzsche says that when someone is seen as "consistent through and through, homogenous in thought and being," they are likely to receive respect as well as "trust [*Vertrauen*] and power." But, of course, someone could be *seen as* consistent and homogenous without actually being so, and even if someone is consistent and homogenous, they might not be trustworthy in the domain in which they are being trusted. Thus, the stability heuristic is liable to lead us astray, as well as to induce people who want to be trusted to pretend to greater stability of character than they actually possess.[8]

Turning next to *Genealogy*, consider *GM* 2.2. In this famous passage, Nietzsche paints a portrait of a character that he dubs the "sovereign individual." While much ink has been spilled in vain on this character, careful and contextual reading shows that he is an exemplar of what Nietzsche calls the herd instinct (Rukgaber 2012; Alfano 2019a, chapter 11). The herd instinct, in turn, is a drive to act and even to be as others expect one to act and be. In this passage, Nietzsche speculates about the prehistory of promising and contractual relations. In such circumstances, the promisor is expected to do as he is promised, the debtor to repay his debt. What is required for promises to be worth taking seriously is that the promisor has an "enduring and reliable will." In other words, he is unconditionally committed to doing what the promisee expects him to do. Nietzsche goes on to half-parodically describe the attitude of someone who has internalized the herd instinct to this extent:

> The "free" man, the possessor of an enduring, unbreakable will, thus has his own *standard of value*: in the possession of such a will: viewing others from his standpoint, he respects or despises; and just as he will necessarily respect his peers, the strong and reliable (those with the prerogative to promise)—that is everyone who promises like a sovereign, ponderously, seldom, slowly, and is sparing with his trust [*Vertrauen*], who *confers an honor* when he places his trust [*vertraut*], who gives his word as something that can be relied on.

Thus, the paragon of the herd instinct also treats his disposition to trust as a touchstone or divining rod. In a sense, he is right to do so, as it continues to serve as a principle of affinity. Whereas the honorable and noble are disposed to trust only other honorable and noble people, the exemplar of herd morality is disposed to trust only those who have fully internalized the herd instinct.

In a later passage (*GM* 2.5; see also *GM* 2.9), Nietzsche describes the methods that a promisor/debtor might undertake not only to inspire trust but also to ensure that his will really is enduring and unbreakable:

> The debtor, in order to inspire trust [*Vertrauen*] that the promise of repayment will be honored, in order to give a guarantee of the solemnity and sanctity of his promise, and in order to etch the duty and obligation of repayment into his conscience, pawns something to the creditor by means of the contract in case he does not pay, something that he still "possesses" and controls, for example, his body, or his wife, or his freedom, or his life.

Such gruesome practices to assure creditors of trustworthiness and ensure that debtors do not default on repayment date back, according to Nietzsche, to prehistory. They are also dramatized in modern literature, for instance, in Shakespeare's *The Merchant of Venice* through the device of the "pound of flesh." Such practices might seem to be at odds with the picture of trust that emerged above, where trust was portrayed as a gift that implied high regard and esteem. This tension may be due to Nietzsche changing his opinion on trust between *Human, All-too-human* and the *Genealogy*, which was published seven years later. Alternately, it may be that the kind of trust Nietzsche has in mind in *Human, All-too-human* does not involve promising and debt, and thus does not operate through the same punitive regime that he describes in *GM* 2.

In any event, the final passage to consider in this section is *GM* 3.15. In it, Nietzsche characterizes the psychological profile of the "ascetic priest" who perpetrates the revaluation of values described in the first essay of *Genealogy*. The ascetic priest, like the warrior class that he undermines, is noble. But, according to Nietzsche, he must also be "sick himself, he must really be a close relative of the sick and the destitute in order to understand them . . . but he has to be strong, too . . . so that he has the trust [*Vertrauen*] and fear of the sick and can be their support, defense, prop, compulsion, disciplinarian, tyrant, God." Once again, we see the idea that the dispositions to trust and to inspire trust operate through a principle of affinity. In particular, Nietzsche here seems to think that establishing a trusting relationship requires a kind of perspective-taking or empathy, which is enabled by psychological affinity. The ascetic priest is able to inspire trust in the sick because—being sick himself—he understands their point of view.

Self-trust

Perhaps Nietzsche's most interesting thinking about trust occurs in the context of *self*-trust. He is especially concerned to ensure that people do not lose trust in themselves without justification, which he seems to think occurs all too frequently, and he actively invites his readers to restore their self-trust, as McKiernan (2016) points out. Before turning to the relevant passages, it is worth reviewing some contemporary research on the nature and value of self-trust. There is a remarkable near-consensus that, unless you have particular reasons to the contrary, you ought to trust yourself. For example, Pasnau (2015) argues that self-trust justifiably influences how we should react to peer disagreement. Lehrer (1997) argues that self-trust grounds reason, wisdom, and knowledge. Govier (1993) argues that self-trust grounds autonomy and self-respect. Jones (2012b) positively evaluates self-trust from a feminist perspective. And Goldberg (2013) argues that self-trust is a good model for trust in others. If trust in others involves a positively tinged affective attitude toward them and their disposition to do as we are relying on them to do because we are so relying on them, then trust in oneself involves a positively tinged affective attitude toward oneself and one's own ability and commitment to carry through with commitments diachronically. If this is right, self-trust could be undermined in two distinct ways. First, one could lose confidence in one's abilities or capacities. For instance, if you have had a few drinks, you probably should not trust yourself to operate a car. Second, one could lose confidence in one's own persistence, diligence, self-control, or patience. If you cannot suffer fools for more than a minute, you probably should not trust yourself to chair tedious committees. Nietzsche is interested in both of these ways in which people lose self-trust, but is especially concerned with cases in which people lose faith in their own affective responses, that is, cases in which they no longer trust their intuitions and evaluative reactions.

Nietzsche's concern with unwarranted loss of self-trust dates back at least to *HL* 5, where he says of the contemporary German: "he has lost and destroyed his instincts and, having lost his trust [*vertrauend*] in the 'divine animal,' he can no longer let go the reins when his reason falters. . . . Thus the individual grows fainthearted and unsure and dares no longer believe in himself." As I have shown elsewhere, Nietzsche understands virtues and vices as drives that interact with the rest of an agent's psychic economy in characteristic ways (see Alfano 2019a, chapter 4). In particular, a drive becomes a virtue when it is integrated with the agent's other drives, and a vice when its possession or expression leads the agent to condemn fixed or immutable aspects of themselves. For Nietzsche, instincts are innate drives, so when he says here that the contemporary German has destroyed his instincts and no longer believes in himself, this constitutes a charge of vice (even if, as Nietzsche argues elsewhere in the passage, this vice is acquired through German education and not directly attributable to the agent). Later, in *HL* 10, Nietzsche laments the state of his contemporaries, saying that they are "[f]ragmented and in pieces, dissociated almost mechanically into an inner and an outer, sown with concepts as with dragon's teeth, bringing forth conceptual dragons, suffering from the malady of words and mistrusting [*ohne Vertrauen*] any feeling of [their] own." This is again a charge of vice and a rejection of any claim to virtue. Instead of being integrated, Nietzsche's contemporaries are fragmented and dissociated; instead of affirming or at least accepting their feelings, they mistrust them. In *SE* 2, Nietzsche continues this theme, criticizing his past self for embodying a certain kind of heteronomy: "I believed that, when the time came, I would discover a philosopher to educate me, a true philosopher whom one could follow without misgiving because one would have more trust [*vertrauen*] in him than one had in oneself." While he does not go so far as to say that he mistrusted himself, Nietzsche does suggest that trusting others more than one trusts oneself is deeply problematic. Against this tendency, he endorses the following imperative: "Be your self! All you are now doing, thinking, desiring, is not you yourself" (*SE* 2). And of course, this is a theme to which he returns in many other passages, perhaps most notably in the subtitle of *Ecce Homo: How To Become What You Are*. To accomplish this task, one must trust oneself to a significant extent.

Nietzsche returns to this idea in the free spirit works. For instance, in *HH* 141, he says: "Everything natural to which one attaches the idea of the bad and sinful . . . oppresses the imagination and makes it gloomy, because frightening to look upon, causes men to haggle with themselves and deprives them of security and trust [*Vertraue*]." Evidently, one thing that is natural is the fixed aspects of oneself, so the doctrine of original sin, which attributes such badness to the essential self, is calculated to destroy self-trust.[9] Or consider *WS* 278, where Nietzsche says that a noble person ought to go out of his way "to notice everything good about other people and after that to draw a line." He goes on to suggest that one can deal with oneself similarly: "whether or not he has a courteous memory in the end determines his own attitude towards himself; it determines whether he regards his own inclinations and intentions with a noble, benevolent or mistrustful [*Misstrauen*] eye; and it determines, finally, the nature of these inclinations and intentions themselves." As I pointed out above, Nietzsche thinks that instincts and other drives (what he here calls inclinations and intentions) become vices when their expression leads their bearers to condemn fixed aspects of themselves. One way in which such condemnation may manifest is through self-mistrust, as this passage illustrates.

Nietzsche's reflections on the value of self-trust continue in his mature and late works. For instance, in *GM* 1.10, he says: "While the noble man lives in front of himself with trust [*Vertrauen*] and openness [γενναῖος/noble-born, which underlines the nuance 'sincere' and probably also 'naive'], the man of resentment is neither sincere nor naive, nor honest and straight with himself." The man of resentment, as Nietzsche puts it here, is driven to undermine the values of healthier, more noble people, but he also needs to think of himself as morally upstanding, which makes it difficult or impossible for him to admit his true motives, even to himself (see Katsafanas 2013). Whereas the noble trusts his own drives and evaluative dispositions, the man of resentment cannot do so without losing the benefits that expressing those drives and dispositions deliver. Worse still, Nietzsche suggests that the self-flagellating self-mistrust of the resentful can spread through emotional contagion. He voices this worry most vividly in *GM* 3.14, saying: "The *sickly* are the greatest danger to man: *not* the wicked, *not* the 'beasts of prey' . . . most undermine life amongst men, who introduce the deadliest poison and skepticism into our trust [*Vertrauen*] in life, in man, in ourselves." As we saw above, Nietzsche had already affirmed in *Untimely Meditations* that "nothing is so beneficial to the soul and body of man" as a sense of "trust [*Vertrauen*] in the future" (*WS* 190). The resentful, by contrast, spread mistrust in life, in humanity, and in the self. They do so by spreading negative sentiments about essential aspects of the self. Nietzsche ventriloquizes their grievance later in *GM* 3.14: "If only I were some other person! . . . but there's no hope of that. I am who I am: how could I get away from myself? And oh — *I'm fed up with myself!*"

THE FUNCTIONS OF MISTRUST

As we have already seen in the previous section, Nietzsche contrasts trust and mistrust. While he is especially worried about the self-mistrust induced by the Christian revaluation of values chronicled in *Genealogy* and elsewhere, he also seems to think that being universally mistrustful is a sign of bad character (*HH* 614; *D* 407; *BGE* 260). But he also has a lot to say about the mistrust of Christian morality itself, as well as the way in which scientific inquirers can harness mistrust in their pursuit of truth and eradication of error. In this section, I catalog Nietzsche's remarks on these two partially overlapping functions of mistrust.

Mistrust of Christian Morality

As early as *Human, All-too-human*, Nietzsche explicitly says that his writings aim to induce a mistrust of morality—especially of Christian morality.

Note that this does not so much aim to *disprove* the premises of Christian morality as to weaken the affective bonds his readers have to it.[10] The goal is to replace blind trust with caution, suspicion, and mistrust. But mistrusting Christian morality does not necessarily entail rejecting all its premises and claims outright. Instead, Nietzsche seems to want to free up his readers to question their default moral assumptions. What they do next is up to them. For example, in *HH* P 1: "What? *Everything* only—human, all too human? It is with this sigh that one emerges from my writings, not without a kind of reserve and mistrust [*Misstrauen*] even in regard to morality." In *HH* 36, he speculates: "perhaps belief in goodness, in virtuous men and actions, in an abundance of impersonal benevolence in the world has in fact made men better, inasmuch as it has made them less mistrustful [*misstrauisch*]." It is important to understand the sarcasm in this passage. Nietzsche is saying that belief in goodness and virtue has made people morally better only in the sense that it makes them less mistrustful and therefore more naïve. Once people start to pay more attention to the reasons for and against belief—including religious belief—such naïvety becomes impossible: "the growth of the Enlightenment undermined the dogmas of religion and inspired a fundamental mistrust [*Misstrauen*] of them" (*HH* 150).

Turning next to *Daybreak*, in the second section of the preface, Nietzsche characterizes his own project thusly: "I commenced an investigation and digging out of an ancient *trust* [*Vertrauen*], one upon which we philosophers have for a couple of millennia been accustomed to build as if upon the firmest of all foundations." Which ancient trust does he have in mind? "I commenced to undermine our *trust in morality.*"[11] Later in this section of the preface, Nietzsche returns to the same theme, saying: "*this* book is pessimistic even into the realm of morality, even to the point of going beyond trust in morality . . . in it morality is denied trust—why is it? *Out of morality!*" Again, it is important to understand the sarcasm here. Nietzsche says that he denies trust in morality out of morality itself because his own will to truth is ultimately grounded in a commitment to inquiry even at great costs. That he is willing to give up so many of his positive illusions about humanity is evidence that, for him, the will to truth is a fundamental commitment.

Mistrust of morality, especially of Christian morality, is also prominent in *The Gay Science*. For instance, in the very first passage, Nietzsche says: "One might quickly enough, with the usual myopia from five steps away, divide one's neighbors into useful and harmful, good and evil; but . . . upon further reflection on the whole, one grows mistrustful [*misstrauisch*] of this tidying and separating and finally abandons it." This idea—that a Manichean divide between good and evil is untenable and oversimplifying—is common in Nietzsche's mature writings and is reflected in the title of a later book, *Beyond Good and Evil*. And of course, this is precisely the dichotomizing perspective he criticizes in Christian morality. Later, in *GS* 214, Nietzsche remarks: "Virtue gives happiness and a type of blessedness only to those who have not lost faith in their virtue—not to those subtler souls whose virtue consists in a deep mistrust [*Misstrauen*] of themselves and of all virtue." No doubt Nietzsche considers himself one of those subtler, mistrustful souls. But does he mistrust himself? Given his criticism of self-mistrust as we saw it above, one might find this passage puzzling. However, this apparent tension can be resolved if we bear in mind that when Nietzsche objects to self-mistrust, he does so because it leads to condemnation of fixed aspects of the self. Milder self-mistrust that simply leads one to be more cautious in drawing inferences is not problematic in the same way.

Next, in *GS* 343, Nietzsche explains what he means by the notorious phrase "God is dead": "the belief in the Christian God has become unbelievable." He then goes on: "To those few at least whose eyes—or the suspicion in whose eyes is strong and subtle enough for this spectacle, some kind of sun seems to have set; some old deep trust [*Vertrauen*] turned into doubt: to them, our world must appear more autumnal, more mistrustful [*misstrauischer*]." Importantly, Nietzsche here points out that what has happened is not simply that mistrust has arisen. Instead, "some old deep trust" has been *replaced* with mistrust. Given that, the object of the old deep trust can finally be called into question, as it is no longer protected by a positive affective halo. The destruction of this barrier, the affective protection afforded by trust, opens space for new questions and inquiries. Nietzsche goes on to say that "we philosophers and 'free spirits' feel illuminated by a new dawn; our heart overflows with gratitude, amazement, forebodings, expectation . . . every daring of the lover of knowledge is allowed again; the sea, *our* sea, lies open again; maybe there has never been such an 'open sea.'"[12] In this metaphor, the sea represents a domain of inquiry that had previously been off limits. Nietzsche uses related imagery to describe the *terra incognita* opened up by mistrust in *BGE* 12: "By putting an end to the superstition that until now has grown around the idea of the soul with an almost tropical luxuriance, the *new* psychologist thrusts himself into a new wasteland and a new mistrust [*Misstrauen*]."

The destruction of trust and its replacement with a nuanced mistrust lifts the embargo to this sea. To venture into such forbidden inquiries requires intellectual courage, curiosity, and a willingness to mistrust where long tradition has inculcated trust. Such dispositions might be seen by defenders of Christian morality as evil, but they are precisely the Nietzschean virtues (see Alfano 2019a, chapters 6–10). Or, as Zarathustra declaims:

> Everything that the good call evil must come together, in order to give birth to one truth; oh my brothers, are you also evil enough for *this* truth?

Audacious daring, long mistrust [*Misstrauen*], the cutting into what is alive—
how rarely *this* comes together! But from such semen—truth is begotten!

While it is always fraught to interpret the sayings of Zarathustra as the
unfiltered thoughts of Nietzsche, this passage is from the third book of *Zarathustra*, where the character has reached his full maturity. Moreover, the
interpretation is borne out by later passages in which Nietzsche speaks with
his own voice. For instance, in *GM* P 6, he says: "This problem of the *value*
of compassion and of the morality of compassion . . . seems at first to be only
an isolated phenomenon, a lone question mark." But, he goes on, "whoever
pauses over the question and *learns* to ask, will find what I found:—that a
vast new panorama opens up for him, a possibility makes him giddy, mistrust
[*Misstrauen*], suspicion and fear of every kind spring up, belief in morality,
all morality wavers." The wedge of mistrust expressed by questioning the
value of compassion opens the door to a whole range of further questions.
Eventually, Nietzsche says, "a new demand becomes articulate. So let us
give voice to this *new demand*: we need a *critique* of moral values, *the value
of these should itself, for once, be examined.*" Later, in *GM* 3.20, Nietzsche
says that there is reason enough "why we psychologists of today cannot get
rid of a certain mistrust [*Misstrauen*] *towards ourselves*" Why? "Probably
we, too, are still 'too good' for our trade, probably we, too, are still the victims, the prey, the sick of this contemporary taste for moralization, much as
we feel contempt towards it—it probably infects *us* as well." As before, the
self-mistrust advised in this passage is not one that induces negative emotional evaluations of fixed aspects of the self. Instead, it is a sort of caution,
an insistence on double-checking the deliverances of intuitions that might be
overly generous and thereby lead one astray. Nietzsche goes on: "What warning did the diplomat give when he spoke to his peers? 'Above all, gentlemen,
we must mistrust our first impulses!' he said, '*they are nearly always good.*'"
In the very next passage (*GM* 3.24), Nietzsche remarks: "We 'knowers'
are positively mistrustful [*misstrauisch*] of any kind of believers; our mistrust [*Misstrauen*] has gradually trained us to . . . presuppose, wherever the
strength of a belief becomes prominent, a certain weakness, even *improbability* of proof." Once again, Nietzsche advocates replacing dogmatic belief and
deep, long-held trust with mistrust. He does so especially when such trust is
bound up with Christian morality, which entices people with a range of positive illusions. He goes on: "Even we do not deny that faith 'brings salvation':
precisely for this reason we deny that faith *proves* anything."

Finally, in *A* 13, while talking about "we free spirits," Nietzsche says: "We
have had the whole pathos of humanity against us—its idea of what truth
should be, of what serving the truth should entail: so far, every 'thou shalt'
has been directed against us. . . . Our objectives, our practices, our silent,

cautious, mistrustful [*misstrauische*] nature." As before, Nietzsche associates cautious mistrust, especially mistrust of what has been traditionally been considered good in Christian morality, with his own epistemic dispositions, his own pursuit of truth. As we will see in the next section, in other passages he turns this cautious mistrust into a scientific methodology that, in his view, harnesses motivated reasoning in the service of inquiry.

Mistrust as a Scientific Methodology

In the previous section, we saw that when mistrust displaces long-held trust in dogmas such as Christian morality, it opens new domains of inquiry that were previously under embargo. In this section, I argue that Nietzsche envisions an even more dynamic role for mistrust in the context of science (*Wissenschaft*, including not just natural sciences such as physics but also social sciences such as psychology, and even humanities such as philosophy). In particular, he adopts a proto-, quasi-Popperian position on severe testing.[13] Nietzsche denies the possibility of disinterested inquiry; in its place, he suggests taking advantage of motivated reasoning. Those who promulgate a theory are positively encouraged to trust their intuitions and cognitive abilities, with the result that they are disposed to find evidence and make inferences that support their theory. But this is only one step in the process. Either they at a later time, or other inquirers in their field, are encouraged to approach the same theory with deep mistrust, with the result that critics are disposed to find counterevidence and draw inferences that contradict the theory. When this diachronic, socially distributed process is complete, both the evidence in favor of and the evidence against the theory should be available to all parties. It is only then that a firm, though still tentative, judgment can be made about the theory.

Nietzsche first formulated this view in *Human, All-too-human*. In *HH* 22, he contrasts religion, which, as we saw, relies on deep trust of traditional dogmas, with science, which "needs doubt and mistrust [*Misstrauen*] for its closest allies." But he does not stop there. Instead, he goes on to suggest that "the sum of unimpeachable truths—truths, that is, which have survived all the assaults of skepticism and disintegration—can in time become so great . . . that on the basis of them one may resolve to embark on 'everlasting' works." Thus, scientific conclusions remain tentative, but they are still a firm enough foundation on which to attempt to build. Much later, in *HH* 633, Nietzsche says that, since the Enlightenment, "we no longer so easily concede to anyone that he is in possession of the truth: the rigorous procedures of inquiry have propagated mistrust [*Misstrauen*] and caution, so that anyone who advocates opinions with violent word and deed is felt to be an enemy." A couple passages later, in *HH* 635, he says that there are "people of intelligence who can *learn* as many of the facts of science as they like, but . . . lack the spirit of science: they have not that instinctive mistrust [*Misstrauen*] of devious thinking that . . . has put its roots down in the soul of every scientific man." What distinguishes the scientist from the nonscientist, on this understanding, is not whether their theories are falsifiable but whether, motivated by mistrust, they go out of their way to try to falsify theories. Those who lack the scientific spirit, by contrast, are too easily satisfied and become lackadaisical as soon as they have a half-plausible solution. "For them," he says, "it is enough to have discovered any hypothesis at all concerning any matter. . . . To possess an opinion is to them the same thing as to become a fanatical adherent of it and henceforth to lay it to their heart as a conviction."[14] True scientists, by contrast, "know what is meant by method and procedure and how vital it is to exercise the greatest circumspection."

In the books subsequently appended to *Human, All-too-human*, Nietzsche returns to these themes. Perhaps the most impressive statement of his philosophy of science is *AOM* 215, which I quote in full:

> Regular and rapid progress in the sciences is possible only when the individual is not obliged to be *too mistrustful* [*misstrauisch*] in the testing of every account and assertion made by others in domains in which he is a relative stranger: the condition for this, however, is that in his own field everyone must have rivals who are *extremely mistrustful* and are accustomed to observe him very closely. It is out of this juxtaposition of "not too mistrustful" and "extremely mistrustful" that the integrity of the republic of the learned originates.

In this passage, Nietzsche makes clear that scientific inquiry is essentially a distributed social process. Those close enough to a given topic are the only ones who are well positioned to evaluate and criticize a given piece of work. If it passes muster through this peer review, then others with less expertise in the relevant field are licensed to accept and build on it. Of course, this process is not infallible, but it is the best that can be achieved by finite creatures such as ourselves. Whether actual scientific practice adheres to this idealized methodology is another question—one which the ongoing replication crisis calls into doubt. In any event, in *The Wanderer and His Shadow*, Nietzsche offers further thoughts on the emotional attitudes of practicing scientists. In *WS* 145, he points to the "aversion to images and similes within science." Such images and similes are all too "persuasive and convincing," which is why they find a home in religious discourse. By contrast, in science "that which makes *credible*, is precisely what is *not* wanted; one challenges, rather, the coldest mistrust [*Misstrauen*] . . . because mistrust is the touchstone for the gold of certainty." Nietzsche puts the point even more starkly (and, ironically, with a metaphor) in *WS* 319: "we mistrust [*mistraut*] everyone who believes in himself; in former ages it sufficed to make others believe in us. The recipe for obtaining belief *now* is: 'Do not spare yourself!

If you want to place your opinions in a believable light first set fire to your own house!'"

Nietzsche continues to associate the scientific spirit with a calculated mix of trust and mistrust in *The Gay Science*. For instance, in *GS* 33, he asks: "Why should man be more mistrustful [*misstrauischer*] and evil now" than ever before? The answer: "Because he now has a science—needs a science." Later, in *GS* 110, Nietzsche claims that only in recent history has it become the case that "not only faith and conviction, but also scrutiny, denial, mistrust [*Misstrauen*], and contradiction were a *power*." Note, again, that he is not advocating unconditional mistrust any more than unconditional trust (see also *BGE* 154). Rather, both attitudes are needed, and in a way that is socially or diachronically distributed. He goes on: "all 'evil' instincts were subordinated to knowledge and put in its service and took on the luster of the permitted . . . the innocence of the *good*." As we saw above, according to Nietzsche, mistrust has traditionally been regarded as an evil attitude, but in science this evil is required, at least instrumentally. Finally, in *GS* 296, Nietzsche questions the value of demonstrating a firm, unchanging character. As we saw earlier, he thinks that this is often treated as a sign of trustworthiness even though it is not so reliable. However, when it comes to inquiry, rejection of those who are less rigid "is the most harmful kind of general judgment, for it condemns and discredits the willingness that a seeker after knowledge must have to declare himself against his previous opinion and to be mistrustful [*misstrauisch*] of anything that wishes to become *firm*." Here Nietzsche demonstrates his version of fallibilism. Someone who possesses a truly scientific disposition knows that he might turn out to be wrong, even if his inquiry was diligent; he also knows that others can turn out to be wrong, even if their inquiries are diligent. For this reason, he must be willing to change his mind and also to mistrust those who dogmatically refuse to admit that they could ever be wrong.

Nietzsche's association of mistrust and science also continues into his mature works, especially *Beyond Good and Evil*. He begins in *BGE* 1 with a discussion of the will to truth, saying: "questions this will to truth has already laid before us!" Nietzsche associates asking questions with mistrust. After all, if one were trusting and confident, many questions would not arise. He then asks rhetorically: "Is it any wonder if we finally become mistrustful [*misstrauisch*]. . . . That we ourselves are also learning from this Sphinx to pose questions?" Continuing this line of thought, in *BGE* 34 Nietzsche admits that in bourgeois society "a mistrustful [*Misstrauen*] disposition might be a sign of 'bad character.'" But, he asks, "what is to stop us from being unwise and saying: 'As the creature who has been the biggest dupe the earth has ever seen, the philosopher pretty much has a *right* to a "bad character." It is his *duty* to be mistrustful these days.'" Again, not everything that the philosopher mistrustfully questions is guaranteed to turn out to be false, though much will. Nietzsche recommends mistrust because it is the best way to test claims and opinions that have hitherto enjoyed only blind trust. It is a way, as he puts it in the subtitle of *Twilight of the Idols*, to pose "questions with a *hammer* and, perhaps, [hear] in reply that famous hollow sound" (*TI* P). Later still, in *BGE* 192, Nietzsche claims that in the history of science, as in all cognition: "there as here, rash hypotheses, fictions, the dumb good will to 'believe,' and a lack of mistrust [*Misstrauen*] and patience develop first—our senses learn late and never fully learn to be refined trusty, careful organs of knowledge." Note again that Nietzsche does not recommend replacing all trust with mistrust. Instead, he suggests that what is needed is a balance between these two, and that striking this balance actually results in "trusty, careful organs of knowledge." Far from being a skeptic, then, Nietzsche appears to be a realist who thinks that we need to harness the motivated reasoning characteristic of both trust and mistrust to reveal as best we can the true nature of things.

Finally, let us return to *The Gay Science*, specifically to a section that Nietzsche added in the fifth book of 1887: *GS* 344 (though see also *GS* 375). In this famous passage, Nietzsche begins by saying: "In science, convictions have no right to citizenship." Instead, "only when they decide to step down to the modesty of a hypothesis, a tentative experimental standpoint, a regulative fiction, may they be granted admission and even a certain value in the realm of knowledge—though always with the restriction that they remain under police supervision, under the police of mistrust [*Misstrauens*]." As we have seen above, this is an expression both of fallibilism and of the need for both trust and mistrust in scientific inquiry. Nietzsche then asks whether this means that "a conviction is granted admission to science only when it *ceases* to be a conviction? Wouldn't the cultivation of the scientific spirit begin when one permitted oneself no more convictions? That is probably the case." Nietzsche then turns a reflexive, mistrustful eye on the very practice he just described, saying:

> We need still to ask: *in order that this cultivation begin*, must there not be some prior conviction—and indeed one so authoritative and unconditional that it sacrifices all other convictions to itself? We see that science, too, rests on a faith; there is simply no "presuppositionless" science. The question whether *truth* is necessary must get an answer in advance, the answer "yes," and moreover this answer must be so firm that it takes the form of the statement, the belief, the conviction: "*Nothing* is *more* necessary than truth."

He goes on to ask whether this unconditional will to truth is the will not to let oneself be deceived or the will not to deceive even oneself. Then his mistrustful skepticism prompts two new questions: "But why not deceive? But why not allow oneself to be deceived?" As he notes, the reasons for these two imperatives are very different. "[O]ne does not want to let oneself be deceived because one assumes it is harmful, dangerous, disastrous to be deceived; in this sense science would be a long-range prudence, caution, utility." But, he follows up, this is an assumption that has not yet been supported. He then asks, "Is it really less harmful, dangerous, disastrous not to want to let oneself be deceived? What do you know in advance about the character of existence to be able to decide whether the greater advantage is on the side of the unconditionally mistrustful [*Unbedingt-Misstrauischen*] or the unconditionally trusting [*Unbedingt-Zutraulichen*]?" As we saw above, Nietzsche rejects both unconditional trust *and* unconditional mistrust. And in this passage he again does so explicitly, saying that both are necessary: "a lot of trust *as well as* a lot of mistrust [*Misstrauen*]." In the remainder of the passage, Nietzsche suggests that there are multiple reasons why someone might adopt this unconditional will to truth. One, which he associates with his own "gay science," is "a quixotism, a slight, an enthusiastic folly." But another, which he associates with life-denial, is the affirmation of truth at any cost, including the condemnation of fixed aspects of oneself that he associates with vice and life-denial. Science, then, turns out to be a dangerous endeavor that only those lucky enough to have no immutable despicable traits should engage in.

CONCLUSION

In this chapter I have set out the first systematic review and interpretation of Nietzsche's thinking on trust and mistrust. He turns out to have a range of views about both attitudes. In *Human, All-too-human*, he discusses how interpersonal trust can be built up and undermined. In later works, he discusses the sometimes-unreliable heuristics that people use to assess others' trustworthiness. And across his philosophical career he is concerned to foster self-trust and dispel self-mistrust, especially when it is directed at fixed or immutable aspects of the self. But Nietzsche does not condemn all mistrust. In many passages, he promotes mistrust of the Christian morality that tends to undermine self-trust. It is a matter of mistrust versus mistrust. And in his reflections on the psychology of scientific inquiry, he recommends a perspectivist approach that harnesses mistrust in the pursuit of truth and eradication of error.

NOTES

1. The following abbreviations will be used to refer to Nietzsche's works: *A* = *The Antichrist*; *AOM* = *Assorted Opinions and Maxims* (in part two of *HH*); *BGE* = *Beyond Good and Evil*; *CW* = *The Case of Wagner*; *D* = *Daybreak*; *DS* = *David Strauss, the Confessor and Writer* (in *UM*); *EH* = *Ecce Homo*; *GM* = *On the*

Genealogy of Morals; *GS* = *The Gay Science*; *HH* = *Human, All-too-human*; *HL* = *On the Uses and Disadvantages of History for Life* (in *UM*); *SE* = *Schopenhauer as Educator* (in *UM*); *TI* = *Twilight of the Idols*; *WS* = *The Wanderer and His Shadow* (in part two of *HH*); *Z* = *Thus Spoke Zarathustra*.

2. This is not to claim that the English word "resentment" perfectly translates the German, which sometimes connotes envy. However, such slight mismatches are common in translation and certainly not unique to *Ressentiment*.

3. These methods were pioneered in Alfano (2018a, 2018b, 2019a, 2019b, forthcoming a, forthcoming b) and made accessible to scholars with no coding background in Alfano and Cheong (2019). For that reason, I do not explain them at length in this chapter.

4. Of course, for reasons of space, not all these passages are explicitly discussed in this chapter. For instance, I leave out those passages in which Nietzsche seeks to establish a confidential rapport with his readers by saying that he is speaking confidentially [*im Vertrauen*] (*DS* 4, *SE* 2, *D* 130, *GS* 93), or by calling them "my friends" [*meine Freunde*] (twenty-four passages, not including an additional fourteen in which Zarathustra says "my friends"). I also leave out his scattered remarks on the relationship between trust and governance (*HH* 473, *AOM* 318, *WS* 190, *WS* 248, *WS* 285, *GM* 2.9).

5. There are many, slightly different, versions of this account of trust. See, among others, Baier (1986), Jones (2012a), and Alfano and Huijts (2020).

6. For more on the esteem implied by trusts, see Pettit (1995).

7. Here and throughout the chapter, italics within quotations are the authors, not my own.

8. For more on the (in)stability of character in Nietzsche's writings, see Alfano (2015, 2019a, chapters 3–5).

9. Nietzsche levels the same accusation against the doctrine of original sin in his last writings: "The concept of 'sin' invented along with the associated instrument of torture, the concept of 'free will,' in order to confuse the instincts, in order to make mistrust [*Misstrauen*] of the instincts second nature!" (*EH* Destiny.8).

10. For more on Nietzsche's use of affective induction to shake loose dogmatic assumptions in his readers, see Alfano (2018b).

11. Note that the Cambridge University Press translation here translates *Vertrauen* as "faith" rather than "trust." But if Nietzsche had wanted to talk about faith, he could very easily have used *Glaube*, a word he uses plenty of times elsewhere.

12. Dawn is of course also the metaphor behind the title of *Daybreak*. Reflecting on that book in *EH* Books.D1, Nietzsche asks where the dawn alluded to in the book's title is to be found and answers "in a *revaluation of all values*, in an escape from all moral values, in an affirmation and trust [*Vertrauen-haben*] in everything that had been forbidden, despised, cursed until now."

13. For more on Nietzsche's interest in harnessing emotions such as trust and distrust as aids in systematic inquiry, see Alfano (2017, 2019b, chapter 6, 2019c).

14. This distinction is borne out by recent work in the field of vice epistemology; see Meyer et al. (2021a, 2021b).

TRANSLATIONS OF NIETZSCHE'S WORKS:

Nietzsche, Friedrich. 1986. *Human, All-too-human*. Translated by R.J. Hollingdale. Cambridge: Cambridge University Press.

———. 1997a. *Daybreak: Thoughts on the Prejudices of Morality*. Edited by M. Clark and B. Leiter. Translated by R.J. Hollingdale. Cambridge: Cambridge University Press.

———. 1997b. *Untimely Meditations*. Edited by D. Breazeale. Translated by R.J. Hollingdale. Cambridge: Cambridge University Press.

———. 1999. *The Birth of Tragedy and Other Writings*. Edited by R. Geuss and R. Speirs. Translated by R. Speirs. Cambridge: Cambridge University Press.

———. 2001a. *Beyond Good and Evil: Prelude to a Philosophy of the Future*. Edited by R.P. Horstmann and J. Norman. Translated by J. Norman. Cambridge: Cambridge University Press.

———. 2001b. *The Gay Science: With a Prelude in German Rhymes and an Appendix in Songs*. Edited by B. Williams. Translated by J. Nauckhoff. Cambridge: Cambridge University Press.

———. 2005. *The Anti-Christ, Ecce Homo, Twilight of the Idols, and Other Writings*. Edited by A. Ridley and J. Norman. Translated by J. Norman. Cambridge: Cambridge University Press.

———. 2006a. *On the Genealogy of Morality*. Edited by K. Ansell-Pearson. Translated by C. Diethe. Cambridge: Cambridge University Press.

———. 2006b. *Thus Spoke Zarathustra: A Book for All and None*. Edited by A. del Caro and R. Pippin. Translated by A. del Caro. Cambridge: Cambridge University Press.

REFERENCES

Alfano, Mark. 2015. "An Enchanting Abundance of Types: Nietzsche's Modest Unity of Virtue Thesis." *Journal of Value Inquiry* 49(3): 417–35.

———. 2016. *Moral Psychology: An Introduction*. New York: Polity.

———. 2017. "Twenty-First Century Perspectivism: The Role of Emotions in Scientific Inquiry." *Studi di Estetica* 7(1): 65–79.

———. 2018a. "Digital Humanities for History of Philosophy: A Case Study on Nietzsche." In *Handbook of Methods in the Digital Humanities*, edited by L. Levenberg, T. Neilson, and D. Rheams. London: Palgrave.

———. 2018b. "The Epistemic Function of Contempt and Laughter in Nietzsche." In *The Moral Psychology of Contempt*, edited by M. Mason. Rowman & Littlefield.

———. 2019a. *Nietzsche's Moral Psychology*. Cambridge: Cambridge University Press.

———. 2019b. "Nietzsche's Affective Perspectivism as a Philosophical Methodology." In *Nietzsche's Metaphilosophy*, edited by P. Loeb and M. Meyer. Cambridge: Cambridge University Press.

———. 2019c. "Nietzsche's Affective Perspectivism as a Philosophical Methodology." In *Nietzsche's Metaphilosophy*, edited by P. Loeb and M. Meyer. Cambridge: Cambridge University Press.

———. forthcoming a. "Nietzsche on Humility and Modesty." In *Humility: A History*, edited by J. Steinberg. Oxford: Oxford University Press.

———. forthcoming b. "The Functions of Shame in Nietzsche." In *The Moral Psychology of Shame*, edited R. Rodogno and A. Fussi. London: Rowman & Littlefield.

Alfano, Mark, and Marc Cheong. 2019. "Guest Editors' Introduction: Examining Moral Emotions in Nietzsche with the 'Semantic Web Exploration Tool: Nietzsche.'" *Journal of Nietzsche Studies* 50(1): 1–10.

Alfano, Mark, and Nicole Huijts. 2020. "Trust and Distrust in Institutions and Governance." In *Handbook of Trust and Philosophy*, edited by J. Simon. London: Routledge.

Baier, Annette. 1986. "Trust and Antitrust." *Ethics* 96: 231–60.

Dannenberg, Jorah. 2015. "Promising Ourselves, Promising Others." *The Journal of Ethics* 19(2): 159–83.

———. 2017. "Promising by Right." *Philosophers' Imprint* 17(22): 1–18.

Goldberg, Sanford. 2013. "Self-trust and Extended Trust." *Res Philosophica* 90(2): 277–92.

Govier, Trudy. 1993. "Self-trust, Autonomy, and Self-esteem." *Hypatia* 8(1): 99–120.

Jones, Karen. 2012a. "Trustworthiness." *Ethics* 123(1): 61–85.

———. 2012b. "The Politics of Intellectual Self-trust." *Social Epistemology* 26(2): 237–51.

Katsafanas, Paul. 2013. *Agency and the Foundations of Ethics: Nietzschean Constitutivism*. Oxford: Oxford University Press.

Lehrer, Keith. 1997. *Self-Trust: A Study of Reason, Knowledge, and Autonomy*. Oxford: Oxford University Press.

McKiernan, Amy. 2016. "Nietzsche's Prefaces as Practices of Self-care." *Epoché: A Journal for the History of Philosophy* 20(2): 447–63.

Meyer, Marco, Mark Alfano, and Boudewijn de Bruin. 2021a. "Development and Validation of the Epistemic Vice Scale." *Review of Philosophy and Psychology*. DOI: 10.1007/s13164-021-00562-5.

———. 2021b. "Epistemic Vice Predicts Acceptance of Covid-19 Misinformation." *Episteme*. Online: http://dx.doi.org/10.2139/ssrn.3644356.

Pasnau, Robert. 2015. "Disagreement and the Value of Self-trust." *Philosophical Studies* 172(9): 2315–39.

Pettit, Philip. 1995. "The Cunning of Trust." *Philosophy and Public Affairs* 24(3): 202–25.

Risse, Mathias. 2003. "Nietzsche's 'Joyous and Trusting Fatalism.'" *International Studies in Philosophy* 35(3): 147–62.

Rukgaber, Matthew. 2012. "The 'Sovereign Individual' and the 'Ascetic Ideal': On a Perennial Misreading of the Second Essay of Nietzsche's *On the Genealogy of Morality*." *Journal of Nietzsche Studies* 43(2): 213–39.

Chapter 9

Løgstrup and the Sovereignty of Trust

Patrick Stokes

It is only in the last decade or so that anglophone moral philosophers have begun to pay serious attention to the works of K. E. Løgstrup (1905–1981), a Danish philosopher and theologian whose outsized influence on Nordic thought has not been replicated elsewhere. To be fair, Løgstrup is, in many ways, an awkward figure to work with. Even while he was still a student, his work tended to be regarded as too philosophical to be theology and too theological to be philosophy. Stylistically, Løgstrup reads as more analytic than continental, yet his touchstones are phenomenologists such as Heidegger and, especially, Hans Lipps, while his self-described "ontological ethics" sit uncomfortably alongside most trends in twentieth-century thought. Yet Løgstrup is nonetheless an engaging and accessible thinker, with deceptively complex things to say about the experience of moral encounter and a talent for presenting everyday ethical life free of some of the theoretical distortions that moral philosophy imposes on it.

One topic of enduring interest throughout the course of Løgstrup's career is that of trust (in Danish, *tillid*). While the ways in which Løgstrup talks about trust evolve over time, reflecting a move away from his earlier, more orthodox Lutheran commitments toward a more explicitly metaphysical account of moral phenomena, he develops a consistent view of trust as a foundational condition for human life. This leads Løgstrup to make some surprising claims: that trust is primary and distrust secondary, and that trust is a "sovereign" life phenomenon that commands our surrender rather than being a relationship that arises between—and within the power of—agents. These claims might sound outlandish at first glance, but Løgstrup's phenomenology of trust illustrates in a striking yet familiar manner the ways in which trust is something not of our making or under our control.

TRUST AS A CONDITION OF LIFE

From the beginning of his work on trust, Løgstrup approaches trust as a question directly related to the conditions under which human life can flourish. In this earliest phase, the emphasis is on trust as a social phenomenon; for all his later emphasis on the encounter with the other (one of the reasons Løgstrup is frequently compared to Levinas), Løgstrup's discussions of trust begin with trust as a condition of communal success rather than of individual ethical responsiveness.

Trust features as a key aspect of Løgstrup's moral philosophy as early as the mid-1940s, during the Nazi occupation of Denmark. In his polemic against the appeasement of the occupying power, "Everyday Life and Foreign Affairs" (*Folkeliv og Udenrigspolitik*), Løgstrup identifies trust as essential for various forms of human good to be realized. Human affairs are subject to certain laws of life, such as "[t]he law of honour that says that we must trust each other in advance to act humanely" (Løgstrup 1943, 11). On Løgstrup's telling, human life is always social life, which means that "each of us has our life's roots in our fellow humans' primitive human trust in us that we will behave humanely" (Ibid., 10). We operate under, and in fact depend upon, a default assumption that the people around us mean us well. Løgstrup is not so naïve as to imagine that nobody ever betrays or swindles anyone else, but our occasional suspicions or localized distrusts take place against a background of unreflective and non-calculative confidence that we do not have to fear what others plan to do to us.

Or at least, that is how things proceed in normal circumstances. Things are different in wartime. Like Levinas two decades later, Løgstrup interprets war in essentially metaphysical terms, though unlike Levinas he thinks of war as a delimited state of human affairs rather than a standing feature of being. Peacetime provides the background conditions, such as trust, that allow certain forms of social institution such as work and family—recognizably a reference to the Lutheran "orders of creation"—to operate successfully.[1] In conditions of war and occupation, however, these background conditions are suspended, if not destroyed. We can no longer simply assume that those around us are not collaborators or informers who will betray us to the occupying power.

What plays out in this situation is not simply a difficult set of circumstances but a metaphysical drama in which we are compelled to defend the conditions under which life, understood roughly as coterminous with individual and collective human flourishing, can actualize itself. When someone seeks to attack foundational trust, even in peacetime, we are compelled to adopt an agonistic attitude to that person which would not be permissible under normal conditions:

> If someone attempts to steal our honour, we must therefore also defend ourselves, and if necessary, defend ourselves by making him into our enemy, for what he is trying to do is nothing less than to cut through the roots of our life and cause it to wither and be stunted in the wretchedness of mistrust, just as surely as each of us has our life's roots in our fellow humans' [*Medmenneskers*] primitive human trust in us that we will behave humanly. (Ibid., 10)

Making someone an enemy, even going as far as organized violent resistance to occupation, becomes necessary because it is the very basis of life that needs to be defended in such a case. Appeasement, even if intended to preserve as much of communal life as possible, instead "eats away at the trust that countrymen must have in each other if they are to live a life together as a people" (Ibid., 18). This in turn can legitimate resistance against those responsible for this state of affairs—a topic that was far from merely academic for Løgstrup, who was actively involved in the Danish Resistance even as he wrote those words, and would shortly have to go into hiding (Brown and Stokes 2020).

It should therefore come as no surprise to find trust playing a central role in 1956's *The Ethical Demand*, a text that is still very much haunted by the experience of occupation and the troubling necessity of resistance. Early in the book, Løgstrup says that trust is so integral to human life that to "meet each other with natural trust" is in fact our standard way of being. If we find ourselves in a context where we distrust strangers in advance, then "[t]he country must be at war, or people who have no respect for law and order must have taken control" such that natural trust has been "stifled through the rise of informants, so that relationships have become strained" (Løgstrup 2020, 9). The reference to the occupation is unmistakable, but already Løgstrup is pointing out that our experience of life in society is quite different to what a certain conception of human prudence might take it to be. *The X-Files'* notorious dictum, "trust no one," may seem like good advice for not getting betrayed, swindled, or let down. Certainly, we might think that not trusting strangers is good advice in general. Yet, as Løgstrup explains, the phenomenology of lived experience shows us that life simply does not work like that:

> By contrast, in normal circumstances we trust the stranger's word and only begin to doubt when we have some special reason to do so. We never believe a human being is lying in advance, but only when we have caught them in a lie. If we are sitting in a train carriage chatting with someone who we are meeting for the first time in our life and who we know nothing about, we believe in advance what they say, and only begin to distrust their word if they make themselves guilty of exaggerations that are too grotesque. Nor do we expect someone to be a thief, if we meet them under normal circumstances: they must first behave suspiciously before we suspect them. In advance, we believe one another's word, in advance we trust one another. (Ibid.)

We assume strangers wish us no harm *unless* we are in exceptional circumstances where we have to be on our guard. Without this openness to strangers, life simply cannot operate, as shown by the distorted and denuded way in which people live during wartime. To distrust in advance "would be hostile to life," and, were we to do so, "our life would wither away and become stunted" (Ibid.).

This is still very much the language that Løgstrup uses during the occupation: war as sowing an unnatural distrust that stunts and deforms the proper actualization of "life." Yet Løgstrup now makes the stronger claim that trust is not simply foundational in the sense of being a requirement of successful life, but in the sense of being prior to distrust. On Løgstrup's picture, distrust is a merely secondary and derivative phenomenon. This claim that trust is primary has proven controversial in multiple ways. Robert Stern (2019) suggests four possible interpretations of this claim:

- psychological: children start out with a trusting attitude and learn to distrust.
- transcendental: trust is a necessary condition of language and society, and so must be the default attitude.
- axiological: trust is an intrinsic good while distrust is a privation.
- ontological: trust is essential to the proper functioning of human life itself, and as such cannot be a norm or a practice that we have instituted for ourselves.

That all these readings are possible and indeed persuasive only enhances the ambiguity of the claim. It is not entirely clear if Løgstrup means that trust is primary ontogenetically, phylogenetically, or both. The discussion of children learning to distrust certainly suggests that trust is ontogenetically primary: each one of us starts off trusting and only gradually learns distrust. But if that is the case, it is not clear that our "default" position before we learn distrust should even be called trust at all. Løgstrup notes explicitly that the child's trust is not voluntary:

> The child, unlike an adult, cannot display a merely reserved form of trust. In order to do so, one must have learnt to hold oneself in reserve. But the child has precisely not learnt how to reserve themselves in this conscious and self-controlled way. For them, their reservations are under the power of an automatic psychological process. (Ibid., 15)

That being the case, we could question whether there can be enough volition in infant trust for it to be recognizable as the same phenomenon as adult trust. If the child is not consciously and deliberately trusting, are they really trusting at all? As we will see, this way of framing the problem ultimately points to an important feature of Løgstrupian trust: namely, that it is not simply a willed action. But the problem remains as to whether spontaneous trust of this sort is worthy of the name if there is no alternative.

The ontogenetic claim about the primacy of trust is also controversial insofar as it implies a sort of lapsarian picture in which childhood development is a gradual falling away from an Edenic state of trust into a corrupted state of distrust, and that, all things being equal, we would be better off if we could remain in the immediate trust of infancy. Alasdair MacIntyre (2007, 2010) in particular has taken Løgstrup to task for this claim. For MacIntyre, our untrained infant trust would, in adulthood, amount to a vice of credulity. The raw material of infantile trust must be trained over time so that the child develops the phronetic judgment to know whom to trust, when, how much, and to what purpose. Proper trust is therefore always reflective or at least open to reflective interrogation and rejection, endorsement, or modification. To go through the world trusting everybody automatically would leave us prone to constant injury and exploitation and would make us less capable of successfully serving others.

We can also read trust as phylogenetically primary: that is, trust is conceptually prior to distrust. Trust is a positive phenomenon, while distrust is merely derivative. Think of this as Augustinian trust: like evil for Augustine, distrust is simply the privation of trust, which is good in itself. As we will see, this coheres with Løgstrup's later insistence that trust qua sovereign expression of life is an intrinsically and incorrigibly good thing just insofar as it promotes life, and distrust is destructive of life. Yet this reading too seems to lay Løgstrup open to MacIntyre's charge that sometimes trusting the other simply *is* the wrong thing to do. Indeed, this problem attends other descriptions of the sovereign expressions of life in Løgstrup, in which Løgstrup presents cases where we are morally required to actively thwart certain sovereign expressions of life, such as "openness" (i.e., spontaneous, uncalculated sincerity) of speech. Løgstrup himself acknowledges that trust can be abused and that there are circumstances where children should be taught not to be too trusting; his explanation that this can only happen *in spite of* the inherent goodness of trust does not so much explain anything as simply redescribe the problem (see Løgstrup 2007, 115). We will return to this issue of trusting the untrustable later. For now, we can simply note that the primacy of trust is in tension with two things we might assume to be essential to trust, particularly given its importance to moral life. First, foundational trust understood ontogenetically is in tension with the idea that trust is centrally linked to rational agency; second, the conceptual priority of trust is in tension (at least without further qualification) with the idea that trust can be misplaced, misguided, or simply wrong. We will now turn to consider where we might place Løgstrupian trust in the standard ways of conceptualizing trust as a two- or three-part relation.

RELATIONAL MODELS OF TRUST

While trust may be foundational for successful life in society as such, trust is nonetheless very much an interpersonal phenomenon for Løgstrup. In *The Ethical Demand*, Løgstrup describes trust in terms of individuals having expectations of each other and thereby making themselves vulnerable to disappointment. Løgstrup tells us that "to show trust is to deliver oneself up" or to "lay oneself open" (*udlevere sig selv* or *selvudlevering*). This laying oneself open is a function of the fact that in interacting with another person we present them with an implicit expectation. This could be something specific, but it can also be as general as expecting sincerity or delicacy:

> It is quite another thing, however, to deliver oneself up in the kind of trust one person shows the other through which something is always required of them, insofar as this does involve an expectation of them. In the expectation of the other, one undertakes something, and this is what the delivering up of oneself consists in. But what one does, and what form this delivering up of oneself takes, does not necessarily mean that one confides in the other person—although of course, it could take this form—but it can take all sorts of other forms too. For example, the delivering up of oneself which consists in trusting the other person to be truthful, or in adopting a particular tone in speaking with them. (Løgstrup 2020, 16)

Simply in speaking to another person, we place an expectation on them to respond with what Løgstrup calls "new" words—that is, to respond sincerely and spontaneously rather than meeting us with "old," that is, predetermined, insincere, or manipulative responses. We deliver ourselves into the power of the other, and thereby form an expectation that the other will deal with us in a way that is responsive to our vulnerability. When the other fails to respond in this way, we tend to act as if the other has committed some moral wrong against us, whereas what we are really doing, according to Løgstrup, is trying to hide from ourselves the painful fact that we laid ourselves open and were rebuffed. Such a reaction makes no sense if we think of trust purely as a calculative prediction as to what the other is going to do, but neither is it properly a moral judgment about the other (see Stern 2019). We "invent a wrong one has suffered in order to justify one's strong and entirely emotional reaction . . . it is the emotional aspect of the situation that causes one to grasp at the moral reproaches and accusations which, precisely because of their moral character, are emotionally charged" (Løgstrup 2020, 11). Hence much moral outrage, according to Løgstrup, turns out to be disguised embarrassment.

On this account, trust is presented as a way of responding to the giving-over of ourselves to others that life requires, while the ethical demand is the corollary that we are required to act for the sake of the other who has been placed in our power. We live, in ways both trivial and fatal, at each other's mercy. Yet that self-delivering also generates an expectation, and that expectation is more or less concrete. "Whatever its form," Løgstrup tells us, "whether spoken or silent, the expectation is expressed on the assumption that the other person will fulfil our expectation. This means that, in the expression of the expectation, one delivers oneself up to the other person's fulfilment of it—even before it is established that there will be any such fulfilment" (Ibid., 10).

At this point, the question arises as to where Løgstrup might fit into the models of relational trust that have been offered by contemporary philosophers. Ever since trust first became a topic of interest among analytic philosophers with Annette Baier's seminal paper "Trust and Antitrust" (1986), an ongoing topic of discussion has been whether we should interpret trust as a two- or a three-place relationship. For Baier, trust is generally a three-place relation: A trusts B with C, where C is, broadly, something A values (Baier 1986, 236). Hence it is not simply that we trust someone, but that we trust someone to act in some particular way in some specific domain.

At first glance, Løgstrup's account of trust may appear to be irreducibly three place. Trust as it is presented in the pre-*Ethical Demand* writings is essentially trust to act in certain ways, namely, those that preserve the communal bases of successful life. Trust being linked to expectation also fits well with the account of trust sketched by Karen Jones, among others: "If A's attitude toward B (in a given domain of interaction) is predominantly characterized by optimism about B's goodwill and by the expectation that B will be directly and favorably moved by the thought that A is counting on her, then A has a trusting relationship with B (within that domain)" (Jones 1996, 6). Key to this account, on Jones's view, is not just that I am optimistic that the other will act favorably toward me, but that the other will be motivated to do so by the fact I am counting on them to act in this way. This accounts for our distinctive offence at being let down, which for Løgstrup, as we have seen, tends to find expression in putatively moral reproach which for Jones is best summed up by the pained retort "But I was counting on you!" (Jones 2017). (Interestingly, Jones too frames the normativity that is violated by someone letting us down not as a moral violation but as a violation of norms linked to our interest in effective agency.)

Yet two-place accounts of trust have their adherents too. According to the two-place account, to say that I trust someone is not necessarily to say that I trust them to do anything in particular; rather, trust can simply be a pro-attitude that I hold toward another person. To say that I trust you is thus not simply shorthand for the set of things I trust you to do, but rather a holistic attitude on the basis of which I may then place more specific forms of trust in you. This may seem like a reasonably thin distinction, and indeed Jacopo

Domenicucci and Richard Holton (2017) point out that whether we think of trust as a two- or three-place relation may be influenced by which language we use, as much as anything. "A trusts B to C," where "C" is an infinitive verb, is perfectly standard in English but awkward or ungrammatical in Romance languages.

One might think that Løgstrup's account is straightforwardly three place: I place myself at the mercy of the other, and thereby create an expectation that the other will act mercifully, in whatever ways mercy might demand. But therein lies an important complication: while I might create an expectation for the other by being placed in their power, *what* the other is now expected to do is not thereby determined. This is so for two reasons. First, to anticipate, trust is a sovereign expression of life, and Løgstrup tells us in later work that these expressions of life never determine in advance what is to be done: they are not principles or decision procedures. Second, the asymmetrical character of the ethical demand would seem to preclude us from saying we trust the other to do any particular thing. Why? Because, while the ethical demand is that we act for the sake of the other, we do not get to then claim that the other should act for *our* sake. Moreover, acting for the sake of the other may in fact look very different to what the other expects it to look like. Acting for the sake of the other need not mean doing what the other asks, and in fact may mean doing exactly the opposite. So, it starts to look as though Løgstrup's account is not a three-place relation account because the third place will be radically under-determined.

This radical under-determination becomes even more serious when we come to look at the account of trust given in Løgstrup's 1967 book *Controverting Kierkegaard*.[2] It is in this work that we are first introduced to the concept of the "sovereign expressions of life." Løgstrup offers a remarkable example of trust interpreted as one such sovereign expression of life, taken from Sartre's play *The Devil and the Good Lord*. The play retells the story of the fifteenth- and sixteenth-century Swabian warlord Götz von Berlichingen, who at one point is depicted dealing with the duplicitous knight Weislingen in a remarkable way:

> He will neither trivialize nor disguise the fact, neither from Weislingen nor from himself, that it is a traitor he is dealing with. He will discover Weislingen's traps, thwart him whenever he is able, and take all precautionary measures. He will take up the challenge, acting prudently and shrewdly, narrowing the scope for Weislingen's treachery as far as he can. He will let Weislingen know that he is aware of what he can expect from him. Yet in all of this, he will still be giving him a chance—the chance which consists in his not washing his hands of him; and in so doing Götz von Berlichingen will realize trust and openness—on his own terms and not on Weislingen's treacherous terms. The opportunity he offers Weislingen is that of being won over to his side against his own treacherous self.

No matter how convinced Götz von Berlichingen may be that this opportunity, too, Weislingen will abuse—he is to have it all the same. But he cherishes no illusions. (Løgstrup 2007, 57–58)

As a description of trust, this is quite astonishing. It is strange, to say the least, that someone would trust an untrustworthy person absent some further aim or extrinsic motivation (Simpson 2017, 179). Yet is also a recurring theme in philosophical discussions of trust that trust is importantly different to mere confident prediction: to trust someone is not simply to be able to predict their actions to a high degree of certainty based on their personality or history. In one sense, then, this passage simply pushes this point to its logical extreme. In Götz's relation to Weislingen, the connection between trust and trustworthiness has been completely severed, making any lingering sense of trust as calculative prediction impossible. Götz knows Weislingen cannot be trusted, and yet trusts him anyway. He knows that whatever he does will be met with yet more underhandedness and deception, so his trust can in no sense be regarded as a *confidence* in Weislingen—indeed, the only confidence he can have is that Weislingen will abuse Götz's trust.

Is this three- or two-place trust? The answer must be: "neither." The complete unreliability of Weislingen, coupled with Götz's awareness thereof, makes a three-part trust relation impossible. It is clear that Götz does not trust Weislingen to do some specific thing, however broadly construed—except, perhaps, to act duplicitously, but this is no trust at all. There is nothing that can occupy the third place. Götz may trust Weislingen, yet he does not trust him to *do* anything at all.

Might we then consider this a paradigm example of two-place trust, whereby Götz trusts Weislingen, but does not thereby trust him to do anything in particular or in any specific domain? That might seem attractive at first, but here too we run into problems. If trusting someone is, to use Jones's term, an "optimism" (which is affective but also cognitive) that the trusted person is well disposed toward my reliance upon them, nothing like that can be said to be the case with Götz's attitude to Weislingen. The only things in Götz's comportment toward Weislingen that can be said to be a response to anything *about* Götz are precisely the things we would normally think of as *dis*trust. Götz is alive to Weislingen's tricks and deceptions and makes no pretense that Götz is trust*worthy*. Nor is it clear that Götz is showing Weislingen what is sometimes called "therapeutic" trust, in which someone is shown trust in order to make them more trustworthy than they already are (Frost-Arnold 2014; Pace 2020). Therapeutic trust presumably requires more promising material to work with than Götz takes Weislingen to be. Götz will show Weislingen trust despite there seemingly being *nothing* in Götz that would justify this. As I have noted elsewhere in discussing this example, all trust is modestly fideistic to at least some degree (Stokes 2020), yet Götz looks to be fideistic in the manner of the phrase wrongly attributed to Tertullian: *credo quia absurdum*, "I believe it because it is absurd."

Yet it would also be wrong here to say that Götz's trust has nothing to do with Weislingen—that is, Weislingen as a concrete person, with a specific character, standing in relation to Götz. Götz's trust is not *mis*placed in that it is not based on a mistaken assessment of Weislingen's character, but equally, it is not an attitude that does not respond to Weislingen at all. Rather, as the passage above makes clear, trust is here presented as a sort of *receptivity*, an openness to Weislingen *despite* his mendacity. As Løgstrup makes clear, the trust that is being extended to Weislingen is best thought of as his being given a chance to act honorably *despite* himself. And this is not an attempt to manipulate Weislingen into mending his ways—for this would require material amenable to such manipulation, which Weislingen, it seems, is not. Götz's trust amounts to a refusal to totalize his understanding of Weislingen's character. By not allowing his judgment of Weislingen to close off the possibility of Weislingen's acting in a trustworthy way, Götz opens the space for a redemption that neither Götz nor Weislingen have it in their direct power to bring about.

We find this thought a decade earlier in *The Ethical Demand*, where we are warned about the dangers posed by the pictures we form of others in our minds. The risk is that once we have formed a picture of a person, it can impede our openness to the other themselves. Our preconceptions or prejudgments of others, if we allow them to get between us and the other, corrupt and corrode our life together. As Løgstrup puts it:

> Not to let the other come forward in words, works, and conduct, but to seek to hinder this with the picture we have formed of him or her through our suspicion and our antipathy, is a denial of life. It is at one and the same time a denial of both the other's and one's own life. It is integral to human existence not to want to reduce oneself to reactions, which—being merely "sensible"—are determined only by what has already happened. It is inherent to human existence that we are as new as the other's new words, new deeds, and new conduct. It is as if we assume that because these are in the present, they are new, and for this reason we want to renew our attitude to them. This could be called a trust in life itself, a trust in its ongoing renewal. (Løgstrup 2020, 14)

In forming a picture of someone, we implicitly take what they *have* been, said, and done to represent the totality of what they *are*. This closes off the possibility of "new" speech and action by reducing the other to the sum total of their past and what we know of them. This is not to say that our assessments of others are inherently wrong or misguided, but that they can obscure the other in a way that shuts down any possibility for spontaneous action. By acting in a way that presupposes a certain totalizing understanding of the other—as a being whose actions and responses are ultimately predetermined—I limit how the situation with the other can unfold. If Götz treats Weislingen *solely* as duplicitous and untrustworthy and simply seeks to contain or restrict him, no better outcome will be possible.

Yet if Götz is right, Weislingen himself is also incapable of bringing about his redemption by himself here. It is not that he is a trustworthy person who is being situationally constrained by others' distrust in him; rather, he *is* every bit as untrustworthy as Götz sees him. In placing trust-as-openness in Weislingen, then, Götz is trusting not just his enemy, but acting from "a trust in life itself, a trust in its ongoing renewal." Trust here opens up a field of possibilities that are available to *neither* Götz nor Weislingen on their own. And this points us toward trust not simply a two- or three-place relationship between agents, but a relationship to something outside of and *between* both parties: a relationship to life itself.

TRUST AS A SOVEREIGN EXPRESSION OF LIFE

For all their importance in the later phase of his work, Løgstrup never actually gives us a clear definition of what the "sovereign expressions of life" (*suveræne livsytringer*) are, nor does he provide an exhaustive list of which life phenomena are to be understood as sovereign expressions of life. When the term first appears, Løgstrup draws a contrast between what he calls "obsessive" or "encircling" phenomena and sovereign ones. The obsessive phenomena—things like jealousy or offense—are "encircling" in the sense that they lock us in with our own ruminations and fixed ideas. They therefore take us out of the realm in which we are able to act for the sake of others, locking us into our own inward-looking concerns in a way that prevents the sorts of mutual goodwill and support that, as we have seen, are requirements for communal flourishing. Against these, the sovereign expressions of life are presented as phenomena that serve to transform the situation of the other person. Hence Løgstrup claims that pity is *not* a sovereign expression of life, but simply a form of other-directed concern, whereas mercy (*barmhjertighed*) *is* a sovereign expression of life because it aims to transform the situation of the person one finds within one's power and "draws its impetus from the thought that the other has received his or her life in order to realize it and is now hampered in so doing" (Løgstrup 2007, 52). Note that this will also distinguish the sovereign expressions of life, at least on an immediate level, from phenomena of the sort that moral philosophers generally like to trade in, such as justice and fairness. To be just or fair will typically involve the application of intersubjectively understood principles or rules which will determine what is to be done, whereas a sovereign expression of life "cannot be applied, but can only be realized, as I realize myself in it," and "does not rigidify the situation but frees it up, transforms it, which is why the individual must involve himself in it throughout" (Ibid., 53).

Central to this contrast is the sense that the sovereign expressions of life come from outside of us. They are not an application of some internal motive, nor are they driven by a concern for one's own dutifulness or virtue. The expressions of life do not call us to engage with our own moral status; instead, "the call to us is to engage with the situation—through the corresponding sovereign expression of life" (Ibid., 76). Løgstrup offers the Good Samaritan as a paradigm case of mercy: the Samaritan is not "engaging with his own mercifulness in his exercise of it as his duty," but instead, "in his mercifulness, he took charge of the man who had been set upon and lay wounded by the roadside" (Ibid.). The sovereign expression of life is thus directed outward at the needs of the other, rather than proceeding from a concern for one's own righteousness.

Crucially, the sovereign expressions of life wear their goodness on their face, as it were. We do not need to ask if trust or sincerity is good: they simply present themselves *as* good. Their sovereignty consists in their not depending upon us for their goodness. We know simply from our engagement with life that trust, openness of speech, and mercy all serve to secure the flourishing of life, while their opposites are destructive of life. Yet the phenomenal corollary of this is that trust and its fellow expressions of life present themselves as coming from *without*. For Løgstrup, trust does not originate from agents themselves. Rather, trust somehow arises from the ground of life—and we then all too frequently impede its operation with our suspicion and distrust. Trust opens the situation up in ways that allow for life to flourish, while distrust shuts the situation down and closes off possibilities.

In that sense, trust still operates *between* agents, but it does not come *from* agents. It comes, in the context of Løgstrup's self-described "ontological ethics," from life itself, a sort of metaphysical principle rather than a behavioral option. Trust imposes itself upon us in a situation and in that sense is not simply something that we control. Indeed, Løgstrup makes precisely this point well before he has formulated the idea of the sovereign expressions of life:

> If trust and the delivering up of oneself that goes with it were just down to our discretion, so that without any loss to ourselves we could choose not to bother with them, then in our lives there would be no other demands than those which one human being might decide for themselves to place on the other, whether they be conventional, sentimental, or megalomaniacal. However, this is not the case. Trust is not down to us. It is given. Our life is simply created over our heads, such that it cannot be lived in any other way than that one human being, through trust that is either shown or desired, delivers themselves up to the other

human being and thereby puts more or less of their life in the other's hands. (Løgstrup 2020, 17)

While Løgstrup's point here is clearly theological (even if his stated aim in *The Ethical Demand* is to provide a purely secular grounding for a theological premise), the point is, I think, compelling even on purely phenomenological grounds. We do not need to buy into a barely concealed creation theology to find something compelling in Løgstrup's descriptions of phenomena such as trust. In particular, Løgstrup's account of trust captures something that analytic examinations of trust tend to leave out: the way in which trust very often appears to us as something that imposes itself upon us in our encounters with other people. It is not so much that we deliberate on whether to trust someone as that we have to reflectively make ourselves *withhold* trust in specific situations. In a well-known passage, Løgstrup describes the irresistible imposition of the sovereign expressions of life, describing a woman having to resist the force of openness of speech in trying to evade the clever questioning of a Gestapo officer looking for her husband. (The scene is autobiographical, and the woman depicted is Rosemarie Løgstrup, during the period when Løgstrup had to go underground due to his resistance activities.) Openness toward the other is not a decision the woman has to make, but a force that seems to come from without and that she, with considerable effort, has to repel under these highly unusual circumstances. Trust, I suspect, is more often like that than we assume. It is not something we deploy, but something that appears *between* us and the other, and we can either frustrate it or let it have its way. Yet to frame things in this way is already to start to distort the very distinctive kind of (non-)agency that is involved here.

TRUST AND AGENCY

This account of trust as something that arises *between* parties, rather than being an action or attitude one takes to another, pushes us toward a very different understanding of the sort of agency involved in moral action. The sovereignty of the sovereign expressions of life consists partly in their capacity to displace the agent, making the achievement of goodness a function of life rather than of the people who populate it.

Løgstrup's focus on the importance of spontaneous action is at once distinctive, attractive, and unfamiliar. Throughout his work, Løgstrup presents effortless and spontaneous concern for the other as a sort of regulative ideal (Stokes 2017), with the ethical demand only appearing to us *as* a demand when this spontaneous response to the needs of the other has failed—that is, when the sovereign expressions of life have already been frustrated:

> The demand is unfulfillable, the sovereign expression of life is not produced by the will's exerting itself to obey the demand. The sovereign expression of life is indeed realized, but spontaneously, without being demanded. The demand makes itself felt when the sovereign expression of life fails, but without engendering the latter; the demand demands that it be itself superfluous. (Løgstrup 2007, 69)

It is important not to misunderstand what "spontaneity" means here. The expressions of life do not preclude deliberation; indeed, because they do not legislate specific actions, it can require considerable reflection and argument to determine what we are required to do (Ibid., 130–31). What they do preclude, however, is deliberation on the normative force of the sovereign expressions of life themselves. Because they wear their goodness on their face, it is not up to us whether to see them as normative or not. Confronted with such phenomena, "my sovereignty, in appraising their goodness or badness, is disabled. Sovereignty devolves on the phenomenon" (Ibid., 115). In the specific case of trust, we do not add our evaluative judgments to phenomena that are themselves neutral, but note evaluations that "inhere in the phenomena themselves" (Ibid.).

As noted above, the sovereign expressions of life cannot be applied in the manner of a principle or decision procedure. In fact, Løgstrup goes further than this, claiming that any attempt to use the sovereign expressions of life instrumentally or calculatively turns them into their opposite (Ibid., 70). To be selectively sincere is simply a way of being insincere, and to trust strategically or manipulatively is in fact a form of distrust: instead of giving myself over to another, I hold myself back, except for carefully calculated gambits. This therefore raises the question of just what, if anything, we actually *do* when we trust someone. We use "trust" as a verb and also talk of "placing trust," "trusting in," and so on, yet Løgstrup's account makes it seem that we do not actually *do* anything in trusting—and certainly do nothing *with* trust.

For Løgstrup, even the idea of "deciding" to trust is an altogether too volitionally loaded expression. We can use the term, but this "decision" is really one of giving up volition: "To decide to show trust or mercifulness is to decide to surrender oneself to trust or mercy." This is not something we can do under our own power, for if trust and mercy are not already given as possibilities in the given situation, then "no decision can elicit them." Even then, realizing trust is not something that lies directly within our power. All that we can do is renounce "attitudes or movements of thought and feeling that are incompatible with trust and mercifulness—such as, for example, aloofness, guardedness, reticence, glibness, vengefulness, arrogance." We do not decide to trust, but simply decide "to give free reign" to the sovereign expressions of life (Ibid., 79–80).

Robert Stern has recently and helpfully drawn upon Béatrice Han-Pile's use of the grammatical concept of medio-passivity to explain what is going on with Løgstrup's understanding of moral volition here. Certain actions, like falling in love or falling asleep, centrally involve the agent but require a letting-go or letting-happen on the agent's part (Stern 2019, 322). We need to will to let go of our will, a state of affairs no less paradoxical for being familiar.[3] As Stern notes, this raises the Løgstrupian agent out of mere animal immediacy, for it makes no sense to speak of renunciation among nonhuman animals, yet also retains the sovereignty of the sovereign expressions of life. They are not choices we make, but phenomena we accede to. We cannot make trust happen; we can only try to clear away the things that block trust's progress through the situation. Not all commentators on Løgstrup agree on this: even medio-passivity may be too active and risk diluting the sovereignty of the sovereign expressions of life. But the term does at least capture a certain volitional ambiguity at the heart of trust itself.

CONCLUSION

At the end of this account of Løgstrupian trust, we find ourselves in a fairly unfamiliar place. Instead of trust as an affective-cognitive orientation toward the other, we find a fairly tendentious picture of trust as a metaphysical and intrinsically normative force connected to "life itself." Instead of a two- or three-place attitude I can take toward another based on their attitude toward me, trust is now a sovereign force that will open up possibilities for living if only we get out of its way. Needless to say, this picture will strike many of us as simply too theological, if not utterly mystical. At the very least, the suspicion arises that Løgstrup has reified a purely relational property into a substantial, self-standing entity.

Yet I do not think we need to share Løgstrup's theological commitments to find that this picture also speaks persuasively of how we actually experience trust, at least much of the time. We need not buy into the idea of expressions of life in order to agree that trust appears to us as something intrinsically good and hard to resist, something that seems to come from outside and that we can either accept or deny. Much has been said about the gratuity of trust, that trust must be a confidence that goes beyond mere calculation or objective evaluation of the other. What Løgstrup brings out is the way in which trust has its own impetus in bridging that gap. To trust is not simply a leap of faith, but to willingly be drawn out of ourselves in the direction of the other. In bringing our attention to these dimensions of trust, Løgstrup points to part of why trust is so important to us that is perhaps not visible without this sort of phenomenology. Trust may or may not be a force that arises from the ground of life itself and demands our acquiescence if our lives are to succeed, but the very fact that it *seems* like this is worth attending to, so as to see what we can learn from it.[4]

NOTES

1. On the Orders of Creation in Løgstrup, see, for example, Kees van Kooten Niekerk's introduction to Løgstrup (2017) and Brown and Stokes (2020).
2. This has increasingly become the standard English name for this work among Løgstrup commentators, but it is rather unidiomatic. *Opgør med Kierkegaard* might be better translated as "Confronting Kierkegaard" or even "Showdown with Kierkegaard."
3. As I have argued elsewhere, we can find analogues to Løgstrup here in thinkers as different as Zhuangzi and Eckhart (see Stokes 2016).
4. My thanks to an online audience at the University of Aarhus for their feedback on an earlier version of this chapter, and in particular to Bjørn Rabjerg and Robert Stern for their insightful comments and suggestions. Thanks too to David Collins for helpful further suggestions on the final version.

REFERENCES

Baier, Annette. 1986. "Trust and Antitrust." *Ethics* 96(2): 231–60.
Brown, Petra, and Patrick Stokes. 2020. "Bonhoeffer and Løgstrup: the Ethics of Disclosure in a State of Exception." *Sophia* 59(2): 229–46.
Domenicucci, Jacopo, and Richard Holton. 2017. "Trust as a Two-Place Relation." In *The Philosophy of Trust*, edited by Paul Faulkner and Thomas Simpson, 149–60. Oxford: Oxford University Press.
Frost-Arnold, Karen. 2014. "The Cognitive Attitude of Rational Trust." *Synthese* 191(9): 1957–74.
Jones, Karen. 1996. "Trust as an Affective Attitude." *Ethics* 107(1): 4–25.
———. 2017. "But I Was Counting On You!" In *The Philosophy of Trust*, edited by Paul Faulkner and Thomas Simpson, 90–108. Oxford: Oxford University Press.
Løgstrup, K.E. 1943. *Folkeliv og Udenrigspolitik*. Copenhagen: Tidehverv.
———. 2007. *Beyond the Ethical Demand*. Translated by Susan Dew and Heidi Flegal. Notre Dame: University of Notre Dame Press.
———. 2017. "The Anthropology of Kant's Ethics." In *What is Ethically Demanded? K.E. Løgstrup's Philosophy of Moral Life*, edited by Hans Fink and Robert Stern, 19–34. Notre Dame: University of Notre Dame Press.
———. 2020. *The Ethical Demand. Selected Works of K.E. Logstrup*. Oxford: Oxford University Press.
MacIntyre, Alasdair. 2007. "Human Nature and Human Dependence: What Might a Thomist Learn from Reading Løgstrup?" In *Concern for the Other: Perspectives on the Ethics of K.E. Løgstrup*, edited by Svend Andersen and Kees van Kooten Niekerk, 147–66. Notre Dame: University of Notre Dame Press.
———. 2010. "Danish Ethical Demands and French Common Goods: Two Moral Philosophies." *European Journal of Philosophy* 18(1): 1–16.
Pace, Michael. 2020. "Trusting in Order to Inspire Trustworthiness." *Synthese* 198(12): 11897–923.

Simpson, Thomas. 2017. "Trust and Evidence." In *The Philosophy of Trust*, edited by Paul Faulkner and Thomas Simpson, 177–94. Oxford: Oxford University Press.

Stern, Robert. 2019. *The Radical Demand in Løgstrup's Ethics*. Oxford: Oxford University Press.

Stokes, Patrick. 2016. "The Problem of Spontaneous Goodness: from Kierkegaard to Løgstrup." *Continental Philosophy Review* 49(2): 139–59.

———. 2017. "Spontaneity and Perfection: MacIntyre vs. Løgstrup." In *What is Ethically Demanded? K.E. Løgstrup's Philosophy of Moral Life*, edited by Hans Fink and Robert Stern, 275–99. Notre Dame: University of Notre Dame Press.

———. 2020. "To Trust the Liar: Løgstrup and Levinas on Ethics, War, and Openness." *The Monist* 103(1): 102–16.

Chapter 10

Iris Murdoch
Trust in the World
Silvia Caprioglio Panizza

In her seminal essay "Trust and Antitrust," Annette Baier (1986) complains about the neglect of the concept of trust in Western moral philosophy and suggests that the lack is due to patriarchal reasons: Western moral philosophy, being male dominated, has also been concerned with problems faced by men, which traditionally revolve around the public rather that the private sphere, and around relationships based on promise-giving and contract-making as opposed to the more vulnerable and less freely chosen relationships of dependency and trust. While seeking to instate the importance of trust in contemporary philosophical conversations, Baier also diagnoses the relative lack of interest in trust through a political analysis, showing the hidden interests and power relations that lie within a tradition of moral philosophy that has as one of its central structuring claims that of having universal validity.

From her early essays collected in *Existentialists and Mystics* (1999), and continuing in the three essays contained in *The Sovereignty of Good* (1970), Iris Murdoch (1919–1999) situates her reflections within a broad philosophical aim of showing that we need to rethink the very ways in which we do moral philosophy, issuing a challenge to her contemporaries in the English-speaking world. Contemporary moral philosophy, she writes, has as its central hero "the man" of liberal culture who experiences himself very much as an individual, who moves in a world which is separate from him and within which he freely chooses, whose morality is identified with his will, and whose acts are public. In this "man," Murdoch sees crystallized a whole culture and its philosophical offspring, "a happy and fruitful marriage of Kantian liberalism with Wittgensteinian logic solemnised by Freud" ("The Idea of Perfection," 305–6),[1] also traceable in existentialist and utilitarian philosophies. The pervasiveness of such an idea of the moral "agent" is seen in the fact that this man is considered by Murdoch to be not only the hero of philosophical texts but also of "almost every contemporary novel" (IP, 304).

The above description of contemporary thinking opens the pages of "The Idea of Perfection," one of Murdoch's best-known essays, and in the very beginning she claims that she wishes "in this discussion to attempt a movement of return, a retracing of our steps to see how a certain position was reached" (Ibid., 299). The position, and the picture of morality that comes with it, is problematic according to Murdoch not so much because it is false (sometimes it is not), but because it excludes other pictures, because it pretends to be neutral, and because what it ignores are certain important and fundamental "facts," such as: "that an unexamined life can be virtuous and love is a central concept in morals" (Ibid.).

Both in method (asking: "How was a certain philosophical position reached?" and "What moral, psychological, and political factors contributed to reaching that position?") and in content (shifting the attention from public to private, or rather including the private as well as the public, and taking seriously, in ethics, those factors that one does not control through the will), Murdoch's project has significant points of overlap with Baier's, and more generally with feminist epistemologists. In *What Can She Know?* (1991), for instance, Lorraine Code argues not only that women are less likely to be taken seriously, but that the very model of knowledge which excludes women's expertise and testimony is based on patriarchal structures (see also Alcoff 1995). This is the system of knowledge creation and acceptance which, according to Baier, has pushed trust to the boundaries of public and philosophical discourse, despite its actual centrality in people's lives.

The lives of those with less power, the ones to whom things are done or whose control on the world around them is slight or irrelevant, are not traditionally central to the Western philosophical paradigm that both Baier and Murdoch are engaging with (as argued convincingly, for instance, by Soran Reader (2007)). In that tradition of moral philosophy, it is the agent rather than the patient, or more simply the subject, that is the real object of concern. The fact that trust's importance is greater in the lives of those who are not, primarily, moral "agents" explains why "the man of modern moral philosophy" described by Murdoch is more likely to talk about respect and contracts, and less likely to talk about passivity and trust. But, as Trudy Govier (1992) argues, trust can be supplemented—but cannot be replaced—by the recourse to contracts or legal institutions. The two, as Murdoch shows, operate on different levels of morality, and we need both. In fact, as frequently noted, the more urgent the call for laws (including moral laws) and contracts, the more likely it is that trust is weak or absent.

These reflections and parallels apply mostly to Murdoch's criticisms of moral philosophy. But the positive, constructive side of Murdoch's philosophy, too, has important elements in common with feminist philosophy, especially, in this case, with care ethics. Murdoch's proposal is that we take seriously "the inner life of the individual": that instead of only focusing on outer, public acts, we also restore the importance of the inner, which on her view has been "theorised away" along with other important facts (IP, 299). Murdoch's ethics, then, is concerned with the more intimate, private dimension of morality, not at the expense of the public sphere but in order to provide a fuller picture of what we are talking about when we talk about goodness. This is a concern that clearly animates care ethics, in different ways.[2] In *Caring* (2013), Nel Noddings puts emphasis on the importance of "engrossment," which she understands to involve a receptive, empathetic attention, where "attention" is one of Murdoch's key concepts. Indeed, Noddings later goes on to prefer the word "attention" as required by caring. Similarly, Sara Ruddick invokes both Murdoch and Simone Weil in emphasizing "attentive love," showing the ethical importance of finding a stance that is at the same time epistemic and affective (Ruddick 1989, 119).[3] The domain of caring and of intimacy, where attentive love finds a paradigmatic expression, is one where trust has a central place, as many feminist philosophers besides Baier have noted (see also, e.g., Govier 1992 and Held 1987).

TRUST IN MURDOCH

This dual connection of Murdoch with feminist philosophy and her investigation of domains where trust operates in fundamental ways would make it seem that Murdoch can be studied as a helpful philosopher of trust. And yet: on the one hand, Murdoch say little, explicitly, about feminism, and does not draw, from her analysis of "the man" of contemporary moral philosophy, the consequences that feminist philosophers—epistemologists in particular—have. Indeed, Murdoch's relationship to feminism is contentious and ambiguous. Some readers, such as Sabina Lovibond (2011), are in fact critical of Murdoch's stress on attention and "unselfing" precisely on feminist grounds. For Lovibond, the withdrawal of the self required in attention and love has a suspicious connection with the self-abnegation that has been traditionally expected of women. Therefore, Lovibond worries that being fascinated by selfless attention as an ethical ideal may reinforce rather than dismantle the patriarchal structures that expect women to be, or become, "nothing."

On the other hand, Murdoch also never explicitly touches on the topic of trust. Nonetheless, her interest in personal relationships is strong, as evidenced not only by her emphasis on love and attention but also by her most prominent examples: as in the much-cited story of M and D, where a mother-in-law changes her perception and description of her daughter-in-law thanks to the exercise of attention with no outer change occurring; or, in less extended examples, where a change in objects of attention is illustrated through falling out of love, or where selflessness is shown through the person who knows when to let another go even if they would rather do otherwise. Murdoch also frequently uses personal relationships and intimate situations not only as examples of moral dynamics but also as the place in which morality is born, first experienced, first negotiated. As she writes in *Metaphysics as a Guide to Morals* (1992):[4] "Human relationship is no doubt the most important, as well as the first, training and testing-ground of morality" (*MGM*, 17).

At this point, we have reasons to wonder what place, if any, trust can have in Murdoch's philosophy, and whether analyzing Murdoch's philosophical work through the lens of trust can be helpful in itself or as a way of connecting it with the feminist theories that she came close to but that she did not explicitly embrace. In the rest of this chapter I will propose a reading of Murdoch that brings out an implicit commitment to trust, part of which also helps to strengthen her connection with feminist concerns from a different angle.

There is, I suggest, a general dimension of Murdoch's work for which reflecting on trust can help expand and deepen our understanding. This dimension is not that of personal relationships, where trust is typically considered to be at home in the philosophical literature. It is, however, a dimension that underlies personal relationships and colors them as instances of moral experience in the way Murdoch sees them but is not limited to them. This dimension of trust is that of *trust in the world*. By combining the shift toward moral psychology and first-personal experience in ethics, which the study of trust has emphasized, with the more impersonal dimension of trust in the world, exploring the role of trust in Murdoch's philosophy may help at the same time to understand the non-straightforward placing of her thought in relation to the main pillars of feminist thinking.

Even through this reading, trust is, as we have seen, only implicitly present in Murdoch's philosophy. Yet this form of trust underlies some of Murdoch's most central and original ideas. It is required, for instance, by Murdoch's suggestion that we shift our focus from principle-based, impersonally applicable ethics to a form of ethics that revolves around the inner life and moral perception. It is particularly in moral perception that trust in the world is an important albeit silent element.

Murdoch appeals to the possibility of moral perception repeatedly throughout her work. Her most significant positive proposal, indeed, is that we need to develop the capacity for attention, which will allow us to see things justly and is therefore prior to, and arguably more important than, principle-based ethics. Murdoch talks about "moral perception" and, more frequently, "moral vision" to refer both to the (successful) outcome of attention—the moral reality or facts that we see or perceive—and to the moral quality of perception and vision themselves.[5] This potentially confusing double usage of "moral perception" and "moral vision" has been noted in the literature.[6] Here, I will focus on the first meaning of moral perception and vision in Murdoch: the perception or vision of a reality that contains moral elements.[7]

In order to shift our hopes for moral improvement away from an exclusive reliance on impersonally and publicly determined principles toward moral perception (which can include both the intuition and understanding suggested by a more metaphorical understanding of "moral vision") which, by definition, relies on no such external check outside of our own perception, we need to be able to trust that what our perception reveals is true. In moral perception we lose some of the security that principle-based theories offer: shared rules that allow us to analyze our actions and give reasons that anyone possessed with the same faculty of reason will be able to understand.[8] Moral perception requires trust because there is nothing outside of the act of perception that allows us to be certain that what we are perceiving is true.[9]

This form of trust extends beyond moral perception to perception in general, and it is one that we exercise all the time, without realizing (such is the nature of trust, according to Baier: like air (Baier 1986, 234).) In moral perception, however, greater trust is required because what perception reveals is not always "on the surface," and it is clearer that more than functioning sight, smell, or touch are needed.[10] To perceive the moral qualities of a situation we may need to be correctly attuned and possess the right sensibility, the right motives. That is why Murdoch uses the vocabulary of attention, as opposed to "mere looking," to refer to moral perception. Attention, for Murdoch, is a state which is itself morally valuable and which allows us to perceive justly what we may not perceive in an inattentive state. But, once again, to think of attention and what it reveals in terms of moral achievement, which Murdoch understands platonically as a progressively closer approach to the truth, we need trust: trust that the reality we are attending to will reveal the features we need to see, and trust in ourselves and our capacity to perceive correctly and not be subject to misperceptions and illusions. These are nonstandard forms of trust, which may explain why Murdoch does not explicitly discuss the concept.

TRUST IN THE WORLD

Murdoch's alternative vision of morality is explicitly opposed to a conception of ethics that is too exclusively focused on outer, observable action, psychological sources that can in principle be made public, and the freedom of the will (see especially "Vision and Choice in Morality" and "The Idea of Perfection"). Instead, she offers a vision of morality that is less easily codifiable, not only by denying that principles are always necessary to guide us and that they can capture all that is needed in a given situation, but also by denying that the moral subject can be reduced to whatever about her is publicly available (IP, 319ff.). "We are obscure to ourselves," Murdoch notes ("The Darkness of Practical Reason," 200), and this means that moral understanding requires a sensibility which is attuned but also patient in its deepening, in the course of attempting to discover what is real.

The world, in this picture, is not presented as inert and separate from us. Rather, reality is something that we are "immersed" in: something of which we are part, which we partly determine, but also to which we must pay attention and to which we must obey. In "The Idea of Perfection," Murdoch declares her view to be "a kind of inconclusive non-dogmatic naturalism" of which she says elsewhere: "The true naturalist (the Marxist, for instance, or certain kinds of Christian) is one who believes that as moral beings we are immersed in a reality which transcends us and that moral progress consists in awareness of this reality and submission to its purposes" (VCM, 96).[11]

The metaphor of immersion in reality is an important image to understand Murdoch's metaphysical view, repeated in the more famous quote from "Vision and Choice":

> There are people whose fundamental moral belief is that we all live in the same empirical and rationally comprehensible world and that morality is the adoption of universal and openly defensible rules of conduct. There are other people whose fundamental belief is that we live in a world whose mystery transcends us and that morality is the exploration of that mystery in so far as it concerns each individual. (VCM, 88)

In the first vision of the world described here by Murdoch, all that we need are functioning senses and well-developed rationality. "All," of course, should be in inverted commas, and Murdoch shows no disrespect to theories based on such a view of the world, accepting them as helpful and even in some cases necessary parts of morality. The problem, for Murdoch, is that they tell a limited story about human morality, and hence a distorted one. That is why she combines moral psychology and metaphysics in a way that makes them inseparable: we experience the nature of reality to be such that reality is available not immediately but to a patient, honest, *moral* sensibility; the Good is absolute and therefore always "beyond," and yet we must strive to get closer to it; in fact, human life is dominated by its (erotic) tension toward the Good, which is at the same time a tension toward the real, in progressive degrees. Plato's ascent and St. Anselm's ontological argument inspire this view (see *MGM*, 391ff.).

This metaphysical picture of reality removes the distance between the individual and the world, not only in the trivial sense that the individual is part of the world, but insofar as, on the one hand, reality is to be constantly and creatively pursued through subjective engagement, and on the other, the answer to the questions of how to live and what to do will come not only from an exercise of reason and will, but from reality itself, revealed to the attentive individual. These two features of our engagement with the real, central to Murdochian metaphysics and ethics, rely on two sets of concepts—mystery, perfectionism, attention, and moral perception on the one hand, and obedience, passivity, and interdependence on the other—which contain trust in reality as an inescapable, although silent, element. The idea that we are immersed in a reality which transcends us implies that we must trust that reality, not only because we are powerless to do otherwise, but also because our task, as Murdoch sees it, is to move in synch with reality, understanding its nature and its demands on us, rather than act as independent agents upon it. This notion of reality requires a passivity and a vulnerability that are central elements of trust.

This is, of course, as I have noted, a nonstandard domain of application of the concept of trust, which the philosophical literature has mostly placed within the domain of interpersonal relationships. Yet some voices have been raised against this restriction. Recently, C. Thi Nguyen (2022) has argued against this focus and has proposed a model of trust which can be applied beyond relationships, as well as beyond the human. According to Nguyen, trust is to be construed as an "unquestioning attitude" which allows us to integrate other objects or people into our agency. Nguyen writes that "trust . . . is about . . . letting something inside, about uniting with it. Closeness and unification are some of the key markers of intimacy" (Nguyen 2022, 240).

Nguyen's account provides a helpful point of connection between Murdoch's unspoken trust in reality and the more systematic contemporary philosophical literature seeking an understanding of the pervasiveness of trust. For Nguyen, trust is an "attitude" of refraining from questioning that which we trust, and which requires greater reasons to do so. That does not mean, as Nguyen notes, that we never questioned what we trust, or that we may never be in a position to do that should the situation arise. That would be particularly incongruous with a trust of reality, such as Murdoch's, that aims to be at the same time morally answerable. But like Nguyen's view, Murdoch's dependence on a reality of which we are part and which we need to see more and more clearly is grounded, not on a discrete act of will or positive action (which would be self-defeating), but on an attitude of attention which we must cultivate and which includes a necessary passivity: attention, which allows us to enter into contact with the real, is receptivity rather than assertion. As Simone Weil, Murdoch's great inspiration on this point, writes: "Attention is an effort, the greatest of all efforts perhaps, but it is a negative effort" (Weil 1951, 111).

Central to Murdoch's idea of the way in which we should approach reality is the idea of "unselfing," which removes the distortions generated by the ego which make it difficult for us to see things clearly (see, e.g., IP). Unselfing is connected with the passivity of attention, refraining from imposing our will or our interpretations on reality. By removing the veil between us and reality, unselfing is also connected with a greater unity with reality, moving closer to the embeddedness into the real which allows for our perceptions and actions to be truly responsive to what the situation calls for, as opposed to being self-generated. This entails giving up a certain degree of control and allowing reality, as it reveals itself to us, to guide us. This is an "integration," in Nguyen's words, that is part and parcel of trust, and that does not need any beliefs in the goodwill of the one trusted, nor indeed does it require any agency in what we trust. Differently from Nguyen, however, we can read Murdoch's trust in the world as operating in a parallel fashion but in an opposite polarity: in Nguyen, we integrate the world into our agency; in Murdoch, we integrate our agency into the world.

ONTOLOGICAL TRUST

To mark the specificity of the role of trust in the world in Murdoch, then, we need to appreciate the abstract nature of the discourse by observing once again that trust operates in Murdoch not only as an ethical stance but also as an ontological one. This distinction is drawn by Josef Früchtl (2018), who, in a study of how film may help restore our "trust in the world," writes that: "Trust is a resource that is as fundamental as it is precarious. It is fundamental socially, especially in a moral, political, economic or psychological sense, but also in an ontological or existential sense" (Früchtl 2018, 2). Früchtl goes on to connect the ontological-existential meaning of trust with philosophers as diverse as Kierkegaard, Nietzsche, James, Heidegger, Merleau-Ponty, and Wittgenstein, who, through a leap of faith, the affirmation of life, or the acknowledgment of a lack of further grounding for our beliefs, variously remind us that some degree of trust in the world is required and, indeed, already present in our engagement with reality, and that uncovering it and embracing it can illuminate a different path for philosophy to take. It is not surprising, then, that all of these philosophers had an impact on Murdoch, who shares the idea that we will not get at what is real, especially in the moral sense, by closer intellectual scrutiny, but that we need to acknowledge the mystery of life for what it is, through imagination, moral effort, and indeed, once all resources have been deployed, through trust.

This form of trust, as I said, is different from the standard, interpersonal understanding of trust, although it is not unrelated. Like Nguyen's unquestioning attitude, trust in the world is more pervasive but also less identifiable. For these reasons, it establishes a way of relating to reality which can be found, with due differences, in ways of relating to others. Karen Jones's (2004) notion of "basal security" is offered as that which does not accommodate the widely accepted model of three-place trust, yet *explains* three-place trust. This notion helps us to further understand the aspects of Murdoch's philosophy which imply an attitude of trust in the world. For Jones, the way we live in the world requires an unspoken sense of trust that things will work in certain ways, that we do not need to constantly check everything—that the earth will support us, that strangers will not shoot us in the streets. These are not beliefs insofar as we do not think about these possibilities (Jones 2004, 7). We show our trust precisely by not thinking about them. Yet when these forms of security are shaken—in Jones's example, by terrorism—we feel that something fundamental has been taken away and our reaction is not merely one that would follow wrongly placed reliance. As Jones writes, our reaction, in line with the nature of basal security, is affectively laden and properly expressed in terms of the betrayal of trust.

Jones notes that, while it may be disputed that the concept of trust applies in these cases, that is exactly the concept that the victims of terrorism or other world-shaking cases reach for (Ibid., 13). And while that is not enough to secure the right application of trust, it is both an important fact that we do conceptualize trust this way and an invitation to revise excessively restrictive conceptions of trust. Nguyen explains the expression of betrayed trust, in these cases, as instances of failed integration into our agency. Jones suggests that these are cases in which our sense of security in the world as such is shaken, a sense that is undefined but also fundamental to our ability to function despite knowing that we have no absolute guarantee that we will not be harmed nor full control over that possibility. Trust is implicit in our very "framework for interpreting the world," and this is closer to the ontological sense of trust that Früchtl talks about, which underlies Murdoch's moral ontology. Murdoch discloses such fundamental trust, however, not by talking about threats but about "the authority of the real" (SGC, 374).[12]

TRUST AND THE GOOD

In different ways, Nguyen, Jones, and Früchtl emphasize cases in which trust is betrayed, with Jones and Früchtl discussing radical cases when such betrayal leads to a shattered sense of reality. It is easy to see why that focus is important: trust, as we saw, becomes visible when something goes wrong. But the emphasis on more radical reconfigurations of our sense of reality after a betrayal of trust indicates a further dimension, more intriguing and more relevant for our purposes. In cases of terror as discussed by Jones, it is not a specific object of trust, nor a specific domain of trust, that is broken. It is one's sense of the world as such that shifts due to the impossibility of continuing with the same affective sense of safety and related behaviors (non-checking) that mark the presence of trust. Früchtl reads this phenomenon through a moral lens, not just insofar as occurrences like terrorism may shake one's trust in the goodness of others, but more interestingly insofar as an attitude of trust as such goes hand in hand with a sense of goodness, and hence, he concludes "evil is what shakes to the very foundations our trust in the world, not only our moral trust but also—and perhaps even primarily—our ontological-existential trust. Evil is the moral opposite of trust" (Früchtl 2018, 3).

Murdoch's moral realism, and the importance of trusting both her philosophy and that which her philosophy suggests, can be understood as building a trust in the Good such that no instance of terror can shake it. For Murdoch, the Good is good with a capital "G," because it is "a single, perfect, transcendent, non-representable, necessarily real object of attention" ("On 'God' and 'Good,'" 344). The Good is the idea of perfection which guides all encounters with reality and which provides motivation for progressing in one's perception and understanding of it. If the Good is thus omnipresent, and its operations in our lives are received with trusting certainty as Murdoch suggests, then when the ontological trust in the world is broken, the certainty of the reality of the Good is also put into question. It is with this Murdochian thought in mind that we can explain and give further depth to Früchtl's observation that "evil is the moral opposite of trust" (3). The experience of evil, then, is not an experience of a specific act or occurrence but a loss of the Good, and hence loss of that which, according to Murdoch, sustains our experience of life and the world. This Murdochian interpretation agrees with, and adds a dimension to, Jones's statement that the victims of terror and those whose trust in the world has not been thus broken live "in different worlds" (Jones 2004, 7).

THE AUTHORITY OF REALITY

"The authority of morality is the authority of truth, that is, of reality" (SGC, 374), Murdoch writes. If we are to accept the real as authoritative, we need to trust that the real is not betraying us. This is both a cognitive and an action-guiding point: a clear-eyed perception of reality is what, for Murdoch, is fundamental to morality, but reality in her sense is not inert. It is experienced by us as posing limits, as inviting to action, or to contemplation. This conception is grounded on the metaphysical difference we have seen between Murdoch's conception of ethics and one that sees the world as independent of value, and as morality dependent on the will. On that model, trust is irrelevant. But if we are to be determined in our being and guided by the real, then we have to trust that the real is something that is inextricable from goodness, and we have no independent way of verifying that—no way that is independent from our sense that what is good cannot be deception, that truth is revealed progressively, and that such progress is also moral progress. St. Anselm's ontological proof, which Murdoch takes as important for illuminating her idea of moral realism, proceeds in such a fashion: the ontological argument is not compelling for everyone, because it appeals not to the intellect, but to faith; Anselm's beginning is *credo ut intellegam*. The parallel to Anselm is twofold. On the one hand, Murdoch describes a love for reality that is not the outcome of but the prerequisite for a clear understanding, and truthful vision as something we should, in our moral life, exercise. This is a form of trust in the world understood as the starting point of the moral pilgrimage (an image dear to Murdoch). On the other hand, her own philosophy has such an "invitational" character. Like Anselm's proof, Murdoch's metaphysical arguments are not to be logically or empirically proven but invite the reader to notice something about life, to see it in a certain light, and if that way of seeing it illuminates and explains something about it, then it is worth pursuing.

The idea of faith is invoked, by Anselm and by Murdoch, not as an irrational surrender in order to make any claim one feels like making, but as an attitude of the mind bent on discovering something that it only darkly intuits, akin to Plato's love or *eros*, the desire to apprehend the Forms that it does not yet see. As Simone Weil notes, "the proof does not address itself to the understanding but to love" (Weil 2013, 375, quoted in *MGM*, 505). Here we observe again how Murdoch is practicing, and inciting us to practice, philosophically, the same attitude that she holds as central to the moral life more generally: attention, as the desire to discover something that one does not yet fully comprehend, that nevertheless presents itself compellingly to consciousness through a process in which we need to surrender ourselves through a trust that is however not blind.[13]

OBEDIENCE

A more extreme reading of the idea that reality has authority over us is its action-guiding interpretation, which in Murdoch's thought, as I hope has become clear, is not the idea that reality provides the data from which we act; rather, it is the striking idea that, if we pay attention, reality will indicate what to do in such a way that choice and will may be rendered irrelevant. This is the idea of "obedience," another concept that Murdoch takes from Weil. According to Weil, obedience refers to the self-surrender that occurs when we allow ourselves to be led by reality, which she takes, like Murdoch, to be displaying what is required for us if we are able to pay attention. The capacity to pay attention is fundamental, because it allows us to distinguish between "low" obedience to the base forces of the ego and "high" obedience to the demands of the real. Attention and "decreation" ("unselfing" for Murdoch) go hand in hand in removing the pernicious influence of the self and acting out of the recognition of a need instead of will or self-assertion. As Weil writes:

> Obedience. There are two kinds. We can obey the force of gravity or we can obey the relationship of things. In the first case we do what we are driven to by the imagination which fills up empty spaces. . . . If we suspend the filling up activity of the imagination and fix our attention on the relationship of things, a necessity becomes apparent which we cannot help obeying. Until then we have not any notion of necessity and we have no sense of obedience. (GG, 48)

A thought which Murdoch echoes very closely, for instance, here in "The Idea of Perfection":

> If I attend properly I will have no choices and this is the ultimate condition to be aimed at. This is in a way the reverse of Hampshire's picture, where our efforts are supposed to be directed to increasing our freedom by conceptualising as many different possibilities of action as possible: having as many goods as possible in the shop. The ideal situation, on the contrary, is rather to be represented as a kind of "necessity." This is something of which saints speak and which any artist will readily understand. The idea of a patient, loving regard, directed upon a person, a thing, a situation, presents the will not as unimpeded movement but as something very much more like "obedience." (IP, 331)

If we are to act out of obedience to reality, we need to trust that reality is authoritative. The idea of obedience, then, is the most radical application of the idea of trust in reality where, as Murdoch argues, reality acts as a normative term in more than one sense: as something constantly to be pursued, and as something to be followed.

CONCLUSION

In this chapter I have been asking why Murdoch does not explicitly address the concept of trust, despite her philosophy containing elements that are strongly connected with trust. One is the concern with interpersonal relationships. Another is Murdoch's aim to move away from a philosophical model based on public acts and promises, contracts, and respect. These two concerns link Murdoch with feminist philosophy through the implicit role that trust has in Murdoch's thinking. However, I have argued, it is in Murdoch's metaphysics and in a broader application of the concept that trust is most at home in Murdoch's philosophy. That is the idea of trust in the world. Trust in the world, I have suggested, is required for Murdoch's ideas of moral perception, the reality of the Good, and moral obedience. While trust in reality is necessary if moral perception is to be both cognitive and action guiding, Murdoch's arguments for the reality of the good require a sense of trust in reality in order for these arguments to be understood. Hence trust is an element both of Murdoch's philosophical ideas and of her methodology.

If trust, as Baier famously stated, is "accepted vulnerability" (Baier 1986, 235), Murdoch's philosophy exhibits precisely such acceptance by delineating a picture of reality that acts upon us instead of being simply a field for us to act on, in which we are immersed in ways which we cannot control, and which nonetheless we must accept as such, not only because we have no choice but because doing otherwise would be a pointless and morally pernicious self-assertion, substituting truth with the self. Murdoch's normative concept of reality is one in which trust is necessary because there is no harder certainty outside our best perceptions and reflections, we are always "in medias res," and it is only out of the affective-cognitive attitude of trust—or faith—that we can hope to get the kind of clarity that morality, specifically, requires.

NOTES

1. Hereafter IP.
2. See, for instance, the foundational work of Carol Gilligan (1982) and Nel Noddings (2013); Virginia Held (1993) and Joan Tronto (1993) have applied considerations of care from the intimate to the social-political domain.
3. Joan Tronto, in *Moral Boundaries* (1993), also takes attention to be central to care, but she draws mostly on Simone Weil for that concept. For a comparative analysis of Murdoch, Noddings, and Tronto on the theme of moral attention, see Gendron (2016).
4. Hereafter *MGM*.
5. For the sake of this discussion, I take moral perception and moral vision to refer broadly to the same phenomenon. On the interpretative difficulties surrounding Murdoch's use of perceptual vocabulary and metaphors, see Lawrence Blum (2012), who attempts to disentangle the use of "attention," "seeing," "looking," and "vision" in order to differentiate between three notions: perception considered neutrally as to its moral quality and its truthfulness; successful, that is, clear and just, perception; and the attempt to achieve such perception. As Blum notes, Murdoch sometimes refers to the first notion by using "seeing" and "vision," taken as activities that present to us the world we have partly created for ourselves through the use (either good or bad) of the imagination. Blum calls this the "subjectively perceived." This idea is also expressed in verb form by the use of "looking," which Murdoch contrasts directly with attention

(IP, 329). Frequently, however, "moral vision" refers to the content of that vision (a moral reality) and "attention" both to the morally praiseworthy effort and to the successful achievement of moral perception; the reason being, for Blum, that "there is a sort of tendency . . . for outward focus to become attention—to successfully grasp another's reality" (Blum 2012, 311).

6. See Clifton (2013, 211) and Panizza (2019, 275–76) on moral perception; see Gomes (2022, 144) on moral vision.

7. On Murdochian moral perception, see especially Blum (1991), Mylonaki (2019), and Cooper (2021).

8. This can give rise to the sense of giddiness addressed by McDowell (2001), who, reading the later Wittgenstein on rule following, proposes that the experience is due to the assumption that a concept has been correctly applied only if one follows universal rules, independently of human practices and the set of responses and attitudes that we typically have as participants in the practices (McDowell 2001, 203). On Wittgenstein's influence on Murdoch, see Hämäläinen (2014), Søndergaard Christensen (2022), and Forsberg (forthcoming).

9. Murdoch herself mainly gives negative criteria for attention: the absence of the self or of self-interested distorting filters between us and reality. Bridget Clarke (2012) has worried about the lack of criteria for checking attention and has proposed that we address it by trying to compare our perception with that of others and identify patterns of perception.

10. I write "it is clearer that" because, according to Murdoch, all perception requires more than functioning senses and sensibility, conceptual skills, and experience, which she considers as moral: "all just vision . . . is a moral matter" ("On God and Good," 357).

11. Hereafter VCM.

12. Hereafter SGC.

13. "Credo ut intellegam (I believe in order to understand) is not just an apologist's paradox, but an idea with which we are familiar in personal relationships. . . . I have faith (important place for this concept) in a person or idea in order to understand him or it" (*MGM*, 393).

REFERENCES

Alcoff, Linda Martín. 1995. "Is the Feminist Critique of Reason Rational?" *Philosophical Topics* 23(2): 1–26.

Baier, Annette. 1986. "Trust and Antitrust." *Ethics* 96: 231–60.

———. 2004. "Demoralization, Trust, and the Virtues." In *Setting the Moral Compass: Essays by Women Philosophers*, edited by Cheshire Calhoun, 176–90. Oxford: Oxford University Press.

Blum, Lawrence. 1991. "Moral Perception and Particularity." *Ethics* 101(4): 701–25.

———. 2012. "Visual Metaphors in Murdoch's Moral Philosophy." In *Iris Murdoch, Philosopher*, edited by Justin Broackes, 307–24. Oxford: Oxford University Press.

Clarke, Bridget. 2012. "Iris Murdoch and the Prospects for Critical Moral Perception." In *Iris Murdoch, Philosopher*, edited by Justin Broackes, 227–54. Oxford: Oxford University Press.
Clifton, Scott W. 2013. "Murdochian Moral Perception." *The Journal of Value Inquiry* 47: 207–20.
Code, Lorraine. 1991. *What Can She Know?: Feminist Theory and the Construction of Knowledge*. Ithaca: Cornell University Press.
Cooper, Andrew. 2021. "Iris Murdoch on Moral Perception." *Heythrop Journal* 62(3): 454–66.
Forsberg, Niklas. Forthcoming. "Murdoch's Wittgenstein." In *Wittgenstein and Other Philosophers: His Influence on Historical and Contemporary Analytic Philosophers, Volume II*, edited by Ali Hossein-Khani and Gary Kemp. New York: Routledge.
Früchtl, Josef. 2018. *Trust in the World: A Philosophy of Film*. Translated by Sarah Kirkby. New York and London: Routledge.
Gendron, Claude. 2016. "Moral Attention: A Comparative Philosophical Study." *Journal of Moral Education* 45(4): 373–86.
Gilligan, Carol. 1982. *In a Different Voice*. Cambridge: Harvard University Press.
Gomes, Anil. 2013. "Iris Murdoch on Art, Ethics, and Attention." *British Journal of Aesthetics* 53(3): 321–37.
Govier, Trudy. 1992. "Trust, Distrust, and Feminist Theory." *Hypatia* 7: 16–33.
Hämäläinen, Nora. 2014. "What is a Wittgensteinian Neo-Platonist?: Iris Murdoch, Metaphysics and Metaphor." *Philosophical Papers* 43(2): 191–225.
Held, Virginia. 1987. "Non-Contractual Society: A Feminist View." *Canadian Journal of Philosophy*, supplementary volume 13: *Science, Morality and Feminist Theory*, edited by Marsha Hanen and Kai Nielsen, 111–37. Calgary: University of Calgary Press.
Jones, Karen. 2004. "Trust and Terror." In *Moral Psychology: Feminist Ethics and Social Theory*, edited by Peggy DesAutels and Margaret Urban Walker, 3–18. Lanham: Rowman & Littlefield.
Lovibond, Sabina. 2011. *Iris Murdoch, Gender and Philosophy*. London and New York: Routledge.
McDowell, John. 2001. "Non-Cognitivism and Rule-Following." In *Mind, Value and Reality*, 198–218. Cambridge: Harvard University Press.
Murdoch, Iris. 1970. *The Sovereignty of Good*. London: Routledge and Kegan Paul.
———. 1992. *Metaphysics as a Guide to Morals* [MGM]. London: Penguin.
———. 1998. *Existentialists and Mystics: Writings on Philosophy and Literature*. Edited by Peter Conradi. Harmondsworth: Penguin.
——— "The Darkness of Practical Reason" [DPR], 193–202.
——— "The Idea of Perfection" [IP], 299–336.
——— "On 'God' and 'Good'" [OGG], 337–65.
——— "The Sovereignty of Good over Other Concepts" [SGC], 363–85.
——— "Vision and Choice in Morality" [VCM], 76–98.
Mylonaki, Evgenia. 2019. "The Individual in Pursuit of the Individual; A Murdochian Account of Moral Perception." *Journal of Value Inquiry* 53(4): 579–603.

Nguyen, C. Thi. 2022. "Trust as an Unquestioning Attitude." In *Oxford Studies in Epistemology*, vol. 7, edited by Tamar Szabó Gendler, John Hawthorne, and Julianne Chung, 214–44. Oxford: Oxford University Press.
Noddings, Nel. 2013. *Caring: A Relational Approach to Ethics and Moral Education*. Berkeley: University of California Press.
Panizza, Silvia. 2020. "Moral Perception beyond Supervenience: Iris Murdoch's Radical Perspective." *The Journal of Value Inquiry* 54: 273–88.
Reader, Soran. 2007. *Needs and Moral Necessity*. London: Routledge.
Ruddick, Sara. 1989. *Maternal Thinking: Toward a Politics of Peace*. Boston: Beacon.
Søndergaard Christensen, Anne-Marie. 2022. "Murdoch and Wittgenstein." In *The Murdochian Mind*, edited by Silvia Caprioglio Panizza and Mark Hopwood, 318–30. London and New York: Routledge.
Tronto, Joan C. 1993. *Moral Boundaries: A Political Argument for an Ethic of Care*. New York: Psychology Press.
Weil, Simone. 1951. *Waiting for God*. Translated by Emma Craufurd. New York: Harper and Row.
———. 2013. *The Notebooks of Simone Weil*. Translated by Arthur Wills. London: Routledge.

Index

Analects, 15–16, 18–19, 29–30
Anselm, 207
anthropology, 3, 98, 101, 137
Aristotle, 3, 5–6, 8, 11, 35–53
attention, 10, 30, 113, 119, 199–204, 206–10
Augustine, 183
authority, 3, 6–7, 55, 57–58, 60, 67, 69, 90–91, 95–101, 106–7, 113–14, 116–17, 123, 125, 133, 146, 148, 151–52, 205–7

Baier, Annette, 11, 79, 81, 84, 91, 127, 185, 197–99, 201, 209
Baumgold, Deborah, 95
Behemoth, 95, 98, 100, 107–8
Bergson, Henri, 2
betrayal, 4, 35, 40, 48–50, 83, 205
botho, 77
Bruni, Luigino, 126
Buddha, the (Siddhārtha Gautama), 5–6, 55–74
Buddhism, 5, 55–56, 65–69, 73; Buddhist modernism, 66, 68, 73; Theravāda, 55, 69, 72–73

Calhoun, Cheshire, 84
Carrasco, Maria, 128
character, 8–9, 35–42, 44–53, 71–72, 81–82, 85–88, 90, 93, 99, 134, 136, 141–42, 144, 147, 149, 153, 158, 162, 166, 169, 172, 174, 175, 184, 188, 207; moral, 8, 81, 85–86. 90, 136, 141–42, 184; noumenal, 134, 141–42, 144, 147, 153
cheng, 4, 15–16, 20–24, 30–31
child/children, 17, 85, 90, 92, 113, 128, 155, 182–83
choice, free, 138–41
church, 96, 98, 144, 146, 149–50; invisible, 149; visible, 150
citizen, 6–8, 36, 43, 50, 79, 96–97, 102–6, 111, 124–26, 133, 149, 151
Code, Lorraine, 198
Collingwood, R.G., 11–12
communalism, 6, 77–85, 87
community, 3, 6–7, 36, 52, 56, 62, 77–86, 88–93, 144, 149–50
Confucius, 1, 4–6, 8, 11, 15–21, 23–30
convention, 114–16, 127–28
cooperation, 3, 7, 12, 78–81, 83, 93, 114, 121, 128, 136
credulity, 7, 95–99, 101–2, 106–7, 183

decorum, 29, 137, 141, 151
decreation, 208. *See also* unselfing
demand, ethical, 181, 184–86, 188, 191
dependence, 79, 82, 84, 90–91, 101, 203
Descartes, Rene, 2
Devil and the Good Lord, The, 186

213

diffidence, 7, 95, 97–102, 106, 108
disposition, 4, 7, 30, 78, 83, 89, 100,
    112–13, 116–18, 120–25, 128–29,
    139, 141–44, 147–48, 150, 152–53,
    159–61, 163–64, 172
distrust, 2, 4, 7, 9–10, 39, 43, 52, 97–98,
    126, 142–43, 157, 175, 179, 181–83,
    187, 189–90, 192
Domenicucci, Jacopo, 186

elderhood, 77, 85–90, 93
enlightenment, 7, 63, 145–48, 167, 170
epistemic access, 26–27, 29, 52
eudaimonia, 35
Eudemian Ethics, 35–38, 41–42, 47,
    51, 53
evil, 43, 97–98, 103, 138–41, 143, 148,
    153–54, 167–68, 172, 183, 206

faith, 4, 8, 59, 65–69, 79, 83, 95–96,
    101–3, 107, 133, 150, 169, 172–73,
    175, 193, 204, 207, 209–10
feminism, 199; feminist epistemology,
    198
Fleischacker, Samuel, 128
focus imaginarius, 135, 147, 154
freedom, 3, 12, 29, 135, 140–41, 145–
    47, 149–50, 153, 163, 201, 208
friendship, 3, 5, 8, 35–53, 78, 80–83,
    93, 121, 152–54
Früchtl, Josef, 204

Gadamer, Hans-Georg, 11–12
Gambetta, Diego, 81
Genovesi, Antonio, 126
Goffman, Erving, 17
good, the, 42–43, 51–52, 80–81, 143,
    148, 155, 168, 172, 202, 205–6,
    209
goodwill, 5, 7, 8, 35, 41–44, 58, 70, 77–
    79, 81, 83–85, 87, 91, 93, 116–20,
    123, 150, 185, 189, 204
government, 8, 96, 105, 122, 124, 146
Govier, Trudy, 164, 198
Gyekye, Kwame, 82, 86–87

Han-Pile, Béatrice, 192
harambee, 77
Hardwig, John, 90–92
harm, 9, 43–44, 58, 104, 114, 138, 182
harmony, 4–6, 77, 90, 141
Hawley, Katherine, 31, 129
Heidegger, Martin, 179, 204
history, importance for philosophy,
    11–12
Hobbes, Thomas, 1, 6–7, 11, 95–109
Holton, Richard, 186
Hume, David, 7–8, 11, 109, 111–18,
    121, 124–29

impartial spectator, 119–20, 122, 126
integrity, 20, 81–90, 92–93, 171
invisible hand, 125

James, William, 204
Jones, Karen, 104, 164, 185, 205–6
justice, 1, 7, 58, 79, 103–5, 111–27,
    129, 189

Kant, Immanuel, 4, 8, 133–55
Kierkegaard, Søren, 2, 186, 194, 204
knowledge, 2, 5–7, 10–11, 19, 22–23,
    35, 39–40, 44–45, 47–49, 51–53, 55,
    60–61, 67, 71–72, 83, 85–86, 90–93,
    97, 101–2, 105–6, 142, 164, 168,
    172–73, 177, 198; self-, 5–6, 11, 22,
    35–36, 44–45, 47, 51–53

language, 55, 62, 67, 69, 72, 127, 182, 186
Leviathan, 96, 99–101, 103–5, 108
Levinas, Emmanuel, 180
Lewis, David, 83, 127–28
Lipps, Hans, 179
Locke, John, 95, 109
Løgstrup, Knud Ejler, 1, 9–11, 179–94
Longworth, Guy, 133
love, 21, 42–44, 48, 77–78, 80, 82–83,
    85, 87, 93, 104, 116, 119–20, 123,
    152–53, 193, 198–200, 207; self-, 7,
    112–13, 118, 122, 125, 137–44, 154
Lovibond, Sabina, 199

Machiavelli, Niccolò, 96, 107
MacIntyre, Alasdair, 183
Masolo, Dismas, 82
Mbiti, John, 6, 80
McGeer, Victoria, 126
McLeod, Carolyn, 6, 81, 88–89, 91
Mencius, 15–16, 20, 30
Menkiti, Ifeanyi, 78–80, 85–88
mercy, 185–86, 189–90, 192
Merleau-Ponty, Maurice, 204
metaphysics, 64, 67, 135, 202–3, 209
Metz, Thaddeus, 80
mistrust, 2, 8–9, 157–59, 161, 165–75, 181
Mitchell, Lawrence, 79
Murdoch, Iris, 10, 197–210

nature, 96, 103, 118, 122, 134–35, 145; ethical, 148–49; human, 3, 9, 15, 84, 96–98, 101, 107–8, 111–12, 118, 121, 138–39, 143, 145, 147, 161, 170, 175; juridical, 149, 151; social, 51; state of, 7, 97, 99–102, 106, 108, 140, 151
Neurath's boat, 10
Nguyen, C. Thi, 203–5
Nicomachean Ethics, 5, 35–42, 45–47, 49, 51–53
Nietzsche, Friedrich, 2, 8–9, 157–75, 204
Noddings, Nel, 199, 209
Nyerere, Julius, 80

obedience, 95, 99, 203, 207–9
Odzuck, Eva, 95–96
O'Neill, Onora, 133

Pack, Spencer, 127
passion, passions, 7, 97–98, 100–106, 108–9, 113–15, 117, 127, 139, 154
passivity, 192–93, 198, 203–4
peace, 90, 96–99, 102–3, 106, 114, 133, 151; of mind, 59
perception, moral, 10, 200–201, 203, 209–10

personhood, 6, 77, 84–90, 93, 135
philia, 35–36. *See also* friendship
Plato, 2, 202, 207
poor, 102, 122–24, 139
possession/possessions, 4, 7, 40, 46, 114–18, 121–24, 127, 129, 155
praise/praiseworthiness, 120, 210
predisposition, 138–40, 144
propensity, 3, 9, 73, 138, 140, 146–48, 154
property. *See* possession/possessions

quietism, 61, 65

Rawls, John, 78–79
Reader, Soran, 198
reason, 2, 58, 81, 84, 91, 96, 105, 113, 126, 134–36, 138, 140–41, 143, 146, 149–50, 152, 164, 201, 203; practical, 135, 137–38, 144, 147, 153
reciprocal/reciprocity, 5, 7, 9, 36, 39, 42, 46, 49, 77, 81–82, 140, 145–48, 152–53
reliance, 77, 79, 91–92, 104, 187, 201, 205; self-, 9
religion, 7, 9, 56–57, 65, 68–69, 95–101, 106, 133, 144, 147–48, 150, 167, 170–71
Rice, Stephen, 134
rich, 122–24
Ruddick, Sara, 199

saddhā, 59–61, 65, 67–69, 71–73
Sartre, Jean-Paul, 186
Schliesser, Eric, 127, 129
Schröder, Peter, 95–96, 107, 133
science, 9, 67, 98, 138, 146, 158, 170–74; of man, 111; political, 97, 99, 106, 108; replication crisis, 1, 171
self-disclosure, 40, 46, 48
self-presentation, 4–5, 11, 16–18, 22, 24, 28–30, 45
sensible knave, 117–18, 128
Smith, Adam, 7–8, 11, 111–12, 118–29
Smith, Vernon, 126

sovereign, 6, 95–98, 102, 105–7, 109, 123, 129, 162; expression of life, 9, 179, 183, 186, 189–93
spontaneity, spontaneous, 183, 188, 191–92
Stern, Robert, 182, 184, 192–93
Sugden, Robert, 126
Sussman, David, 133
Sutta: Brahmajāla, 70; Caṅkī, 59–61, 63, 69, 71; Cūḷamāluṅkyovāda, 72; Kālāma, 56–61, 65, 68, 70–71, 73; Māgandiya, 71; Pañcattaya, 71–72; Pāṭaliya, 70, 73; Poṭṭhapāda, 61–64, 71–72; Sāmaññaphala, 70; Soṇadaṇḍa, 71; Vīmaṃsaka, 71

Theognis, 37, 39, 46, 52
trust: lazy, 8, 143–45, 147; moral, 149, 153, 206; mutual, 5, 77–80, 82, 93, 96, 124, 150–51; prudential, 8, 137; self-, 8–11, 141–43, 147–48, 150, 157–58, 160, 164–66, 174; in teachers, 5, 55, 59–60, 71
trustworthiness, 1–2, 4–7, 9, 11, 15–16, 23–29, 45, 49, 52, 55, 59, 78–79, 81, 84–85, 87–90, 93, 104–5, 107, 109, 111–13, 116–21, 123–26, 128, 137, 160–63, 172, 174, 187

truthful/truthfulness, 5, 16, 35–36, 45–48, 51–53, 82, 113, 143, 184, 207, 209

ubuntu, 77
ujamaa, 80
unhu, 77
unselfing, 199, 204, 208

Vanderschraaf, Peter, 126
virtue, 5, 35–37, 40, 43, 45–49, 51–53, 78–79, 86–88, 90, 93, 103, 115–16, 118, 120–26, 128–29, 164–65, 167–68, 190; kingdom of, 148–50, 153–55
vision, moral, 200–201, 209–10

war, 9, 97–101, 106, 129, 151, 180–82
Weil, Simone, 199, 203, 207–9
welfare, general, 77–82, 84, 86–87, 92–93
Wiredu, Kwasi, 91
Wittgenstein, Ludwig, 204, 210

xin, 4, 15–18, 20, 22–24, 30
Xunzi, 15, 20, 30

zhong, 4, 15–16, 18–20, 22–24, 30

About the Contributors

Wania Ahmad graduated from Wellesley College with a BA in philosophy and chemistry in 2022. She is currently pursuing a PhD in philosophy at UCLA.

Mark Alfano is associate professor of philosophy at Macquarie University, Australia. His work encompasses subfields in philosophy (epistemology, moral psychology, philosophy of science), social science (social psychology, personality psychology), and computer science. He also brings digital humanities methods to bear on both contemporary problems and the history of philosophy (especially Nietzsche).

David Collins is a postdoctoral researcher in the Faculty of Philosophy at the University of Oxford, funded by the Social Sciences and Humanities Research Council of Canada. His current work focuses on topics at the intersection of philosophy of art, moral philosophy, and philosophical psychology, as well as the thought of R. G. Collingwood.

Christel Fricke has been a professor of philosophy at the University of Oslo since 2003. She works on moral sentimentalism and aesthetics and on the history of modern philosophy. She is the author of two monographs and a number of papers on these topics. She has also edited collections of essays on Adam Smith as a moral philosopher.

Corinne Gartner is associate professor of philosophy at Wellesley College. Her research interests are in ancient Greek and Roman philosophy, with an emphasis on ethics and moral psychology. Much of her work to date has been about Aristotle's accounts of friendship in both *Nicomachean Ethics* and *Eudemian Ethics*.

Polycarp Ikuenobe is professor of philosophy at Kent State University, Ohio. He specializes in philosophy of law, social and political philosophy, moral philosophy, African and African American philosophy, informal logic and critical thinking, and philosophy of race and racism. He has published extensively in these areas.

Antoine Panaïoti is associate professor of philosophy at Toronto Metropolitan University (formerly Ryerson University). Trained as a philologist of Pāli, Classical Sanskrit, and Classical Tibetan, and a historian of Classical Indian and nineteenth-century German philosophy at McGill University and the University of Cambridge, he is the author of *Nietzsche and Buddhist Philosophy* (Cambridge, 2012). His current research focuses on metaphilosophy, particularly in connection to the Anglo-American reception of Nietzsche, early Madhyamaka thought, and transcultural philosophy.

Silvia Caprioglio Panizza is Marie Skłodowska-Curie Fellow in the Centre for Ethics at Pardubice University and senior adjunct research fellow at University College Dublin. She is the author of *The Ethics of Attention: Engaging the Real with Iris Murdoch and Simone Weil* (Routledge, 2022), co-editor of *The Murdochian Mind* (Routledge, 2022), and co-editor and co-translator of Simone Weil's *Venice Saved* (Bloomsbury, 2019) and *Mirror of Obedience* (Bloomsbury, 2023).

Esther Oluffa Pedersen is associate professor of philosophy at the University of Roskilde, Denmark. She works in the intersection between history of philosophy, philosophy of culture, and social epistemology. Her research involves trust, German-Danish philosophy from the eighteenth to the twentieth century, and aesthetics. She is coeditor of *Anthropology & Philosophy: Dialogues on Trust and Hope* (Berghahn, 2018) and has written several articles on trust, including "A Kantian Conception of Trust" (*Sats*, 2012) and "A Two-Level Theory of Trust" (*Balkan Journal of Philosophy*, 2010).

Patrick Stokes is associate professor of philosophy at Deakin University, Australia. He is the author of *Kierkegaard's Mirrors* (Palgrave, 2010), *The Naked Self* (Oxford, 2015), and *Digital Souls* (Bloomsbury, 2021).

Winnie Sung is associate professor of philosophy at Nanyang Technological University, Singapore. Her current research covers three main areas: early Confucian thought, especially pre-Qin philosopher Xunzi's thought; moral psychology, including topics such as hypocrisy, trustworthiness, resentment, and sympathy; and issues at the intersection of epistemology and philosophy of mind, focusing on reasoning and self-knowledge.

Iris Vidmar Jovanović is associate professor of philosophy at the University of Rijeka, Croatia. She is a secretary of the European Society for Aesthetics and an associate editor with *Philosophia*. She works primarily in philosophy of art, with a particular interest in narrative art, poetry, and television aesthetics, and in metaphilosophy.

Erfan Xia earned a PhD in Political Science from the University of Toronto in 2023 and will be joining the School of International and Public Affairs at Shanghai Jiaotong University as an assistant professor. His doctoral dissertation explores Montaigne's and Hobbes's political visions based on their ethics of "mere life," in contrast to the ethics of "the good life" in the Aristotelian tradition. His interest in Ancient and Early Modern political philosophy began during his undergraduate years at Peking University. His articles have appeared in *Interpretation* and *History of European Ideas*.

Milton Keynes UK
Ingram Content Group UK Ltd.
UKHW012106250124
436714UK00002B/8